THE FUTURE OF INDUSTRIAL RELATIONS

Related titles:

Denvir, Ferguson and Walker: *Creating New Clients*
Denvir, Ferguson and Walker: *Managing Key Clients*
Farnham and Pimlott: *Understanding Industrial Relations*, 5th edition
Fell: *An Introduction to Financial Products and Markets*
Pettinger: *Managing the Flexible Workforce*
Roberts: *Dismissal: A Guide to Effective Management Procedures*
Robson: *Essential Accounting for Managers*, 6th edition
Simons and Naylor-Stables: *Effective Communication for Managers*

The Future of Industrial Relations

Richard Pettinger

CONTINUUM
London and New York

Continuum

Wellington House
125 Strand
London WC2R 0BB

370 Lexington Avenue
New York
NY 10017-6503

British Library Cataloguing-in-Publication Data
A catalogue record for this book is available from the British Library.

ISBN 0-8264-4834-8

Designed and typeset by Kenneth Burnley at Irby, Wirral, Cheshire.
Printed and bound in Great Britain by Redwood Books, Trowbridge, Wiltshire.

Contents

Summary boxes and figures

Figures

Preface

All organizations are communities of human beings. Their performance is the performance of human beings. Human communities must be founded on common beliefs, and must symbolize their cohesion in common principles and mutuality of interest. The overriding mutuality of interest lies in the fact that everyone involved has a direct interest in the long-term success of their organization.

The history and reality of this, in the UK at least, is rather different, however. In practice, diversification of interest, short-termism, partiality and expediency have dominated the staff management and employment relations practices of all but the best organizations. Indeed, the trade union movement was founded on the need for workers to band together in order to give themselves both a voice and also a measure of influence in their dealings with their employers. At the same time, employers found themselves able to treat their workers purely as a function of production. This was the basis on which, with some notable exceptions, the adversarial attitudes, values and beliefs of employment practice in the UK grew up.

As such, industrial relations – the means by which the employment relation is regulated – became effectively a sponsored battlefield on which those involved could, and did, fight out their frustrations with each other. Indeed, it is well documented that in many UK public services, nationalized industries and multinational organizations, the management, workers and unions have conspired between themselves at regular intervals to engineer strikes and disputes mainly as a relief from the sheer awfulness of the working situation. Without exception, organizations that followed this line have either vanished altogether or else sharply and irreversibly declined, exactly at the time when demand for commercial products and public services has greatly increased.

This in turn has been reinforced by the polarization of attitudes and values and above all prejudices. In the UK matters came to a head in the 1970s following extensive industrial strife and serious disruption to industry and public services. All the main players in IR – unions, employers and government – adopted narrow, partial and self-serving positions rather than paying any attention to the long-term security of organizations and work that was genuinely being demanded.

Indeed, two general elections were conducted with the national state of IR as the central plank. In 1974, following extensive IR strife in the coal mines, the then Conservative prime minister Edward Heath conducted his election campaign from the standpoint of 'Who runs the country, the government or the unions?'. Heath lost. In 1979, following a series of serious public services strikes and disputes, the Conservative opposition led by Margaret Thatcher won the election from the Labour government by conducting a campaign that focused on the effects of the disputes – closed hospitals, rubbish piled up in parks, graves not dug, and stating that, if elected, they would reform the whole state of UK IR. Both turned out to be battles of political expediency rather than a genuine attempt to reform IR; for nothing was subsequently done to address the structural problems, nor to provide a universal long-term basis for improvement in the area.

There has therefore to be a better way, and this is the standpoint of the content of this book. The heart of the matter lies in acceptance and recognition by those who own and who direct and manage organizations, that effective IR is a key feature of long-term organizational success in delivering high quality products and services. It also asserts that, whatever the prevailing state of organizational IR, there is substantial scope for making it work, or making it work better, so long as the situation is fully analysed and understood.

The structure of the book reflects this. Chapter 1 is an introduction, summary and review of the general state of IR in the UK and elsewhere. Chapters 2, 3, 4, 5, 6 and 7 deal in turn with different perspectives from which IR policies and practices can be seen to derive – a strategic perspective, IR with unions, IR without unions, the Japanese view, the 'Excellence' view, collective bargaining and the alternatives. The rest of the book deals with common principles. Chapters 8 and 9 deal with communications, culture and behaviour in organizations, Chapter 10 with management qualities and styles. Chapter 11 is a short summary and conclusion to the whole.

The book is aimed at those who wish to gain real insights to the future effective management of staff. As such, it is of value to practitioners – managers at all organizational levels; consultants, advisors and business developers. It is also of value to students following academic and professional qualifications or courses of study. It is of especial worth to those on postgraduate or post-experience programmes of study, especially MBA programmes, or those required by the Institute of Personnel and Development and the Institute of Management.

RICHARD PETTINGER
September 1999

Chapter 1

Introduction

The purpose of this chapter is to introduce the total picture of industrial relations, and its key features. This illustrates the piecemeal and ad hoc nature of the development of this part of management and organizational behaviour, and also indicates the source of some of the many quirks and imperfections. However, an understanding of these is essential if lessons are to be drawn, and progress is to be made.

Industrial relations (IR) is the system by which workplace activities are regulated, the arrangement by which the owners, managers and staff of organizations come together to engage in productive activity. It concerns setting standards and promoting consensus. It is also about the management of conflict.

Much of this has its roots in the economic and social changes of the industrial revolutions and the urbanization of the nineteenth century; the inherent conflict between labour and the owners of firms; the formation of collectives, combinations of groups of workers to look after their own interests; and the demarcation lines and restrictive practices that some occupations and trades were able to build up. The influence of these traditions remains extremely strong, particularly in long-established industries such as factory work, transport and mining. However, in recent years there has been a serious attempt to change the attitudes of all concerned in this field, and to generate a more positive and harmonious ethos. Companies and their managers have come to recognize the importance of positive employee relations and the contribution that they make to profitable and effective organizational performance; some trade unions have seen this as an opportunity to secure their future, and to attract new members. Other unions have lost their influence because of the great numbers of jobs that have disappeared in the sectors which they represent.

Perspectives

It is usual to distinguish three approaches as follows.

- *Unitarism:* which assumes that the objectives of all involved are the same or compatible, and concerned only with the well-being of the organization and its products, services, clients and customers. The most successful of unitary organizations (e.g. McDonald's, Virgin,

IMG) set very distinctive work, performance and personal standards, to which anyone working in the company must conform. This is also inherent in the Japanese approach to the management of the human resource.

*   *Pluralism:* admitting a variety of objectives, not all compatible, among the staff. Recognizing that conflict is therefore present – rules, procedures and systems are established to manage it and limit its influence as far as possible. This is the approach taken especially in public services, local government and many industrial and commercial activities, where diverse interests have to be reconciled in order that productive work may take place.
*   *Radicalism:* the view that commercial and industrial harmony is impossible until the staff control the means of production, and benefit from the generation of wealth. Until very recently, this was a cornerstone of the philosophy of many UK trade unions and socialist activists in industry, commerce and public services.

IR strategies

IR strategies ultimately depend on the industrial or commercial sector concerned, whether it is public or government serviced. One of the following positions is normally adopted.

*   *Conflict:* the basis on which staff are to be dealt with is one of mistrust, divergence, irreconcilable aims and objectives; disparity of location; divergence and complexity of patterns of employment and occupations; professional, technical, skilled and unskilled staff. In such cases as this, the IR strategy will be devised to contain the conflicts, to reconcile differences and to promote levels of harmony as far as possible. This has been the basis of much UK employee relations in the past, and remains a key influence today.
*   *Conformity:* where the diversity of staff and technology may be (and often is) as great as in the above scenario, but where the IR strategy rather sets standards of behavioural and operational aims and objectives that in turn require the different groups to rise above their inherent differences. Organizations such as Nissan, Sony, The Body Shop and Virgin have all sought to adopt this view.
*   *Consensus:* where the way of working is devised as a genuine partnership between the organization and its staff and their representatives. Genuine consensus or partnership is very rare.

IR, staff and the organization

Whichever is adopted, there are common threads. Organizations must understand the nature and strengths of the types of staff that they employ. They must recognize that there are divergences of aims, and different priorities that must be resolved if effective and profitable work is to take place. The nature of IR and related staff management activities will vary accordingly, but at the outset all staff, whatever their occupation, must form an identity with the organization that is both positive and complementary to its purposes. Boundaries of performance and behaviour requirements must be established in order that these purposes are achieved effectively and successfully. Issues to do with the nature and style of workplace regulation and staff representation must be resolved. Above all, IR and staff management must be seen both as continuous processes and as an area for constant improvement. If designed and conducted effectively by the organization, it will constitute a major return on the investment made in the workforce as a productive entity.

Whichever IR strategy is adopted must therefore be supportive of, and complementary to, the wider aims and objectives of the organization. This will extend in some measure to the capabilities and qualities of the workforce; but ultimately the workforce must be harmonized to the needs of the organization. Effective IR strategies start from this point. They may have regard to staff who, for example, are highly trained or professionalized; however, the overall direction of IR will seek again to match these with organizational requirements. Where staff have a very strong group identity – because of again, their profession, or because of sectoral traditions or a long history of unionism for example – the organization must work to ensure the harnessing and commitment of this to its own purposes.

The inability of organizations to do this can be seen across the whole range of industry, commerce and public services. In the latter, major conflicts have arisen between the 'professional' commitment to client groups – teachers to pupils; doctors and nurses to the sick; social workers to the disadvantaged – and the management by organizations of these staff. IR in these situations is largely ineffective because of the inability of organizations to direct their professional staff in ways universally understood as effective, and because of their lack of regard for, or ability in, IR matters. It has been compounded by the perceived conflict of objectives between service managers and service professionals. Finally, at no stage have professional people generated an identity with the service organization that remotely touches that which they have with their profession.

Industrial situations are traditionally no better. IR in coal mining across the world has been so bad that miners have adopted loyalties to anyone other than the mine owners. In the UK, the focus of coal mining was the union, which provided welfare, leisure and recreation facilities; support for families in case of death or injury; representation at disputes; and a lobby for increased investment in safety and technology. Endemic throughout hundreds of years of coal mining, the result has been that the first and only loyalty of the staff has been to the union; at no stage has any

SUMMARY BOX 1.1

The boundaries of industrial relations

IR boundaries are established by organizations as follows.

- Organization culture.
- Standards of performance that are required.
- Standards of ethics, behaviour and attitude.
- Parameters of employee relations activity and where those parameters begin and end.
- Organizational and managerial approaches to staff management in general.
- Organizational and managerial approaches to the management of dispute, grievance, discipline and dismissal.
- Procedures for the management of dispute, grievance, discipline and dismissal.
- Consultative, participative and communication structures.
- The precise forms of workforce representation including the recognition of trade unions.
- The desired aura or climate of workplace staff relations.

Note

The *aura* or climate is the backdrop or general impression created. This is reflected in the nature and numbers of accidents, disputes and absences at the place of work; it may also be indicated by rates of turnover of labour or problems with particular staff categories.

Whatever standpoint is adopted, it is important that both managers and staff understand it so that they can identify their mutual expectations. Needless disputes are kept to a minimum as long as everyone understands the position of everyone else.

managing organization, either private or nationalized, been able to provide an identity equivalent to this (nor is there any real evidence that they have tried). Rather they have taken the view that conflict is inherent, and have sought to devise 'safety-valve' IR strategies, to ensure as far as possible that when conflict does blow up, it can be contained without serious disruption to the work in hand.

The strategy adopted will be supported by staff handbooks and rule-books; the procedures used and the ways in which these are promulgated; and any formal structures that are devised and put in place. These are in turn, underlined by the nature of staff representation, induction and orientation programmes, and day-to-day work practices (see Summary Boxes 1.2 and 1.3).

THE FRAMEWORK OF INDUSTRIAL RELATIONS

The UK tradition: the tripartite system

In the UK, it is usual to regard the framework of employee relations as *tripartite*. In this view, the parties are government; employees, their representatives and trade unions; and employers, their representatives and associations. Each has a distinctive role (see Figure 1.1). This is then bounded by a legal framework.

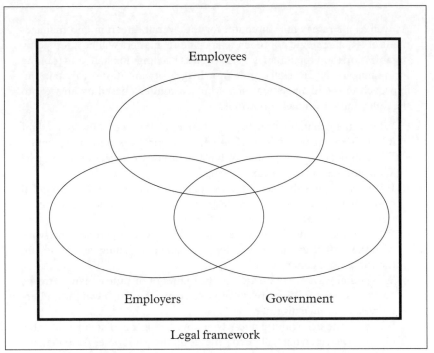

Figure 1.1

The tripartite sys-
tem of industrial
relations

**SUMMARY
BOX 1.2**

**Other
considerations**

- *The structure of the workforce:* operational aspects; dispersion; depart-
  mentalization and groupings; particular ways of working.
- *Staff management aspects:* of core and peripheral work groups; specialist
  sub-contractors, consultants and advisors; those on fixed term or fixed
  project contracts.
- *Technology:* its usage; its effect on the working environment; the rate at
  which it changes; the skills and expertise required.
- *Patterns of work:* attendance patterns; output patterns; job and work
  mixes; the nature and style of supervision.
- *Expertise nature:* the specific nature of the expertise employed; the mix of
  expertises employed; the nature and style of management approach to
  that expertise.
- *Balancing* and *reconciling* a great mixture of conflicting and divergent elements in the basic interests of organizing and maintaining effective
  working methods and ensuring fairness and equity to all.
- Balancing *harmony* and *contentment* with commitment, drive and
  organization purpose.
- The establishment and provision of *standards* and *sanctions* for the
  enforcement of rules.
- *The capability of managers:* one of the greatest advances in the field has
  been the recognition of the qualities, aptitudes and attitudes necessary
  for the promotion and maintenance of effective and harmonious IR; and
  the training of managers and supervisors in the field.

<table>
<tr><td>

SUMMARY BOX 1.3

Problem-solving in industrial relations

</td><td>

As well as a strategy and direction for the overall direction and management of IR, a strategic approach to specific IR matters will be adopted by organizations and their managers. As well as briefings for staff, and training for managers in IR skills and knowledge, organizations will take an approach to the management of workplace conflicts based on answers to the following six strategic questions:

- What is the likelihood of a dispute occurring? If it does, how long might it last? What are the wider consequences to ourselves, and to our staff?
- If it does occur, can we win it? What are the consequences of winning it? What are the consequences of losing it?
- If it does occur, what costs are we going to incur? As well as financial cost, what of the questions of PR, media coverage and local feelings in our community? Is this a price worth paying?
- What happens when it all settles down? How will we interact and work with the staff afterwards? How long will any bad feeling last? What are the wider implications of this?
- What other ways are there around the matter or dispute in hand? Are we able to use these? What are the pros and cons of going down these alternatives, *vis-à-vis* a dispute?
- What are the behavioural and psychological aspects that surround this issue? If we win, what will be the effects on the workforce? And on managers? Are there questions of morale to be considered? If we lose, would loss of face be important? How could we save face, if that were to arise? What would be the response of the workforce and its representatives?

From consideration of the matter in hand in this way, and by establishing the answer to these issues, the answer to the critical question emerges:

- Why are we seeking, entering, or preparing to enter, into this dispute?

This approach will form the basis of any strategic consideration of any conflict, or potential conflict, whether global, organizational, departmental, or divisional; or at team, group or individual level.

</td></tr>
</table>

Government

The government is the single major universal influence on IR everywhere. It invariably is the single largest employer responsible for the pay, terms and conditions of employment of the civil service; the armed services; the police; the emergency services; local government and services; nationalized industries and utilities; health and social services. As dominant employer, it sets standards of employment and IR practice that others will be expected to follow; and there is great scope for setting 'model' terms and conditions. Major public activities (especially large hospitals, government functions, nationalized industry premises) are often the dominant employer of a locality, directly affecting what others have to pay to attract staff to work for them.

Governments make employment and industrial relations laws, as with everything else, and set the standards and boundaries of practice. They also establish codes of conduct, codes of practice and employment protection and encouragement policies. They may also set contract compliance rules, requiring anyone wishing to tender for government contracts to adhere to particular standards of practice. Governments may also use the military police and emergency services in terms of industrial strife to keep essential services open and maintain the general national quality of working life.

Governments codify all aspects of workplace relationships – the rights and limits of trade union activities; the rights of individuals at the workplace; the rights of organizations and their managers; equality of opportunity; the right to strike; and the right to work.

Employees

The interests of employees at places of work are looked after by trade unions, staff associations, some professional bodies, and the individuals themselves. Over the years, the greatest single influence has been trade unions.

Trade unions were first established to protect the interests and standards of living of persons working in particular sectors. A variety of definitions have therefore grown up, and unions may be classified in the following way.

- *Industrial unions:* all members are from one industry (e.g. mineworkers; steelworkers; railway workers).
- *Skilled or craft:* in which all the members have completed a course of training or apprenticeship (e.g. electrical; engineering).
- *White collar:* for example, the civil service and banking unions.
- *Local government:* as a distinctive sector.
- *Professional:* representing such groups as teachers and nurses.
- *Technical:* representing managerial and research staff.
- *General:* representing the unskilled and semi-skilled.

In recent years, trade unions in many parts of the world have lost influence and reputation as the sources of much of their power and membership, the manufacturing and primary sectors, have declined. New jobs created have been in the assembly, service and retail sectors, where no traditions of unionism exist. Legislation has been enacted to ensure that proper procedures are followed before strike action or other disputes take place. Governments have reduced the national influence and reputation of the unions by setting their own IR agenda, and by covering the widest possible range of employee representative bodies (see Summary Box 1.4). Finally, automation and technological advance has eliminated most of the demarcation distinctions between occupations, and the move is now towards multi-skilling and the flexible workforce.

SUMMARY BOX 1.4

The Donovan Commission

Part of the review of the Royal Commission on Trade Unions and Employers' Associations (the Donovan Commission of 1965–7) was to define for the first time what the real roles of unions were. In summary, the findings were that unions:

- bargain for best possible wages, terms and conditions for members;
- lobby for improved share in national wealth for members;
- influence government policy and the legal framework on behalf of members;
- lobby for social security for all;
- lobby for full employment, job security, wage levels, cheap housing for the poor;
- bargain nationally, regionally, locally, industrially, for organizations and individuals;
- represent members at disputes and grievances and for any other reason according to need.

Source: Donovan (1968).

Unions have therefore had to seek new or redefined roles. They have returned from national lobbies to effective action at individual workplaces on behalf of individuals and groups of members. They have engaged in cooperative agreements with organizations, including productivity, training and no-strike arrangements. They have gained benefits for members such as advantageous rates for personal and possessions insurance, and health care. They have engaged in mergers and membership drives in order to maintain and improve on the levels of influence that they have.

Employers

The third party to the framework is the employer, represented by employer and trade federations and associations, individual companies and organizations. The influence of employers is currently at its highest level, and rising, on the conduct of workplace employee relations though (as with the unions) the employers' lobby has declined at national level.

The function of the employer in IR is to set standards of staff management, attitudes, behaviour and performance for the organization or company; to set terms and conditions of employment, and pay levels and methods; to act in a fair and reasonable way towards all employees at the workplace. They may take part in national arrangements to set minimum standards for the sector concerned. They may choose to recognize trade unions or not. They will make representations to government on their own behalf, through their associations and federations.

In recent years, the area of IR has become recognized for the first time as an area of profitable and effective activity. Managers are now being trained in the skills of staff relations and problem-solving. Great emphasis is increasingly emerging in the devising of human resource policies, the tone and style of staff handbooks, the attitudes and approaches to staff and workforces. Companies are looking at fresh and creative approaches to HRM issues, and staff and IR management problems.

The European Union view: social partners and the social dialogue

The European Union (EU) of the present day had its origins in the European Coal and Steel Community (ECSC). The ECSC was formed in 1951 by six countries – Belgium, France, West Germany, Italy, Luxembourg and The Netherlands. The purpose was to abolish import duties on cross-border movements of coal and steel within these six countries, while imposing a common external tariff on supplies of these commodities from elsewhere in the world. From an early stage, however, it was much more than a purely economic arrangement. Employers' associations, trade unions and other employee representative bodies were actively and positively encouraged to contribute to the development of coal and steel community policy. The best interests of the ECSC would be served in the long term, it was deemed, if there was workplace harmony, and security and stability of employment.

Since then, the ECSC has developed – first into the European Economic Community (EEC) or Common Market; and subsequently into the European Community (EC), and finally into what is now known as the European Union (EU). At all stages, the institutions governing the European Community and Union have taken the view that there was a much greater legitimate involvement for all those concerned with workplace management and activities, than the narrow economic – and traditional – view adopted in the UK. In the management of organizations, therefore, the EU enshrines the concept of social partners. The social partners are deemed to be:

- the European Community and its institutions, including the European Parliament;
- trade unions and other employee representative bodies and interests;
- employers' associations, other employer representatives, and individual organizations;
- other expert, quasi-legal and academic bodies with a legitimate or vested interest or expertise in the direction and management of organizations in particular, and IR at large.

It could be argued that the basis of the social partnership is fundamentally similar to the tripartite system. However, the approach adopted is fundamentally different. It cites a partnership rather than a set of parts. It gives both employees and employers a legitimate – and legalized – position as organizational stakeholders equivalent to that of shareholders.

Moreover, it is reinforced by the content of the European Social Charter to which the UK signed up in September 1997 (see Summary Box 1.5).

SUMMARY BOX 1.5

The European Social Charter

The European Social Charter enshrines the fundamental rights of all EU citizens, in society at large as well as places of work (Appendix 2).

- The freedom of movement for workers and self-employed persons across all countries of the EU.
- Adequate protections for employment and remuneration.
- Improvement of living and working conditions.
- Adequate social protection and social security.
- Freedom of association – including the right to join trade unions and associations, and the right not to join trade unions and associations.
- Adequate and continuing vocational and job training.
- Equality of treatment for men and women.
- Information, consultation and participation of workers on key work-place issues.
- Health and safety protection at work.
- Protection of children and adolescents at work.
- The access of elderly persons to labour markets.
- The access of disabled persons to labour markets.

EU social – and IR – policy is still being developed. In general, however, all provisions above apply to all employees regardless of their length of service or hours of work. Specific issues concerning employers' responsibilities in continuous job and vocational training, pension rights, job and workplace security, and the maintenance of other social institutions such as the family (e.g. through parental leave), are still being worked through. At the time of writing, it is clear that organizations and their managers are going to be required to take the broadest possible view of employment, social and human rights.

MULTI-UNIONISM

A large part of traditional IR has been taken up with the reconciliation of differences between trade unions. This has occurred not just between occupational groups within organizations, but also within them. Multi-national corporations, public and health services carry vast, complex and sophisticated employee relations superstructures consisting of committees, sub-groups, working groups and ad hoc groups that all have to be managed and harmonized by the IR managers and departments concerned.

Moreover, they arrive at working practices which the functional managers in the organizations must adopt and respond to.

The complexities of multi-unionism have been compounded by the tradition of setting nationally agreed terms and conditions, wage levels and trade union policies (see Summary Box 1.6). A feature of organizational approaches to IR has been to attempt to reconcile these. A variation of this has occurred (in industry rather than services) where national minima have been agreed across the board and then top-ups offered by employers in relation to their difficulties or otherwise in attracting and retaining staff. This phenomenon is known as *drift* in wages and conditions and is a key feature of local collective bargaining arrangements.

- The teaching profession in the UK is served by the following unions: National Union of Teachers; National Association of Schoolmasters and Union of Women Teachers; Assistant Masters and Mistresses Association; Professional Association of Teachers; National Association of Head Teachers; and Deputy Heads' Association. Some are more specific than others; however, there is nothing to prevent a head teacher from continuing to belong to one of the generic unions.
- A State Registered Nurse (RGN), may choose to belong or not to any of the public service unions. However, his/her qualification will be endorsed by the Royal College of Nursing, a recognized trade union as well as professional body.

SUMMARY BOX 1.6

Multi-union illustrations: UK

Recourse to arbitration

This is open to all those involved at all times in their attempt to resolve disputes at the workplace. Arbitration is available whether these disputes are individual (between a manager and a member of staff) or institutionalized (between an organization and a union or body of employees). Used effectively, it represents a means of resolution that is both considered and subject to internal scrutiny and which may also have the benefit of acceptability on the part of all because a third party has arrived at the conclusion.

Arbitration is not in itself a universal means of problem-solving. It can only be applied where all other approaches have failed, or when there is an issue of presentation concerning the means of delivery of a decision.

It is not an employee relations policy. Regular recourse to arbitration encourages extreme positions on the part of those in conflict so that any middle position recommended by an arbitrator is as favourable as possible. Internal credibility is lost. Continued recourse to arbitration leads to the frustration of those who can, and would, resolve their own problems and this leads to the loss of IR skills, expertise, aptitudes, and therefore, control.

Recourse to arbitration thus becomes an additional tool to be used by managers when the context and situation requires. Its use and value will be pre-evaluated in the light of these situations, the advantages and disadvantages weighed up by managers when they decide on whether to go to arbitration on a particular matter or not.

CONFORMISM AND CONSENSUS

Conformist IR requires the subordination of divergent and conflicting interests at the workplace, in the interests of pursuing common and understood aims. These are set by the organization in advance of any staff agreements. The stance normally taken is that the organization must be successful, effective and profitable, and that the purpose of IR (like all other workplace activities) is to contribute to this.

For the approach to be truly effective, overwhelming obligations rest with the organization and its managers. Standards are preset and prescribed, not the subject of negotiation. Areas of managerial prerogative, matters for consultation, and aspects open to negotiation, are all clearly stated. Conformity leaves much open to consultation, but very little to genuine negotiation.

Procedures are quick and direct. Managers seek to solve problems and promote harmony. Conflicts of interest between groups are kept to a minimum. Disputes (especially those to do with pay and conditions) are resolved within given deadlines. Staff identity with the organization must be strong. The position of trade unions (and any other staff representative bodies such as staff associations) is clearly defined and limited at the outset. The basis of any agreement is set by the organization. The union or representative body is invited to work within it. If it feels unable to do this, it will not be recognized.

The single union agreement (see also Appendix 2: The Sanyo Staff Handbook)

This approach to IR is extensively used by Japanese companies operating in the West. It is a conformist approach. The IR agreement is made between the company and one trade union, along the conformist lines indicated above, with the overriding concern of streamlining and ordering workplace and staff relations, to ensure that their operation is as effective and ordered as any other business activity. Pre-designed and pre-determined by the organization, such agreements are normally limited to a single site or operational division.

Invitations to tender for the rights to representation of the staff are issued to a range of trade unions. The unions then normally present the benefits that accrue to the organization dealing with them. The organization will hear all the presentations, and then decide on one union, which it will recognize, and which will then represent all the staff.

The groundwork for this must be very carefully carried out. There are problems of acceptance on the part of managers, who may not be used to dealing with a particular trade union; and on the part of the staff also, who may have no previous affinity or identity with it. There are also problems of acceptance on the part of highly organized occupational groups for the same reason; and on the part of those unions that are not to be recognized.

To be effective and successful, this strategy for the management of IR must have the following attributes.

- It must mirror the *philosophy, ethos, style and values* of the organization concerned; there must be commitment to it and a willingness on the part of the organization to resource and underwrite it all.
- Managers and supervisors are trained in the *procedures and practices* of IR, the ability to manage staff on a basis free from inherent conflict, and the ability to solve rather than institutionalize problems when they occur.
- *Wage levels* tend to be at the upper end of the sectoral scale, and will also be good in relation to other variables such as regional considerations and the ability to compete for all categories of staff in both the sector of operations and the locality where work takes place. Wage rises are never backdated.
- There is *one set* of procedures, terms and conditions of employment only, operated by the organization in conjunction with the recognized union. The procedures themselves, together with the rest of the IR policy, are devised and drawn up by the company and the union is invited to participate on preset terms.
- The union represents *all members of staff* at the workplace and there is no other IR format.
- *Disciplinary and grievance practices* operate from the standpoint of resolution and prevention of the matters in hand rather than institutionalization. They are aimed, above all, at getting any recalcitrant employee back into productive work in harmony with the rest of the company as quickly as possible. Where recourse to procedures is necessary, these also are designed for maximum and optimum speed of operation. The purpose here is to prevent any issue that may arise from festering and getting out of control.
- The *disputes procedure* is normally that of binding pendulum arbitration (see below) and represents the final solution to the matter in hand. It is only invoked at the point where an official dispute would otherwise take place; there are cultural as well as operational pressures that ensure that this gets used as rarely as possible.

This style of IR is above all designed to be a businesslike approach and arrangement, designed as part of the process of ensuring the success, continuity and profitability of the organization.

Single table agreements

The single table agreement is a variation of the single union agreement (see Summary Box 1.7). The principles, practices and approach are the same. All staff are on the same basic terms and conditions. Representation is allowed from more than one union, and is conducted from the one central standpoint. The advantage is that, within the broad constraint, it gives a measure of choice to the individual member of staff in the matter of representation.

SUMMARY BOX 1.7 **The basis of the single union or single table agreement**	• The standpoint in the first section of the agreement is that of a business venture and the contribution of employee relations to success, continuity and business profitability. • The parameters of employee relations and the extent and limitations of the union's involvement and influence are clearly defined. • Consultative and participative meetings are to take place on a regularized and formalized basis; matters for consideration are prescribed (though there is an in-built flexibility). • The standpoint of grievance and dispute, and disciplinary handling, is clearly stated. The full operation of procedures for these should be kept to a minimum; where they are necessary, they should normally be fully invoked and the issue resolved after a maximum of two weeks. Rights of representation and appeal are clearly indicated. • The arbitration procedure is clearly stated.

Pendulum arbitration

This is the term given to the instrument in most common use in this situation, which is invoked only at the point where a strike or other industrial action would otherwise take place.

An arbitrator is appointed by agreement of both sides to the dispute. The arbitrator hears both sides of the dispute, and then *decides* wholly in favour of one party or the other. Someone therefore always wins (and is seen to win); and someone always loses (and is seen to lose). The concept of pendulum arbitration is based on this – faced with the prospect or possibility of losing a dispute, each party will wish to resort to the negotiating table once again to resolve the differences. In particular, in Japanese companies, there are strong cultural pressures on managers not to get into disputes, and not to lose them if they do.

Pendulum arbitration normally represents the final solution to any dispute, against which there is no appeal; this is clearly stated in handbooks and agreements in which this is the instrument for the resolution of disputes. Those entering into it agree to be bound by the outcome before the arbitrator hears the case.

IR without unions

If industrial relations is to be conducted without unions, the reasons why people join unions must be removed. Trade unions grew to prominence in organizations to represent the employees' interests, to serve particular groups, and as a brake on the worst excesses of management that led to a quality of treatment across the whole of the business sphere that by any standards, commercial or ethical, was unacceptable and untenable. If this arises, once unions have been eased out or de-recognized (or in a new organization, where there is no intention to have them in the first place) the staff will simply join up again *en masse*. So an approach to IR that precludes the need for outside representation is essential.

This normally consists of adopting a benevolent, consultative and open mode of general communications, corporate attitudes to the staff and an enlightened general attitude as the cornerstone of the IR and staff management approach. Operation of procedures and practices must be fair, and perceived as such. Pay, pay rises, working conditions and other operational matters are consulted upon through works councils, organization councils and staff associations.

Responsibility for the style and tone of employee relations rests entirely with the organization. Staff adopt the desired corporate attitudes, values and aspirations.

The single status concept

This concept is based on an ethical stance that all employees should be treated equally, and that the same fundamental terms and conditions of employment are to apply to all. There is, in these situations, a single staff handbook applying to all. Terms and conditions, and elements of the contract of employment, on such matters as holiday accrual, hours of work, the provision of staff facilities, working clothes and safety and protective wear, are the same for all. Participation in such things as profit-related or merit award payment schemes involves everyone.

Behavioural issues reinforce this. Everyone is addressed in the same manner regardless of occupation. The work of each employee is valued and respected. Differentiation between groups and categories of employees is on the basis of work function only; there are no exclusive canteens, or car-parking spaces.

Flexibility

Related to single status is the concept of the 'flexible workforce'; where everyone concerned is both trained and available for any work that the organization may require of them. Staff normally will be made to understand, when they first join, that they may be required to undertake duties away from their normal or habitual occupation. In the wider interests of staff motivation, organizations will endeavour to do this on a positive rather than coercive basis. Nevertheless, it is a fundamental departure from traditional specialization, demarcation and restrictive practices.

Implicit in this are obligations on the part of employees to accept continuous training and development as part of their commitment to the organization – and this applies to all categories and occupations.

Works councils

Many organizations have established works councils in recent years. This is akin to having a board of directors looking after the employee (rather than shareholder) interests. Representatives are drawn from all departments, divisions and functions, as well as any recognized trade unions.

The European Works Council Directive 1994 required all companies to establish works councils as follows:

- *EU Scale Undertakings* – with at least 1,000 employees within the EU and at least 150 employees in at least two Member States.
- *EU Scale Groups of Companies* – groups controlled by a single parent company, with at least 1,000 employees within the EU, and owning or controlling at least two undertakings in separate EU States, each with at least 150 employees.

The Works Council Directive 1994 is certain to have its scope extended by the EU in the next few years. Since the UK signed up to the EU Social Charter in September 1997, this will apply to all UK undertakings, as well as those within the rest of the Member States of the EU.

IR PROCEDURES   These are written and promulgated for the purpose of regulating workplace activities – general employment practices, standards and approaches, general standards of workplace conduct and activity, discipline, grievance, disputes, health and safety, internal opportunities, equality.

They are used by managers, in their pursuit of, and operation of, these aspects of work. They are for guidance, and only where something requires precise operation (such as a safety procedure), or there is a legal restraint (such as with discipline), should they be strictly adhered to. Their purpose otherwise is to set standards of behaviour and practice at work; this also has implications for the more general standards of decency, ethics, and staff treatment that are established at the workplace. Procedures also indicate and underpin the required attitudes, and let everyone know where they stand. More generally, they define the scope and limits of the influence of the workplace. Above all, they have to be understood and followed by all concerned; as long as legal requirements are met, organizations and their managers must follow what they promulgate.

Procedures should always be in writing, and state to whom they apply, and under what circumstances. They should be written in the language of the receiver, so that they are easily and clearly understood and followed.

The best induction programmes will contain both coverage and explanation of them, so that new employees know from the outset where the boundaries lie, and what the expectations and obligations under them, on the part of both themselves and the organization, are.

Procedures should be reviewed and updated regularly, and when they pass from currency, they should be changed to reflect this. Staff groups and any recognized trade unions should always be consulted on the introduction, use and application of procedures and any changes that are made. Ultimate responsibility for both the standards that they set, and their design and implementation, must always remain with the organization.

Summary Box 1.8 compares UK industrial relations practice with that adopted in the USA and Europe.

SUMMARY BOX 1.8

Comparative industrial relations

It is relevant to draw attention here to the uniqueness of the United Kingdom IR system and its variants from others. This is especially true of the trade union movement. Until 1993, all UK trade unions took at least a collective standpoint and most were overtly socialist, at least in their leadership. The Labour Party was originally founded to represent the interests of the unions in Parliament; the major stakeholders in the Labour Party remained the trade unions. Only at present is this relationship being seriously examined for the first time.

The other quirk specific to UK trade unions is their sectoralization and specialization. The titles, National Union of Teachers, Rail and Maritime Trade Union, define spheres of influence and interests. They are drawn from a tradition of demarcation and specialization and, again, this is only being examined for the first time in the last decade of the twentieth century where there are moves afoot among certain sectors to refocus their outlook.

This is to be contrasted with unions elsewhere. In the USA, they are professional lobbies. They work in the same way as any other such lobby to promote and defend their interests – through the media, political representatives and on industrial, commercial councils and committees. They are neither as universal nor as institutionalized as in Europe and the UK, neither do they carry the same influence (indeed, they have lost credence and influence in the wake of corruption scandals in recent years).

In the countries of Europe, unions adopt a much wider brief than their British counterparts, representing 'public services' or 'the car industry' for example, rather than a particular occupation or sub-section of it. They also adopt a much wider variety of stances and affiliations ranging from communism and socialism to conservatism, Christian democracy and Roman Catholicism. Finally, they take a much wider view of IR. Some are militant (e.g. France, Italy); some concentrate as much on welfare benefits as wages (e.g. Holland); while others adopt the stance that a productive, harmonious and profitable undertaking is good for everyone including their members (e.g. Sweden, Germany).

CONCLUSIONS   The general level of understanding and appreciation required of the managers if they are to be truly effective in this field is clearly deep and complex. They must create the basis of an harmonious and productive working environment so that effective work can be carried out. Employee motivation must be maintained. The managers must establish formal, semi-formal and informal chains of communication with workforce representatives (if there are any) and with employees at large.

They may have to bring a range of skills to bear in the day-to-day handling of staff matters. Negotiations, dealing with disciplinary and grievance matters, handling disputes, and other problem-solving activities may have to be undertaken. They may have to balance conflicting demands and may only be able to resolve one issue at the expense of another.

Managers may be fortunate enough to be able to conduct IR in an atmosphere of positivism and industrial harmony. Conversely, they may constantly be working in an atmosphere where mistrust is endemic and outright conflict is just below the surface. In such circumstances, the best strategy may simply be to move from problem to problem if by doing so the manager can at least ensure a modicum of output. The ability to make any progress and shape a more positive and effective future for them in such circumstances will stem from an understanding of the status quo in the first place. A general appreciation of the traditions, history and background of IR is also essential if the managers are to understand both the current general state of IR thinking and also that of their own organization in particular. These traditions are underpinned by mythology, legends and folklore that still engender great pride in certain sectors of the population; this mythology has its roots in real grievances, deprivation and a style of entrepreneurship and management that was very often entirely unacceptable by any standard against which any such practice would be measured in the world of today.

This helps in an understanding of the behavioural and procedural niceties of bargaining activities, and also ensures that their importance in the conduct of IR is not underestimated. In traditional, long-standing and public UK institutions, both staff and unions are comfortable with this way of doing things; taking a little time to ensure that the processes and structures are adhered to may repay dividends in the early, ultimate resolution of conflict or negotiations. It also helps in the understanding of the scale and scope that any intended reform of IR practice must address. It is not enough simply to cut out the behavioural and procedural aspects, as these provide the format in which IR practice takes place. If such reform is to be carried out, either globally or at the workplace, in relation to these traditions, an entire new system of IR must be devised and implemented. That way, any uncertainty, mistrust and conflict inherent in piecemeal tinkering with the status quo is avoided.

This history also explains the attraction to organizations of both the single union and non-union approaches. Both have a ready-made model and a set of principles from which to work. Both have been demonstrated, tried and tested elsewhere with degrees of success and effectiveness in certain circumstances. However, as discussed fully in Chapters 5 and 6, these approaches require special and distinctive understanding, skills and attitudes if they are to be fully effective.

It should therefore be apparent that there are no ready-made solutions to the problems inherent in regulating workplace behaviour and activities. It is essential that as full an understanding as possible is achieved of the current state of IR in the UK; and that is the purpose of the next chapter.

Chapter 2

The old and the new

INTRODUCTION The purpose of this chapter is to draw a distinction between the main factors that hindered or blocked progress in the past, and elements that give the prospect of a much more successful, effective, harmonious – and profitable – approach to IR in the future. The reasons for this are as follows.

- To identify the sheer extent to which the familiar and accepted ways of conducting IR affairs acted as barriers to effective organization performance.
- To identify the direct relationship between these activities and the decline and demise of organization performance.
- To identify the managerial advantage that accrues from their removal.
- To identify the managerial responsibilities and expertise necessary to move from one to the other.

THE TRIPARTITE SYSTEM This was identified in Chapter 1 as the traditional basis of IR in the UK and elsewhere.

Each element is bounded by a legal framework that was greatly enhanced, codified and defined over the period of Conservative government from 1979 to 1997. The Labour government elected in 1997 has done nothing to change the legal basis or to remove the tripartite system from legal regulation, although it has subsequently legislated in the areas of trade union recognition, the minimum wage and individual employment rights.

It is therefore clear that the legal basis is to remain for the foreseeable future. It is also clear that this is contentious to each of the parties in some ways as follows.

- *Trade unions:* trade unions resent both the legislation and perceived political interference in what they regard as their legitimate sphere of activity; and especially resent the implication that this legislation is delivered because of political drives, rather than the search for operational effectiveness.
- *Employers:* employers resent legislation in the areas of minimum wage levels, maximum hours of work, individual rights, because they see this as their legitimate concern. Again, it is strongly perceived in some quarters that the drive is for political reasons rather than to enhance

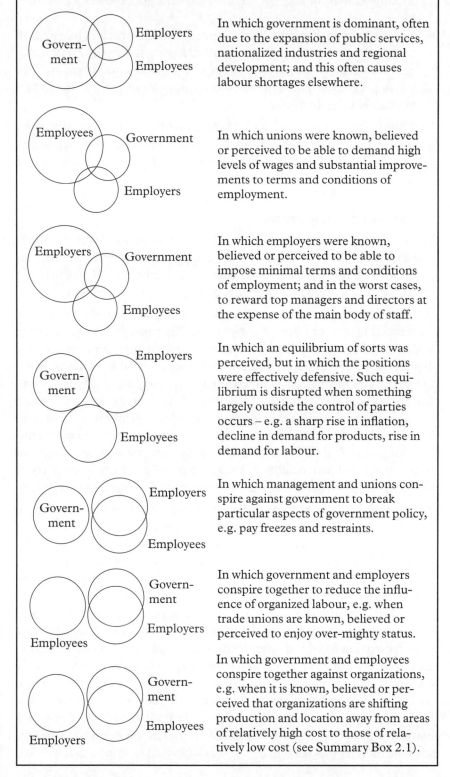

Figure 2.1

Tripartite system operation

In which government is dominant, often due to the expansion of public services, nationalized industries and regional development; and this often causes labour shortages elsewhere.

In which unions were known, believed or perceived to be able to demand high levels of wages and substantial improvements to terms and conditions of employment.

In which employers were known, believed or perceived to be able to impose minimal terms and conditions of employment; and in the worst cases, to reward top managers and directors at the expense of the main body of staff.

In which an equilibrium of sorts was perceived, but in which the positions were effectively defensive. Such equilibrium is disrupted when something largely outside the control of parties occurs – e.g. a sharp rise in inflation, decline in demand for products, rise in demand for labour.

In which management and unions conspire against government to break particular aspects of government policy, e.g. pay freezes and restraints.

In which government and employers conspire together to reduce the influence of organized labour, e.g. when trade unions are known, believed or perceived to enjoy over-mighty status.

In which government and employees conspire together against organizations, e.g. when it is known, believed or perceived that organizations are shifting production and location away from areas of relatively high cost to those of relatively low cost (see Summary Box 2.1).

organizational, industrial, commercial and public service effectiveness.

- *Government:* instruments of government find themselves having staff management problems as the result of having to impose minimum – and now legally supported – wages, terms and conditions, thereby putting up their labour costs during periods of general budgetary restraint and reductions.

Each party from its own particular standpoint therefore adopts the view, from time to time, that government is interfering in its own legitimate sphere of IR influence and activity. However, the picture bears further detailed examination.

Tripartite system operation

In practice, the tripartite system seldom worked as a whole. It was dominated, in turn, by each of the three players, and nobody was ever quite sure of the boundaries of their own legitimate IR activity and influence. The system may therefore be re-presented as in Figure 2.1.

In each of the cases illustrated, the system is in place; but it is in practice dominated by one or other of the parties. They also operate in isolation from each other, rather than with a measure of harmony and coincidence of interest. The problem is compounded when two of the parties conspire together. The problem is compounded also when one party is known, understood, believed or perceived to be acting in the ways indicated because prevailing economic or political conditions allow it to do so. The issue that the UK tripartite system failed to address was to arrive at genuine mutuality of interest. Neither was the system operation effectively or sufficiently regulated to address the problems inherent when one party or the other was able to dominate the situation to the exclusion of the others.

The problem was further exacerbated by the lack of specific regulation. Trade unions always enjoyed immunity from prosecution for business or operational losses sustained as the result of a genuine industrial dispute. Until 1971, it was quite legitimate for employers to discriminate on grounds of race, gender, disability or trade union membership when selecting people for employment or promotion. When required, government would simply use its position as the largest employer to enhance public sector wages, terms and conditions to get over problems of labour requirements in its own domain. This happened especially in the immediate post-World War II period when large volumes of people were required for the rebuilding of infrastructure, delivery of the new nationalized industries, and employment in the new public services (above all, the National Health Service). There was therefore a long history of an essentially divided, divisive and unregulated approach, very much at variance with the model proposal and how it was supposed to work.

In 1998 and 1999, Marks & Spencer were heavily criticized by both the UK government and Trades Union Congress. This was because, following two years of declining performance, and especially a very bad commercial reduction during the Christmas period 1999, the company revised its policy of providing as much work as possible to UK suppliers and instead looked to cut costs by taking supplies from overseas. Many factories that had supplied Marks & Spencer for several years, and who had come to depend on the company, therefore suddenly lost their main customer – and in many cases, were forced to close.

This led to criticism from the Department for Education and Employment, the Minister of State for Industry, and the General Secretary of the TUC. The consensus was that companies adopt a short-term expedient approach to address the problems inherent in long-term organizational malaise. The junior employees were paying for the mistakes of senior managers in establishing effective policy and direction, and as well as short-term job losses, there would be a long-term knock-on effect on the general climate of IR at the company.

Annual cycles

These divisions and conflicts of interest were – and remain – always apparent at least once a year. Company annual reports showed rises or falls in levels of profitability and output, and organizations came to lay off or acquire labour as the result. Government departments spent budgets on an annual basis, and if these were not used up, then the funds provided were clawed back by the Treasury. Acting on behalf of their members, trade unions got into the habit of seeking annual pay rises, other benefits and increased general terms and conditions for their members; and this has been going on for so long that whatever the prevailing economic conditions, people expect an annual increase in pay and rewards (see Summary Box 2.2).

The annual cycle problem is compounded by three further elements.

- Rises in price inflation to levels that meant that the value of wages and salaries was noticeably eroded. In 1978, this reached 26 per cent and had a major knock-on effect on shareholder and capital confidence. It also meant that consumer activities were affected because people no longer had either purchasing power, or the confidence to make purchases. Even where there are low levels of inflation, people still expect to be compensated for these erosions in their purchasing power.
- The fragmentation of the trade union movement meant that some categories of workers were able to command much greater influence than others. In the 1960s and 1970s a pay 'pecking order' or 'league' became apparent. Such groups as printers, miners, power and transport workers gained places near the top of the pay league. One of the

SUMMARY BOX 2.2

The death-knell for the annual pay round

In May 1999, Tony Blair, the UK prime minister, urged employers and unions to end the, what he called, 'often meaningless ritual' of the annual pay round.

He was speaking at a TUC Conference on 'Partnership'. He stated that partnership worked best when it was about 'real goals' which he defined as a strategy to develop the business, to change employee relations, and to end the annual pay round ritual. Doing away with the regular wage round would have profound implications, especially for the government's 1,250,000 employees whose wages and salaries are set by individual and independent pay review bodies.

He went on to castigate the IR climate of the 1960s and 1970s, as having destroyed much of the traditional UK industrial and commercial base; and from this, he called for a new approach to industrial partnership.

In terms of the tripartite system and the IR tradition in the UK, such an approach is certain to be viewed with suspicion – if not downright mistrust – by both other parties, because:

- employees, trade unions and other employee representatives are certain to read into such an approach the beginnings of a dilution of employment rights, and above all, the ability to demand fair wages;
- employers and their representatives are certain to view such an approach with the view that 'a partnership' in this context means the reinforcement of employee involvement and participation rights.

Missing from the statement was any indication of how these particular issues were to be addressed.

problems therefore became to ensure that this position was maintained whenever pay or terms and conditions came to be discussed. Any other group that tried to genuinely better itself, to move up the pay league, would cause conflict between itself and other groups because it was known, believed or perceived to be disrupting the pecking order. As well as bargaining with their own employers, therefore, employee groups had to take account of the views and influence of other employee representatives, and trade unions, when trying to establish the best possible terms and conditions for their own members.

- The need of employers to bargain separately with different groups of staff within their own places of work. This was, and remains, divisive because employees felt that they gained advantage or were disadvantaged, not because of the merits of their case, but because of the relative influence of their representative and trade union. Employers would accede to every demand from one group of staff because they were known, believed or perceived to have industrial muscle; but yet felt able to dictate terms advantageous to themselves with another group of staff.

Industrial muscle

Industrial muscle is the term used to describe the ability of one player in the IR system to force, threaten or coerce the opposite side to accede to their demands (or to be understood or perceived to be able to do so). At different stages, it has been used by all of the parties over the post-war period. It was used by employers on unskilled and semi-skilled staff to force them to accept low and declining rates of pay and worse terms and conditions of employment. It was used by trade unions which would raise the threat of strikes, disputes and disruption, both to employers and their profits, and also to the public at large, to gain large pay rises and substantial improvements in terms and conditions of employment for their members. It has been used by governments of all political persuasions – for example, it was used by Labour governments in the late 1960s and 1970s which demanded that any organization bidding for public work must recognize trade unions; and Conservative governments of the 1980s used rising unemployment as a stick with which to beat the effectiveness and integrity of trade unions.

The language used is self-explanatory. It is confrontational and divisive, a product of the conflicts and mistrust endemic in large parts of UK industry, commerce and public services since the early part of the Industrial Revolution (see Summary Box 2.3).

Many organizations try to get over the problem of having to deal with industrial strife by having specialist IR departments, divisions and functions to manage it. This has the one great advantage of giving staff representatives and trade unions a focal point for the management of IR and the handling of specific problems and conflicts. In many cases, IR officers are highly trained and expert in their field. IR directors are highly paid with bonuses accruing for solving disputes or creating industrial harmony, and containing conflict within the particular organizations. The serious problem is that this approach becomes self-serving and extremely expensive. The organization interest, in many cases, is to a greater or lesser extent excluded. Managerial and specialist careers are made as IR experts. The ideal is to create an organizational IR climate in which the specialist function is purely concerned with maintenance and improvement. In reality, it invariably becomes a vehicle for institutionalizing problems and disputes, and for the containment of conflict, because to resolve such matters would result in the IR function working itself out of a job. Moreover, if IR specialists are to be measured for their success and effectiveness on the resolution of problems and disputes, then they first have to have problems and disputes to resolve.	**SUMMARY BOX 2.3** --- **IR departments, divisions and functions**

Context

Finally, in this section it must be noted that there is no reference at all to organizational effectiveness or profit so far. If this view of IR is adopted, then the organization simply becomes a kind of sponsored battleground on which particular vested interests display their relative strength. Yet everyone is overtly in the same organization for the same reasons – to earn a living, to enhance their standard of living and quality of life, to make and sell products and services that customers will want to buy, or to deliver public services to those who require them. In the tripartite approach to IR, this is almost invariably lost (see Summary Box 2.4).

SUMMARY BOX 2.4 **The tripartite system and industrial muscle: some examples**	Once organizational and work situations become 'industrial battlegrounds', where industrial muscle is flexed, and where the broader context – of providing effective and profitable business and public services – is lost, the results of this approach to industrial relations are not good. For example: • *Frank Lorenzo:* Frank Lorenzo was known in the United States as a tough negotiator, a business hard man and a union hater. He provoked a strike at Eastern Airlines that had the purpose of taking on and defeating the staff trade unions; the end result was to bankrupt the airline. He subsequently was engaged by Braniff, and repeated the process with the same result. • *British Leyland:* British Leyland was the last indigenous mass producer of cars in the UK. The company had extensive labour troubles in the 1980s. In particular, the recognized trade unions were presented as a communist threat, and the phrase 'reds under the beds' was extensively used. The company Chief Executive, Michael Edwardes, was similarly portrayed as an industry hard man who would be 'a match for the unions'. The company effectively ceased trading in 1988 and the component parts – Rover, Land Rover and Austin – were sold on to foreign buyers. The terms used – 'hard man', 'reds under the bed' – should be noted. This approach, reinforced by this use of language, is certain never to sustain long-term profitable viable activity.

Most curiously, the whole is said to be acting in the shareholders' best interests. Clearly, the number of job losses and company bankruptcies sustained in the UK primary and secondary industry over the past thirty years does not support this view. It is therefore necessary to develop the approach further.

As stated in Chapter 1, the EU has enshrined this as the basic concept of effective IR, and drawn the relationship between long-term employee interest and long-term organizational viability.

While the main players are the same, the overriding general approach, and also the attitudes to regulation, are fundamentally different.

Employees

Employees are regarded by the EU as having the same primacy and legitimacy of interest in their organization as the shareholders and backers. Everything that is done is therefore to be assessed from the point of view of employment security and progression, as well as financial and operational viability. It is true that the two coincide in theory. On the other hand, where this view does not prevail, long-term prospects are always going to lose out to short-term shareholder and backer advantage. This is especially true where there is an expectation or anticipation of short-term high levels of dividend, or substantial short-term rises in share prices.

Employers

Employers are required to treat employees with the same principles of human decency and dignity that are enjoyed by everybody in society at large within the EU. This is underpinned by the statutory status of works councils which monitor the standards of employment practice and treatment of employees as a specific aspect of their remit. The works council provides a corporate forum for the identification and resolution of problems and disputes. Works councils are to be required in all organizations with more than 20 employees; and the statutory protection is extended to organizations where there are fewer than 20 employees.

Government and EU instruments

The EU, and its forerunners, always took the basic approach that the interests of backers and employees coincided absolutely in the long run. This has been underpinned and regulated since the early 1950s, and has resulted in two main thrusts:

*   employment social protection of which the instrument is the Social Charter, and which itemizes and details the rights of all employees to job training, employment protection, health and safety standards, fair wages, terms and conditions, equality and fairness of treatment, and regulated hours of work;
*   employers' paternal obligations and duties of care, requiring that a broad and enlightened view is taken of the long-term commitment to employees. This includes continuous job training, retraining and redeployment where required; operationally, short-term working and

short-term lay-offs as alternatives to redundancy, adequate pension arrangements, and attention to other social aspects.

This is underpinned by a fully established and familiar recourse to law. It is directed by the EU through the provisions of subsidiarity – whereby the individual has recourse to local legal remedy; and which allows for access to the European Court of Justice as the final arbiter if matters are not resolved at a lesser level.

The major differences between the tripartite system and the EU approach lie in attitude and perspective. The whole concept was founded on the belief of coincidence (rather than division) of interest. The EU approach requires a fundamental shift in organization and public service governance on the part of many UK organizations. Above all, if it is to work, it requires a shift from short-term and expedient approaches to IR, towards the creation of a climate in which long-term mutuality of interest can be assured. One way of doing this is to broaden the overall perspective and to look in detail at all those who have a legitimate interest – a stake-holding – in long-term and sustained organizational viability.

IR AND STAKEHOLDERS

The stakeholder view of organizations

In recent years, the stakeholder approach to organizations has gained credence. Stakeholders are deemed to be anyone who has an interest in any aspect of the particular organization, its products, services or performance. Stakeholders may therefore be summarized as:

- *the staff:* everyone who works for, and in, the organization and who is therefore dependent upon it for their income and standard of living;
- *the communities:* in which the staff live and work, and in which the organization operates;
- *social customers:* for example, charities, schools and hospitals which may approach the organization for sponsorship and support;
- *shareholders and backers:* the investors of money in an organization in the expectation and anticipation of returns;
- *other financial interest:* including contributors, bankers, loan makers, venture capitalists, city institutions and stock markets;
- *suppliers of components and raw materials:* these have a vested interest in the success of the organization, in terms of continuity of the business relationship, and also in the gaining of a wider reputation for those components and raw materials as they are used in successful, effective and profitable activities;
- *the community sectors and markets:* in which the organization offers its products and services for sale and consumption;
- *distributors and agents:* who rely on their own position between the organization and the end-users of the products or services;

- *government departments and agencies:* with whom the organization comes into contact;
- *trade, market and employers' federations and associations;*
- *competitors and offerers of alternative products and services, substitutes and competition for the organization;*
- *lobbyists, vested interest groups and other influential groups:* related to the location, nature, delivery and distribution of the products and services in question;
- *local, regional, national and global media.*

It is essential to recognize in general the relative position of each in particular sectors. Not all carry the same influence; sometimes one may carry overwhelming influence. They often have conflicting interests. One way of looking at this is to adopt the knowledge–influence spectrum.

The knowledge–influence spectrum
All stakeholders bring with them a combination of knowledge and influence as shown in Figure 2.2.

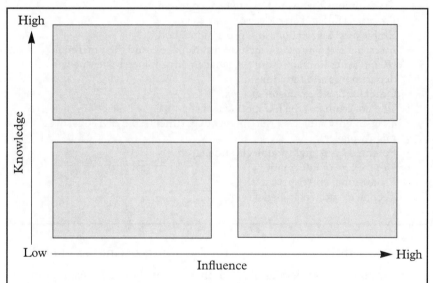

Figure 2.2
Knowledge and influence

Four extremes may then be defined as follows.

- *Low knowledge and low influence:* in which there is a perception that something needs doing, but there exists no wherewithal to do it (especially to do the right thing). In such situations, consultants and independent bodies are normally called in.
- *Low influence and high knowledge:* in which what needs to be done is well known and even understood, but which lacks access to the right media or spheres of influence to get it carried out.
- *Low knowledge and high influence:* in which a point of view prevails purely because of the rank, status, position or privilege of the individual or group that adopt it, in spite of any lack of knowledge that they have in the area.
- *High knowledge and high influence:* in which what is done is the right thing.

- Knowledge and influence are applied to the particular situation by the stakeholder or stakeholders.
- Knowledge is genuine, rational, supported, understood, tried, tested and evaluated.
- Influence arises as the result of rank, status, position, privilege, access to media and public perception.

IR and stakeholders

A more precise stakeholder approach may now be taken related directly to IR. The IR stakeholders of all organizations can be seen in Figure 2.3.

Figure 2.3

IR stakeholders

- Shareholders and other backers.
- Directors and senior managers.
- Other managers and supervisors.
- The staff as a whole.
- Staff groups, departments, divisions and functions.
- Recognized trade unions.
- Trade unions that would like to be recognized.
- Potential staff and employees.
- Employers' associations and professional bodies.
- Internal vested interests: including committees and their members, IR and other human resource management and personnel specialist departments and functions.
- Other lobbies and cluster groups.
- The government, the EU, political parties.
- Over-mighty subjects, over-mighty departments and divisions, over-mighty players.
- Potential over-mighty subjects and players.
- Controllers of information.
- Professional and expert staff.
- Technical and technological staff.

In IR terms, the following views have also to be taken into account.

- Customers, suppliers and distributors may choose to use an organization because of the known or perceived reliability (or lack of it) as the result of the state of IR in a particular organization.

- Media are dependent upon organizations for generating news stories.

The knowledge–influence spectrum may then be applied to IR as shown in Figure 2.4.

The approach gives the basis of understanding why and how different groups of people either may become involved in workplace IR activities, or may affect or be affected by particular issues, especially problems and disputes (see Summary Box 2.5).

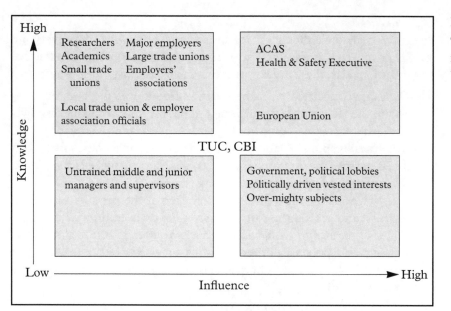

Figure 2.4

The knowledge–influence spectrum and IR

Examples of stakeholder responses to IR activities

- *Customers:* while customers do not necessarily seek out suppliers with good IR, they may very well be put off by suppliers with bad IR. This is for the hard reason that they need to be able to predict their supplies with a fair degree of certainty; and for the soft reason that nobody likes to be associated with organizations that have bad reputations (for whatever reason, and this includes IR).
- *Suppliers:* by the same token, suppliers do not want their own flow of business, or certainty of work, disrupted by customers and clients that are constantly having to adjust delivery volumes and schedules because of bad IR, including stoppages, strikes and disputes.
- *Trade unions:* many trade unions find themselves drawn into supporting legitimate industrial disputes. They then subsequently find that their reputation is tarnished because of the interventions of other stakeholders. This especially applies when politicians use the particular dispute for their own ends; and to the media which may put particular slants on the matter in hand for their own primary purposes (to sell newspapers or journals; to generate interest and therefore viewers and listeners for broadcasters).
- *Politicians:* politicians have a legitimate interest in IR in the management and ordering of public services. They also take an active interest when they have a political (as distinct from operational) axe to grind; and, for example, they will propose legislation when it is (or is perceived to be) in support of a particular political point of view. This sometimes works to operational advantage in, for example, legislation defining individual and collective rights. It always affects – both positively and negatively – the prevailing macro ethos and climate of IR in the country.

Key stakeholders

In spite of all the influences, legitimate and otherwise, that everyone brings to bear, it is essential to recognize that in pursuit of effective organizational IR, there are key interests in all circumstances. These are:

- *Directors:* concerned with the overall direction of the organization, and in the IR context, the ordering of people into departments, divisions and functions, supported by a managerial and supervisory style.
- *Managers:* responsible for directing their own particular aspects, and in IR terms, the maintenance of skills, knowledge, attitudes and behaviour, and harmonious working arrangements.
- *Staff:* responsible for delivering their part of the product or service process, and in IR terms, attending to their own legitimate interests.
- *Shareholders and financial backers:* in whose interests the long-term IR strategy and policy is either designed or else emerges (exactly the same as it does for all other aspects of organization strategy, policy and direction).

This may be represented diagrammatically as in Figure 2.5.

Figure 2.5

Key stakeholders

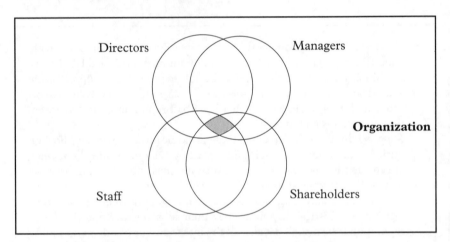

Again, the issue is to ensure the greatest possible area of overlap in each area. Variations may be noted, of which examples are shown in Figure 2.6.

Each of these examples is normally the foundation for adversarial rather than cooperative IR, though it is possible to identify measures of co-operation between different parties in each (see Summary Box 2.6).

The main problem, therefore, lies in recognizing the demands and expectations in IR terms of each, and in comparing these to what is possible, likely and achievable in each set of circumstances. From there again, it is possible to identify the likely potential, and source of, IR problems.

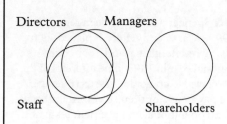

A high degree of internal cohesion, but little attention to long-term direction or backers' interests.

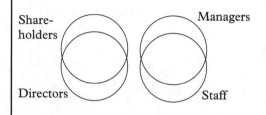

A high degree of coincidence of interest between backers and directors; and between managers and staff; but representative of two distinct and divergent interests.

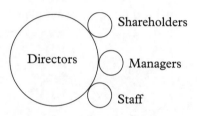

In which the organization exists for the directors' purposes alone.

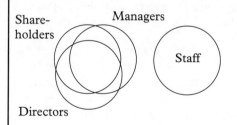

In which the organization is arranged to give the greatest possible advantage to directors and managers, but in which the staff interest is neglected.

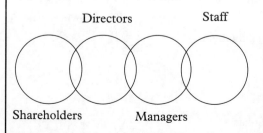

A linear approach, in which the only coincidence of interest is at the hierarchical meeting point.

Figure 2.6
Key stakeholder relationships: examples

SUMMARY
BOX 2.6

Divergence of
stakeholder
interests:
examples

Marks & Spencer
IR and staff management at Marks & Spencer has always been regarded as a model for others to follow. In 1999, Marks & Spencer replaced its top management team in the interests of re-energizing and redirecting the organization, following a bad operational year in 1998. The interests of the backers, managers and staff were perceived to coincide. The top managers, however, negotiated large severance payments for themselves. An hitherto positive and committed workforce and operational management team now perceived that large rewards could be gained for failure.

Public services
In these terms, a public service model may be drawn up as follows.

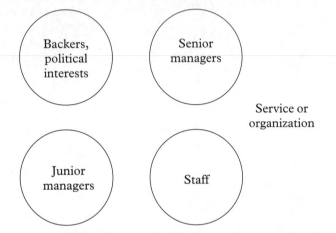

Service or
organization

In this, each group perceives itself to be working more or less in isolation from the others. Communication is formal and restricted. The key identities of staff are, in order of priority: their profession or occupation; their colleagues; their professional body. There is only a passing relationship with the organization.

The Body Shop
Since its foundation in 1976, The Body Shop, the cosmetics organization, had built for itself a reputation of excellent cooperative staff management and IR. In 1999, following a sharp decline in profits, the company announced the closure of its manufacturing division, and redundancies in its retail and marketing activities. The move was very sharp and sudden,

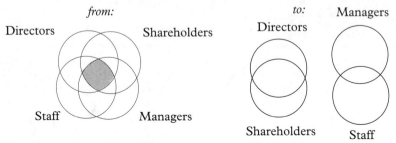

This resulted in a very quick shift to a general perception that, rather than being unique, the company was no different from the vast majority of others – that the staff would be asked to endure the consequences of lack of sensitivity, and that this had first been brought on by errors from senior managers and directors.

The Mirror Group of newspapers
When Robert Maxwell owned the company, it could be summarized as:

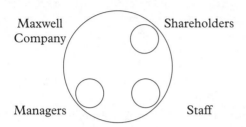

Each group was distinctly subservient to the owner, and worked directly to him, in isolation from the rest. When Robert Maxwell died, the instant result was an immediate cohesion founded on what was perceived to be personal loss and tragedy. When a few days later it became known that Robert Maxwell was a crook who had been stealing from his own companies and their pension fund the result was, in IR terms, the directors looking to salvage the company as best they could. Staff and managers became both alienated and, in many cases, traumatized by the whole affair. However, a genuine bond was felt for the first time between these two groups. This was reinforced in the subsequent months when it came to be perceived that those responsible for clearing up the mess left by Robert Maxwell attended to the backers and directors' interests rather than to those of the staff and other managers. This compounded the effects on the general state and climate of IR, and on individual and group motivation and morale.

CONCLUSIONS

It is essential to understand the points made in this chapter if progress is to be made and steps taken to improve both the quality and delivery of staff management and IR policies and practices.

Far too often, proposals for the development of organizations, changes in direction and ways of working, neglect the importance of ensuring that attention is paid to the IR and staff management aspects, and the effects that these have on effective, productive and profitable activities (see Summary Box 2.7).

This also applies to public services. For the past thirty years, governments of all political persuasions have sought to make all aspects of the public sector as cost effective as possible, as well as seeking to ensure that the services provided are delivered as quickly and as effectively as possible. The failure to recognize the stresses and strains that this places on people in terms of their working lives is invariably a major contribution, when it becomes apparent that, as the result of political initiatives, services are

SUMMARY BOX 2.7

The printing industry in the UK in the 1980s

Traditionally, newspapers had always been printed using the hot metal process. In its own terms, this was a highly expert and technologically advanced activity. It was delivered by men working very often in oppressive conditions. These men – the printers – had both the expertise, and also the command of technology, that ensured that every issue of the particular newspaper was produced on time.

In the early stages of the technological revolution of the 1970s, it became apparent that newspapers could be produced more accurately, quickly and easily using computer technology rather than the hot metal process. The leaders of the two main trade unions, Brenda Dean of the Society of Graphic Artists and Technicians (SOGAT) and Tony Dubbins of the National Graphical Association (NGA), visited Canada in 1978. There they were invited to demonstrations of new technology already in operation in their industry in that country.

Both realized that this technological revolution could not be kept out of their own domain. They accordingly drew up proposals designed to ensure the smooth transition from hot metal to computer print methods. These were agreed with the companies with whom they had dealings.

The process of change at the *Financial Times* (a division of the Canadian Pearson Publishing Group) was managed smoothly. This was because the company understood that the traditional ways of working that had existed for nearly 200 years could not simply be swept aside. People's feelings had to be managed; they had to be made fully aware of what was proposed; and they also required assurances and information concerning what they would be required to do in the future, how they would be required to do it, and what the implications were for retraining, redeployment and job loss. These questions were all fully answered by the company.

This took place in a building in the same road, and in the same week, that there were serious riots outside the offices of News International (now News Corp), an Australian multinational that had acquired *The Times* and the *Sun*. The riots were the product of the failure to consult staff on the proposed changes (as had been carried out by the Pearson Group); and above all, the failure to recognize the importance of the traditional ways of working to the particular group of staff involved. In their defence, News International stated that they only lost one edition of the *Sun*. However, *The Times* suffered serious production difficulties for a period of ten months; and the company as a whole lost many millions in advertising revenues, which it subsequently took many years to fully regain.

delivered to a lower quality standard, and more slowly (see Summary Box 2.8).

The historic effects also require to be recognized when organizations choose to use consultants to appraise their business and to make recommendations for advancement and improvement. Managerial fashions and fads in IR are dealt with later in the book (see Chapter 8). At this stage, it needs to be understood that no board of directors or public ser-

Changes in working hours and shift patterns in the Prison Service
During the 1990s work methods, professional practice and the cost effectiveness of the Prison Service was the subject of scrutiny by both Conservative and Labour governments. In the particular matter of paying attention to the cost effectiveness of the service, there have been many administrative initiatives designed to streamline the patterns of work attendance so that costs are kept to a minimum, and so that, nevertheless, the service can be maintained.

In 1999, a major initiative was proposed in Scotland designed to ensure that, in return for a particular salary, staff would accept full flexibility of working, while at the same time not knowing more than a fortnight in advance what their particular hours of attendance and patterns of work would be.

This was most disruptive to both the working lives, and work team effectiveness, of those involved. It resulted in a great proliferation of individual grievances, as well as both personal and collective loss of morale. This was because the staff were not consulted on the changes, nor were they asked to make any contribution towards identifying, from their own point of view, the best way forward in this matter.

Nursing
At the end of 1999, there were 500 nursing vacancies in the hospitals and health trusts of Kent. This followed major recruitment drives both for student nurses, and also efforts aimed at getting people back into nursing after periods of time away.

At the same time, The Body Shop cosmetics retailer maintained an average waiting list of 90 persons per branch in the same area; while the company asserted that it received anything up to thirty requests per day for recruitment information, and to be placed on these waiting lists.

vice governors should accept any recommendation from consultants or advisors that fail to place a priority on managing the transition of IR and staff management as an integral part of a business plan (see Summary Box 2.9).

Invariably, therefore, it should be clear that both the institutions and also individual organizational IR and staff management have grown in ad hoc, unordered, unstructured ways. Imperfections are always apparent. People, nevertheless, are used to them and comfortable with them. They have got into the habit of working with them – imperfections notwithstanding. Any transition from this that is known, believed or perceived to be more desirable must acknowledge this as the starting point. It is also the only way in which the lessons to be drawn from specific initiatives can be implemented. This applies both to those undertaken by organizations of their own volition, and also to those proposed by consultants, advisors and other experts.

SUMMARY BOX 2.9

Master of the Universe

In its own field, McKinsey Inc. carries both high prestige and reputation as a tough, direct, solution-oriented – and expensive – management consultancy. The company is booked by clients to solve business problems, and to advise on strategic direction, and the future assurance of success.

Whenever the company has been criticized for failing to deliver, either wholly or in part, that which it promised, it has always been because insufficient attention was paid to the traditional ways of working, and IR policies and practices of the particular client. Only when it has become apparent that the business plan changes required – and accepted – by the client organization also require extensive attention to IR and staff management practices, has the scale of disruption been recognized. In one instance, Swedish *Daily News* nearly lost its entire production capacity because the production line was identified as the most expensive part of the business, and redundancies were proposed. This was without reference to the fact that a period of transition was necessary during which it would be essential that the old style printing presses and staffing practices were maintained. The error was only remedied when one of the consultants involved crossed the floor to become managing director of the newspaper. Ensconced in his new job, he immediately undertook a period of extensive consultation with the trade unions and staff representative groups involved.

Source: *Masters of the Universe*, Channel 4, 1999

Chapter 3

Industrial relations with trade unions

At some point, all organizations, except the very small, are faced with the prospect of choosing whether or not to deal with – or recognize – trade unions as representatives of their staff. In many cases, this is an extremely complex choice to have to make, because of both the actual history, and also the reporting, of IR with trade unions in the past.

INTRODUCTION

Primarily, trade unions are a vested interest themselves. Their existence is dependent upon members' subscriptions. Moreover, the position, role and function of trade unions in UK society in industry, commerce and public services is contentious, prejudicial and emotional. This is not helped by the fact that they are used extensively by other vested interests – especially the media and politicians – to advance their own particular point of view. Their genuine role and function, and their contribution to places of work and people at work, is not covered to nearly the same extent (see Summary Box 3.1).

The Royal Commission into the workings of trade unions and employers' associations was the first attempt ever undertaken in the UK to define a set of both legitimate and also actual roles and functions of each. Addressing the particular matter of the legitimate roles and functions of trade unions, the Commission identified the following:

THE ROYAL COMMISSION ON TRADE UNIONS AND EMPLOYERS' ASSOCIATIONS (1965–8)

- to engage in political influence and debate;
- to lobby for full employment;
- to lobby for social security;
- to secure benefits for all those in places of work before, during and after their period of employment;
- to lobby for increased wages and enhanced terms and conditions of employment;
- to lobby for security of employment;
- to represent groups of workers individually and collectively;
- to undertake collective bargaining.

These findings were never questioned. No serious critique of this summary was ever published either by a political party or group, or the mass media (see Summary Box 3.2).

SUMMARY BOX 3.1

———

Descriptions of trade unions by other vested interests

Some colourful and extreme examples are as follows.

- *'The enemy within'* – Ian MacGregor describing the National Union of Mineworkers during his period in office as Chief Executive of the UK National Coal Board.
- *'Reds under the beds'* – Peter Oppenheimer, Conservative Cabinet Minister (1981–5).
- *'Of course we do not consider them to be traitors'* – Margaret Thatcher on the trade union presence at General Command Headquarters (GCHQ), 1985.
- *'The Vanguard of the Revolution'* – Lenin (1921), advocating world socialist revolution.
- *'The foundation for a socialist Britain'* – Arthur Scargill, President of the National Union of Mineworkers, on accession to office in 1980.
- *'If you stop someone in the street and ask them "What do you think about employee relations and trade unions?" the chances are that you will get an emotional response which is either strongly for or equally strongly against them. Unfortunately, it is far less likely that you will get an informed response'* – Julie Baddeley, Industrial Society (1981).

Apart from the last, these phrases are all designed by advisors and presentational experts to ensure that they flowed easily when they were pronounced on the television or in the media, and would fit into a newspaper headline format. Politically effective though they have all been in turn, no lasting IR success has at any stage been achieved as the result. However, each pronouncer gained short-term enhanced credibility among their own followers as the result; and the newspapers, television and radio stations got their stories.

SUMMARY BOX 3.2

———

Role and function of trade unions

The Royal Commission research and inquiry was conducted thoroughly and extensively over the period 1965–8 into the workings and activities of trade unions in the UK.

It never extended its remit to look at any overseas examples or activities. So when it reported, it never considered the social partnership, stakeholder or legitimate interest group perspectives and approaches of what was then the EEC. This was in spite of the fact that each of these had been enshrined in treaty in Member States for twenty years.

At the macro end of the scale, the Commission defined a political role for trade unions and the Trades Union Congress. At the micro end, it defined workplace roles for shop stewards, union officials, national, local and lay officers. It never gave any thought or credence to the idea that either trade unions, or the staff whose interests they were supposed to represent, were a legitimate interest group in organizations, of the same standing as shareholders, customers and backers.

In order to understand this, it is necessary to briefly outline the history and development of trade unions in the UK.

In the UK, trade unions come by two main routes. The first is the medieval trades entry system. In this, anyone wishing to take up a particular occupation – e.g. cooper, wheelright, smith – had to find a practising tradesman willing to take them on. They then accepted a period of articles which was effectively a bond agreement by which the newcomer agreed to serve the master for a period of years before becoming fully qualified and permitted to practise the trade on their own as an expert.

HISTORY AND DEVELOPMENT OF TRADE UNIONS IN THE UK

This gave rise to the two concepts of restrictive practice and restraint of trade. It meant that anyone who was not qualified as a tradesman was not allowed to practise the trade; and it also limited the numbers coming into the trade to ensure that the perception of expertise was maintained. It also meant that prices charged by tradesmen could be kept high.

The second route is the general principle that strength comes from unity, that a collective approach is more effective than the efforts of individuals. In IR terms, bargaining, negotiation, consultation and political power are dependent on the extent to which they are collective and unified. This arose from the excesses suffered at the hands of the worst employers during the Industrial Revolution in the early part of the nineteenth century. By banding together, people were at least able to confront factory, mine and mill owners (see Summary Box 3.3).

This form of bonding together extended into non-industrial groups and came to be known first as black-coated trade unionism; this is now known as white collar trade unionism. Since 1945, this aspect of collectivization has become ever more influential. It now includes banks, finance, computers, shops and retail; and the public service professions of teaching, medicine and social care (see Summary Box 3.4).

The reasons for the decline in trade union influence are as follows.

DECLINE IN TRADE UNION INFLUENCE

- The overwhelmingly adversarial nature of IR that trade unions were known, believed or perceived to bring with them, especially in the 1960s and 1970s.
- The problems caused to organizations by multi-unionism, especially having to try and devise complex solutions to specific problems and issues that were acceptable to every union involved in the matter.
- The damage to motivation, morale and output that extensive and formalized IR procedures and negotiations were known, believed or perceived to bring with them.
- The organization expense involved in complex, protracted and adversarial IR; and this was compounded by the need for attention to the

SUMMARY BOX 3.3

Collectivism in the UK

Cultural background

The ways in which UK trade unions have come about are worth noting. The broad cultural perception was (and to an extent remains) that if people could define themselves as 'a trade' they could then band together, demand collectively agreed pay and terms and conditions of employment, and also organize themselves in such ways as to ensure complete job protection. They sought in other words to take the best of both elements indicated in the text. Some trades remained from medieval times. Others were easy to define – e.g. engineer, builder, railwayman, miner.

Constraints

Others needed a certain amount of creativity. For example, in order to give themselves at least a perception of trade expertise, office clerks invented their own business language or jargon, and this could only be fully understood by another clerk. In this way, the business owner would therefore need to keep clerks in their jobs.

'Mates'

Another approach was the 'mate'. Someone who enjoyed the fact or perception of expert or restricted status would have a 'mate' attached to him. Akin to medieval time serving, the expert and the 'mate' would have their own set tasks divided up among themselves and which only they could carry out.

Demarcation

Collectivization in the UK was reinforced with the establishment of lines of demarcation. These were agreements between different categories and classes of workers who agreed not to do each others' work. Thus, if one group was going on strike, others would refuse to carry out the work of those on strike. The principle of demarcation was first established in the UK in the shipyards in the 1880s, and extended to the rest of industry in the early and mid-twentieth century.

behavioural and ritualized aspects of collective bargaining activities.

- The decline in influence and reputation of the UK Labour Party over the period 1976–97; and the subsequent determination of the Labour Party (1997 onwards) to operate on a consultative rather than contractual basis with the trade union movement and Trades Union Congress.
- The loss of reputation and regard for trade unions, partly fuelled by the adversarial approach taken to them by governments and some large employers over the period since 1978.
- The loss, demise or substantial decline in the UK of those industries and sectors where trade unions were strong, especially coal, iron and steel, engineering, shipyards, national transport systems.

Trade unions may be classified as follows.

- *Industrial:* e.g. Rail, Maritime and Transport Union; National Union of Mineworkers.
- *Expert:* e.g. engineering.
- *Professional:* e.g. Royal College of Nursing.
- *Sectoral:* e.g. Transport and General Workers' Union; UNISON (generic public service union).
- *White collar:* manufacturing, science and finance; banking, insurance and finance (N.B. it should be apparent from this that there is a measure of choice available to those in particular sectors).
- *Elite:* e.g. First Division Association (civil servants); Professional Footballers' Association; Professional Golfers' Association.
- *Public professions:* e.g. National Union of Teachers; Royal College of Nursing (again).

Note
In 1999, there were 229 trade unions registered with the UK Department for Education and Employment.

SUMMARY BOX 3.4

A classification of trade unions

- The growth and development of new industries – especially services and retail – where there was no history or tradition of trade union involvement, either on the part of the unions themselves, or on the part of the staff now working in those sectors.
- The outlawing of the union membership agreement or 'closed shop', in which members of staff were required to become trade union members either before taking on a particular job, or as a condition of taking on a particular job.
- Other legal measures designed to define the boundaries of legitimate trade union activity and involvement, and with especial reference to the conduct of industrial disputes (see Summary Box 3.5).
- The loss of macro political, economic, social and technological influence. If this is related to the Royal Commission coverage (see above), the specific losses are in the following areas:
  - political – compounded especially by the loss of closeness of relationship with the UK Labour Party; and with the ability to command large numbers of the population in the support of an established political point of view. When Margaret Thatcher came to power as UK Conservative prime minister in 1979, she acknowledged that this was due to the support of the large number of trade union members;
  - economic – rises in unemployment in spite of the best efforts of trade unions, together with the loss of those industries in which trade unions had hitherto been strong, meant that it was no longer possible to protect either the standard of living of people in work, or the certainty of work in the future;

SUMMARY BOX 3.5

Conduct of disputes

UK legislation in the 1980s attended especially to the conduct of industrial disputes as follows.

- *Picketing:* picketing was allowed for information purposes only. It became illegal to prevent access to places of work, or to victimize those who crossed picket lines.
- *Secondary picketing and secondary activity:* picketing at any place of work other than that directly affected by the dispute became unlawful.
- *Strikes and other forms of industrial action:* the legal position in 1999 is that all strikes and other forms of industrial action must be agreed through a majority of those taking part in a secret and independently scrutinized ballot. Seven days' notice of intention to hold a ballot must be given to the employer. Once the outcome of the ballot is known, the employer must be informed of this. If industrial action or strike is to take place, at least seven days' notice of commencement of the action must be given to the employer.

- – social – when communities that had grown up around mines, docks, shipyards and steelworks lost these activities, there was a consequent loss in social cohesion and fabric in those communities;
- – technological – present technology is much more dependent upon job training than time serving as in the past; responsibility for job training is much more the prerogative of employers than of trade unions.
- The decline of collectivism has been accelerated through the advent of flexible working, short-term contracts, core and peripheral workforce arrangements and subcontracting. New industries and the service sector have sought to design their own approaches to individual and collective rights, terms and conditions of employment, and wage and salary levels. This, in turn, has meant a designed, rather than emergent, approach to the management of trade unions.

THE MANAGEMENT OF TRADE UNIONS

Historically, this took one or more of the following forms:

- peaceful competition;
- forceful opposition;
- benign neglect;
- neutralization.

Peaceful competition

The strategy of peaceful competition in the management of trade unions includes a variety of tactics. Salaries that are paid are equal to, or better than, those in unionized firms or occupations. Salary increases may be granted during trade union recruitment campaigns. Additional benefits may be offered by organizations including establishing welfare, profit sharing and other benefit schemes. Organizations may differentiate between those who belong to trade unions and those who do not; and from this, offer rewards to those who are not members of trade unions.

The main problem with such an approach is that because it differentiates between staff who are members of trade unions and those who are not, the approach is divisive. There is also a perception of lack of integrity; and this has enduring long-term effects on motivation and morale throughout the organization.

Forceful opposition

The strategy of forceful opposition is implemented through such approaches as:

- overlooking union members for promotion and pay rises;
- transferring active unionists from department to department;
- adopting punitive supervision approaches to active unionists;
- appointing union leaders to managerial and supervisory positions; and victimizing and harassing union officials;
- organization managements may also adopt industrial espionage tactics on their own staff to try and establish who are union members and who are union activists.

This is one of the worst forms of adversarial IR, and is always destructive to productivity, organization performance, motivation and morale.

Benign neglect

This is the approach that is taken whereby organizations ignore the manifestation of problems that arise, preferring instead to concentrate on broader issues.

This invariably means that there is a steady, largely acceptable, generally negative approach to staff–supervisory–managerial relationships overall.

Neutralization

Neutralization arises as the result of the creation of extensive procedural (rather than substantive) IR committees and functions. This ensures that all IR time, energy and resources are used in non-effective, neutral, non-divisive and non-confrontational committees and meetings.

The best that can be said for this is that it may generate sufficient confidence and mutuality to develop matters more positively in the future.

In all of these cases, when serious problems do occur, the organization and its managers normally cannot cope with anything except adopting a particular point of view to the given situation (see Summary Box 3.6).

SUMMARY BOX 3.6

The management of trade unions I

'The memory seared into my skull was of crowds of demonstrators and police on horses and angry pickets who would be screaming at you with wild eyes and big teeth. And it was a dreadful business, for among the 5,000 sacked workers were hundreds and hundreds of decent, mild-mannered librarians, clerks, secretaries, printers and messengers whose only sin was to have joined a union. Inside Wapping throughout that long winter of 1986 while we found our way through a new computerised technology, we could hear chants and turmoil, the muffled clops of passing police horses, the roar and shrieks of a baton charge, but because the building was windowless, we couldn't see anything. It was very odd. We would watch it on the nine o'clock news, then step outside and there it would be in three dimensions – the most bitter and violent industrial dispute yet seen on the streets of London – happening outside the front gate.

'To keep morale up, the company each night brought round boxes of sandwiches and beer, which seemed a cheery gesture until you realised that the largesse was carefully worked out to provide each member of staff with one damp ham sandwich and a six ounce can of warm Heineken.

'It occurred to me that I was about to squander my small life for the benefit of a man who had, without apparent hesitation, given up his own nationality out of economic self-interest, who didn't know who I was, would have as likely discarded me if a machine could be found to do my job, and whose idea of maximum magnanimity was to hand out a six ounce can of beer and a limp sandwich. And eventually the company stopped bringing round free sandwiches and beer.'

Source: Bill Bryson, *Notes from a Small Island*, Black Swan, 1994

Note
Overtly, the approach to the management of trade unions in this particular case – *The Times*/News International dispute of 1986 – was of forceful opposition. However, it also included overt statements of peaceful competition, in that some staff kept their jobs; benign neglect, in that the potential problems had been ignored until there were violent confrontations; and neutralization, in that all IR was conducted on the basis that it was better not to have to face these problems at all.

Problems

The overriding problem with each of these is that they are extremely expensive in terms of finance, resources, staff time, motivation and morale. Each is a trial of strength between two or more warring parties.

The competitive approach means that everything has to be paid for at short notice, because it depends on the capability to keep ahead of the highest payer and 'best employer' in the sector or locality.

The opposition approach requires resources and expertise to be diverted away from supposed primary activities in order to engage in confrontations with the staff whose job it is to carry these out.

Benign neglect is akin to having the car serviced only when it breaks down. It may be possible to neglect problems for weeks or months; but failure to address them other than when they arise, simply means that much more serious issues have to be dealt with later on.

This form of approach can work in the short term where organizations exist in long-term stable and commercially assured or protected markets because the costs incurred can simply be passed on to customers. In the early twenty-first century it is not easy to think of any market that fits that description anywhere in the world. Indeed, in the past, such markets have been largely illusory also – between them the UK docks, mining, steel, transport and car industries have lost nearly 10 million jobs over the period 1945–99, and this was at a time when demands for these products, services and activities delivered on a genuinely commercial basis have been rising very steadily and sharply.

Context

Clearly, the precise context of the future management of IR with unions at particular organizations and places of work will vary. Broadly, however, this has to be seen as follows.

MANAGING TRADE UNIONS IN THE FUTURE

- The influence and direction of the EU, and its identification of trade unions as social partners and a legitimate interest group, mean that organizations are likely to be unable not to recognize them and refuse to deal with them on the same basis as in the past.
- The drives towards openness, availability and access to information, in turn, set standards for consultation, participation, involvement and communication.
- Greater levels of commitment to staff required for the lifetime of their employment. The EU has targeted organizations as having wide-ranging continued responsibilities concerning the rights, occupational health, social security and portable pension of their staff. It is also certain that much greater protection from unfair dismissal will be brought in during the early part of the twenty-first century (see Summary Box 3.7).

On this basis, those organizations that choose to recognize trade unions, or that are subsequently required to do so, have the following distinctive matters to address.

- *The desired standpoint or point of view:* deciding on the overall corporate approach to the trade unions involved.

**SUMMARY
BOX** 3.7

**Ready, willing
and able**

'In the past, we have tried both industrial militancy and macho management. Now is the time for a new approach.

'Partnership is the buzzword in IR today, but some employees view it as another management fad, while others see it as a cynical re-branding of the status quo. Some managers are suspicious too. They suspect a return to the bad old days of 1970s management by expediency, and a new round of demarcation, dispute and inter-union competition. But a look at workplaces where partnership is reality shows them all to be wrong.

'The unions' approach has changed. Our starting point is what our members want. Their top priority is job security followed by a wish for fulfilling work. Most workers do not believe that they work for a bad employer, although many want better managers and a greater say in decision making.

'Employers may find this persuasive in theory but doubt the practice. *Partners for Progress*, the research commissioned by the TUC will convince them otherwise. It has uncovered an extraordinary range of partnerships. And while it has found no simple off the peg model, there are six clear principles at work in such a relationship.

'First, both partners must be committed to the success of the enterprise.

'Second, true partnerships recognise that each side has a legitimate and separate interest, requiring trust, respect and willingness to resolve differences.

'Third, effective partnerships are based on employment security.

'Fourth, partnerships must improve working life.

'Fifth, there must be a real sharing of hard information. Consultation must be genuine with a commitment to listen to the business case.

'Sixth, an effective partnership adds value. It taps into new sources of motivation, commitment and resources.

'Building a relationship requires both sides to invest time and effort. Partnership agreements between employers and trade unions are by definition high trust relationships and, particularly where they superseded antagonism, there is no way to shorten this lengthy process. Partnership provides the basis to make the most of this however, and this way contributes to the competitiveness of the business and the nation. Those who don't believe the hype about the new spirit of partnership between employers and trade unions will soon be able to see evidence that will change their mind. Now is the time for a new approach: partners for progress.'

Source: John Monks, General Secretary of the Trades Union Congress, *People Management*, 20 May 1999.

- *General remit and terms of reference:* those areas in which unions are to operate, and the ways in which these operations are to be established.
- *Specific factors:* where the unions are to be recognized in each or all of the following ways – social partnership, collective bargaining, negotiations, consultation, participation and involvement; and this includes

drawing up the constitution of works councils and supervisory boards, either when required by statute, or when the organization chooses to do so.

- *Choosing the unions to be recognized:* normally in consultation with staff and staff groups.
- *Designing the policies, procedures and practices:* in the same way as all other organization policies, procedures and practices are drawn up.
- *Designing specific remits and terms of reference:* for joint consultative committees, joint negotiating committees, health and safety committees, works councils and other fora.
- *Establishing specific published means of wider consultation and participation:* including facilities for staff meetings, briefing groups and open meetings.
- *Designing and publishing IR procedures:* concerning discipline, grievance, dismissal, disputes, training agreements, health and safety, serious problems, poor performance and bad behaviour.

If this is undertaken as a matter of corporate responsibility and integrated (rather than separated) from the rest of overall policy and direction, then there are distinct advantages to be gained from involving trade unions as follows.

- Trade union expertise in specific IR matters.
- Professional expertise of trade union officials.
- The sectoral knowledge that trade unions bring with them.
- The independent monitor role in which organizations are sufficiently confident of their own basic standing and ethos to allow an outside legitimate special interest group in to be involved in their conduct.
- Staff confidence – especially along the lines of the fact that if something has trade union agreement then it is likely to be acceptable more widely.

There are caveats that must also be noted as follows.

- Those that have had direct involvement in bad unionized IR may take some persuading that any future involvement of trade unions is going to be of benefit.
- Cultural barriers – along the lines of 'This is not the way we do things here' (see Chapter 10).
- The involvement of trade unions can be construed as a barrier or hurdle between management and workforce, and may be perceived to be divisive in itself.
- The formalization of relationships must be designed with the purpose of speeding up progress, not to slow it down.
- Trade unions are vested interests – and will flourish as independent and self-serving vested interests if they are not managed and integrated into the precise purposes for which they have been required.

The continuing role of trade unions

In 1999, 7.5 million people belonged to affiliated trade unions in the UK. This figure was down from a peak of 14.7 million in 1979. According to the workplace industrial relations surveys of 1994 and 1998, the main reasons why people continue in trade union membership are as follows.

- Employment protection insurance so that if, and when, an individual does get into difficulties with their organization they have recourse to expert representation including legal advice and representation where necessary.
- Access to formalized channels of consultation, negotiation, bargaining, participation and involvement.
- Macro-organizational representation where unions continue to be recognized on either an organizational or an individual/sectoral basis.
- There still remains a strong history and tradition of joining trade unions in some sectors (e.g. electrical, engineering, manufacturing) and localities (e.g. North-east, North-west, Scotland, South Wales).
- The fact, belief or perception that there is now the need to join a trade union where previously this did not exist. For example, the Banking, Insurance and Finance Union has enjoyed substantial membership increases in the 1990s.
- Professional indemnity insurance required by nurses, doctors, teachers and social workers; and which is offered by the unions as part of their role as professional body.
- Training agreements, entered into as a part of national joint council arrangements, whereby a union is a signatory of the certification process of occupations such as building, plumbing and electronics.

People also join trade unions for a range of other real and perceived general benefits including:

- other indemnity insurance;
- discounts on shopping;
- visa cards at advantageous interest rates;
- private health care;
- holiday discounts and facilities;
- access to discounted car, home and property insurance.

From the organization's point of view, much of this needs to be drawn up and formalized into collective agreements. These agreements need to be able to cover each of the above points in terms that give the maximum possible benefit to both themselves and their employees, and free up as much management time as possible to be engaging in primary organizational activities.

Collective agreements

A major concern of the conduct of IR between organizations and trade unions, therefore, is the making and sustenance of collective agreements. Collective agreements normally fall into one of two categories.

* *Substantive agreements:* in which the remit, terms of reference and cover of the relationship is defined.
* *Procedural agreements:* in which a procedural format or framework is produced by which the substance is addressed and delivered.

The approach therefore addresses both what is to be covered and also how it is to be covered. At its most effective, the practice of entering into collective agreements means that there is a substantial organization standpoint from which the principles and practices of IR are to be delivered. It also means that those matters are dealt with on a collective, rather than individual, basis (see Summary Box 3.8).

SUMMARY BOX 3.8

Individual agreements

As part of its approach to reforming IR, the UK Conservative government of the 1980s sought to promulgate the concept of individual agreements and contracts of employment, and to dilute the effects of the collective approach to IR. Thus, the Employment Act (1982) enabled employers to offer inducements to individual employees to break collective agreements. The point of view taken was that this would break the stranglehold or straitjacket placed on organizations by the collective approach, which was deemed to stifle creativity, innovation and individual motivation.

Like so many political interventions, the individual agreement approach was found to be seriously lacking in the long term from every substantial and considered point of view. The reasons were as follows.

* It was divisive, because it often meant having individuals doing the same or similar work for different salaries.
* It penalized long-serving employees, because there was a tendency to overpay or offer inducements to new starters.
* It was expensive, because time had now to be taken up with each individual rather than a single agreement.
* In practice, it became open to those aspiring to senior posts and high salaries, but closed to those in more junior posts and on lower salaries. This, in turn, led to the lengthening of the divide between top and bottom of pay scales, and thereby inequality rather than equality was reinforced.
* It required the drawing up of individual contracts and terms and conditions of employment where the collective approach was broken, and this increased overheads.

By the end of the twentieth century most organizations that went down this route in the first place had reverted to a collective approach. Even where this is not conducted as part of a formalized collective agreement with trade unions, the principle of universal or collective basic terms and conditions of employment is widely perceived to be a much more businesslike approach to the management of IR.

This is much more cost effective provided that it is designed and managed. The starting point is therefore to decide which unions will be dealt with and on what basis. The following matters have to be addressed.

- Whether the staff choose their own unions or whether the organization invites particular unions to represent the staff.
- Whether the coverage and extent of recognition extend to each union involved or whether this is to be varied.
- Whether each union is to have equality of influence or whether this is to be dependent on the numbers and proportions of staff represented.
- The means for addressing, conducting and resolving individual and collective problems including serious disputes.

Consideration has therefore to be given to each of the following.

- The composition and remit of joint consultative committees, joint negotiating committees and staff fora.
- Voting procedures and other matters of direct influence.
- Specific activities – e.g. where one union's members are at greater risk of health, safety or welfare problems, the extent to which this union has pre-eminence in these matters.
- Speaking rights in meetings – the extent to which union representatives are allowed time to put their point of view at committees is dependent on the numbers of members and proportions of workforce represented.
- Inter-union relationships: the recognition and management of any internecine strife and its possible consequences (see Summary Box 3.9).

There are advantages and disadvantages to the collective agreement approach.

Advantages
- Provided that the organization format is clear and transparent everybody knows where they stand.
- There is no dispute over the extent, content or coverage of individual terms and conditions of employment because these are the same for everybody.
- It provides a basis for the conduct and resolution of all IR matters and serious disputes.
- Everyone is represented by the union (i.e. the expert) of their choice.
- The unions involved become legitimate organizational stakeholders and provide their point of view on the wider progress of the organization as well as concerning itself with specific IR matters.

Historically, the management of trade unions was overwhelmingly concerned with drawing up policies, remits and, above all, procedural agreements that enabled trade unions to function alongside each other. This was because many unions had their own particular constitutions that would not allow them to accede to any possible variation on the work that its members covered, or the ways in which that work was covered. Many trade unions were also bound by national pay rates and terms and conditions of employment. Many trade unions had also fallen out with each other on a macro-basis following arguments over which categories of staff they were able to represent in particular industrial sectors and localities.

Organizations that take responsibility for their collective agreements now favour one of the following approaches.

Single status or single table representation
This concept is based on an overwhelmingly ethical stance that all employees should be treated equally and that the same fundamental terms and conditions of employment are to apply to all. In these situations, there is a single staff handbook. Terms and conditions, the elements of the contract of employment, provision of staff facilities, are the same for all. Each union that is involved accepts these as a condition of involvement; variations come only when issues concerning a particular staff group have to be addressed.

Single union agreements
This is akin to the Japanese approach. A single union is invited by the organization, or else lobbies the organization, for representation rights. The union represents all members of staff at the workplace and there is no other IR format. There is a single set of procedures, terms and conditions of employment operated by the organization in conjunction with the recognized union.

Each of these approaches requires policies, systems, procedures and practices to be kept simple. All matters can therefore be much more easily understood than long and convoluted policies and procedures; or depend on nationally drawn up policies and procedures which have little or no relevance to specific workplaces.

SUMMARY BOX 3.9

The management of trade unions II

Disadvantages
- It is often very difficult to maintain genuine parity and evenness over extended periods of time. Two forms of this are especially difficult:
  - where one staff group gains or loses currency or influence in relation to others represented by the same union;
  - where one staff group gains or loses currency or influence in relation to others represented by different unions.
- In some cases, organizations may be able to come to agreements with one staff group but not all; or with one or more unions (in a multi-union situation) but not all.

- Distributive agreements, where one staff group is known, believed or perceived to have benefited at the expense of others, always leave enduring wider problems of motivation and morale. This is bad enough if there are sound strategic or operational reasons; it is greatly compounded either when management has used a distributive agreement to 'divide and rule', or when a union has used its individual muscle to gain an advantage that it knows that other groups will not be able to gain or sustain.

- Unions and their officials sometimes gain a known or perceived over-mighty influence. They become a major channel of communication and in some cases are known or perceived to use this to further their own influence or to put a particular point of view on either general IR matters, or specific issues that serve their own interests rather than those of their members at the organization. The best organizations get over this by using all other possible channels of communication alongside the trade union; and this, in turn, tends to reduce any potential or actual issues concerning over-mightiness that may exist.

CONCLUSIONS   It is clear that in recent years trade unions in the UK have had to reinvent themselves. They enjoyed influence over the period until 1980 largely because people were prepared to give it to them. Once it became apparent that in many cases life could go on without them, many organizations chose either to dilute their influence or to do without it altogether. This was compounded by a full understanding of the consequences of adversarial approaches brought to IR by both organizations and trade unions in these situations in previous times.

Some of this reinvention has been fuelled by the intervention and influence of the EU. The drive towards the social partner approach to IR has meant that many unions have had to adopt a much broader consideration of what staff and staff group interests actually are, and to accept the much greater responsibilities that the elevation of staff to the position of major organizational stakeholders brings.

Otherwise, the quality and delivery of individual member services is the key to the future success and effectiveness, and therefore continued influence, of specific trade unions. These services encompass the broad and the general, specifically related to IR, and also bringing the sort of benefits that are available to anybody who joins any club or society. The true key to this lies in the continued ability in the field of individual representation – providing the best possible advocacy, support, case presentation and, where necessary, legal advice and representation to individual members when they find themselves in some form of dispute with their organization, manager or supervisor.

In the broader situation, there is no doubt that employers are going to be required to take a much more constant and cooperative role in their dealings with trade unions. Those organizations and their managers that view this with any sort of trepidation or uncertainty need therefore to understand the complexities and responsibilities involved.

For those that already recognize trade unions for whatever purpose, the assessment of the required future relationship is based on the extent to which the current situation is effective, what aspects of it could or should be changed, and the barriers that prevent, hinder or dilute these changes from taking place.

It is further necessary to understand that when unions are being recognized at first, a sound basis for a mutually beneficial (rather than antagonistic) relationship needs to be put in place (see Summary Box 3.10).

Whatever is drawn up, needs to be considered from the point of view of present, continued, sustainable and future performance. There is no point in drawing up something that will not sustain even a modicum of scrutiny. There is also no point in dreaming up something that is based on historic prejudice or perception. In the past, this problem was always compounded when shareholders' representatives tried to devise their own approach. Having neither genuine understanding nor expertise in the area, these approaches either took the form of general statements that reflected prevailing prejudices, or else tried to cover every possible human frailty and failing through the production of extensive, convoluted – and contradictory – procedures.

The main lessons in the effective management of trade unions for the future therefore lie in the understanding of the totality of the situation. It is necessary to ensure that any relationship is capable of being sustained positively and effectively over long periods of time. If trade unions are going to be recognized then it must, in turn, be recognized that they have legitimate interests in each of the following areas.

*   *Social partnership:* especially in the organization and management of works councils; and as more general partners in participation, consultation and involvement of staff.
*   *Individual representation:* in the conduct of individual discipline, grievance and dispute cases.
*   *Vested interests:* in specific areas of IR management and practice; in related areas, especially health and safety and welfare; and in broader organizational matters in so far as the future prosperity and effectiveness of the organization, and the future employment prospects of the unions' members, coincide.

If unions are recognized, then they have a legitimate interest in the organization overall and in the staff in particular. They have to be treated as such. If the relationship needs developing then there is scope for doing this positively and harmoniously provided that it is actively and purposefully directed and managed.

SUMMARY BOX 3.10

Steelworks

The chief executive of a private steel company in the Midlands was asked by his workforce to recognize their union, the Iron and Steel Trades Confederation. The union had been de-recognized several years before. The company had a history of good profitability and working relationships. Absenteeism and labour turnover were low, output per member of staff high.

The chief executive refused to recognize the trade union. He saw no need – after all, all the issues for which trade union recognition was normally sought were covered. Moreover, he was both surprised and disappointed to find that most of the members of staff had kept up their trade union membership. He had not realized this.

Accordingly, he confronted his staff representatives. Angrily, he demanded what they thought they were playing at. He had worked for years to get the steel company to its present level of profitability and was not going to throw it all away on a return to the bad old days.

Almost overnight, this approach destroyed the extensive positive relationship that had been built up. The company staff tried in vain to point out that they were not seeking a return to bad or adversarial IR. They simply wanted their interests represented by an expert body. The reason that they had kept up their individual membership of the trade union was as a form of employment protection insurance. It therefore seemed sensible to ask the company to recognize the union as a single formal means of conducting IR. Nothing need be changed. Attitudes, commitment, productivity, and organizational performance would all be kept up; indeed, it should be enhanced, because IR would be conducted by a body that knew what it was doing, rather than on a basis of informality.

The chief executive refused to listen. He reported to his shareholders that all of the old IR problems of the past had not gone away, they had merely been suppressed. He asked for resources to force the staff to relinquish their trade union membership; and if they refused to do this, to support him when he dismissed them.

Accordingly, he dismissed those that he perceived to be the ringleaders of this movement. Productivity plummeted; absenteeism and staff turnover soared. Customer complaints increased; and there began a history of poor quality work, bad scheduling and late deliveries.

The company was sold on to an American multinational in 1996. The new owners came in determined to stamp out trade union subversion. Accordingly, they summoned the local ISTC official to a meeting and peremptorily informed him that under no circumstances would the trade union be allowed any involvement in the organization. When the ISTC official mildly pointed out to the new American owners that under UK law, people were allowed to join the trade union of their choice, or not to join any trade union at all, he was ejected. Convinced that they had bought a bad company, the new owners closed it down and sold the assets for property development.

Chapter 4

Collective bargaining

Collective bargaining is a uniquely UK employee relations arrangement. Its purpose is to make collective (as distinct from individual) bargains or agreements on behalf of those involved. Collective bargaining takes place at industrial, organizational, plant, divisional and unit levels.

The key to effective collective bargaining is negotiation. The strength of the approach is that each party comes to the bargaining table with a clear view of what they want – for example, what level of pay is required or on offer; hours of work required or on offer; other terms and conditions of employment required or on offer. Its great weakness is that it tends overwhelmingly to be adversarial and time consuming. It is compounded by facts, beliefs and perceptions on the one hand that what employees and their representatives demand is unreasonable in the circumstances; and on the other hand that what employers and their representatives have to offer is designed to ensure that they keep the lion's share of whatever is available for themselves and their shareholders.

Collective bargaining is overwhelmingly about pay and terms and conditions of employment. It is concerned with the following.

*   *Substance:* what is on offer or demanded; the context in which it is on offer or demanded; any other limiting factors – for example, increased work commitments in return for increased pay rates.
*   *Behavioural:* requiring special attention to the forms, processes, rites and rituals of the situation; matters of media presentation; gaining the known or perceived moral high ground; the use of forms of language in reaching agreement, and in implementing those agreements.

Agreements are made as follows.

*   *At national level:* minimum pay, terms, conditions and performance rates are established, which give a clear guideline to all those in the sector.
*   *At regional or local level:* these may be topped up according to special local needs – the need to compete for scarce labour resources; the inability to recruit at minimum levels; and so on.
*   *At organizational, divisional or plant level:* national minima are accepted; and these will again be topped up through specific attention to productivity, payments and targets, overtime requirements, specific issues concerning other work patterns – for example, shift work; part-time work; short-time work.

Consideration of local factors gives rise to the phenomenon known as *wages drift*. Wages drift upwards when specific local factors are applied. This is always taken into account by employers' associations at national level when they are establishing their agreed minima.

Negotiating

Whenever anyone concerned with effective IR enters into any form of negotiation, they must have their own aims and objectives and understand, above all, what their preferred outcomes are. In such cases, they will have in mind:

- their own dream scenario, in which everything is settled on precisely their terms;
- a baseline – below which they will not drop;
- a field of negotiation in between the two, in which there is scope for agreement.

Those concerned should always pre-prepare their own case, establishing what they are seeking, when, where, how and why. They need to know any constraints within which they have to act. They also need to be aware of any opportunities afforded by a wider consideration of the matter in hand. They must have an understanding (if not sympathy) with the position of the others involved, and of what they want, when, where, how and why; and of the substance, merits and demerits of their case.

Anyone who promises anything in a negotiation must be able to deliver it if it is agreed. If they do not, they simply cause much deeper conflict, and long and injuring mistrust (see Summary Box 4.1).

Conducting effective negotiations also requires a complete understanding of the behavioural norms of the situation. If it is necessary to let

SUMMARY BOX 4.1

Labour negotiations: the education sector in the 1980s

In 1982, teachers in secondary schools and further and higher education colleges were told by the Department for Education that they would have to accept annual performance appraisal as part of their terms and conditions of employment. In return for this, the then Education Secretary, Sir Keith Joseph, promised all concerned a 15 per cent pay rise.

The proposal was accepted lock, stock and barrel by the trade unions representing the school and college teachers.

The offer was promptly withdrawn. To this date, no effective performance appraisal scheme exists in secondary schools and colleges. There was a widely held view – never denied – that the offer was made simply on the grounds that the Department for Education and Secretary of State were absolutely certain that it would be rejected, and that consequently school and college teachers could be portrayed as seeing themselves as above the constraints imposed on other people in other working situations.

someone have their say, and if by doing so, the process is advanced, then this must be allowed. This above all applies where there is a potentially explosive or extreme situation, or a serious crisis in the making.

It is also necessary to be aware of the continuing need to work effectively and harmoniously at the same time as collective bargaining is being carried out. Even where the matter in hand may result in a serious dispute, this should not hide or obscure the basic requirement for the eventual production of an harmonious working environment.

Those concerned in negotiations therefore require:

*   strategic, tactical and situational awareness;
*   empathy;
*   judgement;
*   situational understanding;
*   the ability to communicate in the correct ways according to the nature of the situation.

Collective bargaining is based on mistrust and conflict – that is, that there is a fundamental divergence of interest between employers and employees. At stake initially, therefore, is a basis on which the two can agree to cooperate together at all. This is made more difficult or extreme where there exists a long history and tradition of workplace conflict.

THE COLLECTIVE BARGAINING PROCESS

At its most effective, collective bargaining is a strategy and structure for the management of this conflict. Summary Box 4.2 shows the ritualized nature of labour relations and bargaining. Much of the process is therefore stylized and ritualized, and anyone who wishes to operate it effectively must understand the importance of this. The purpose must be to use both instruments and language to gain workplace agreements that at least contain conflicts that are inherent. It is also formalized, so that everyone concerned and involved understands their particular part or role in the situation.

The bargaining framework

There is a broad bargaining framework to understand (see Figure 4.1).

*   The *first offer or claim* is always made on the basis that it will be rejected (if for any reason it is accepted straight away, it generally causes resentment rather than instant satisfaction).
*   There then follows a process of *counter-offer and counter-claim*, with each party working its way gradually towards the other.
*   The content of the *final agreement* is usually clearly signalled before it is made; and the basis of what is genuinely acceptable to each party is signalled also.

**SUMMARY
BOX 4.2**

**Behavioural
theories of
labour
relations**

Walton and McKersie (1965) distinguish four interrelated processes.
These are

- *Distributive bargaining:* the resolution of conflicts of interest. This is the classical collective bargaining process. It concludes a consideration of the costs, benefits and opportunities afforded by each side of an industrial dispute; the ability and strength of each party concerned; and the bargaining position, tactics and postures to be adopted. The process consists of assessing the opponent's standpoints and likely responses to particular moves; the use of tactics which influence the opponent's perceptions; the manipulation of the opponent's perceptions of his own position of strength, either by changing his views of the value of his own demands or by changing his view of the unpleasantness or unacceptability of the other side's proposals; affecting the costs of the dispute to one's own advantage; setting deadlines, 'final deadlines', 'final, final deadlines' and so on; and manifesting all of this in a degree of commitment that is necessary to ensure victory in the dispute. Finally, in such a situation it may or may not be necessary to demonstrate that one side or the other has won at the expense of the other; in such cases forms of words and other face saving formulae may need to be devised.
- *Integrative bargaining:* this is the process by which common or complementary interests are found and is the means by which problems are resolved in the interests of all parties concerned. In this way, both sides gain; the purpose therefore is not to conduct a dispute but to find a means of resolving it in the interests of all concerned. The confrontational postures and stance indicated above do not form part of integrative bargaining. The process adopted rather uses a problem-solving model – that is, the identifying of the issue or matter of concern; searching for alternative solutions and extrapolating their consequences; and from this, choosing a preferred course of action.
- *Attitudinal structuring:* this is the process by which each side influences the attitudes of the participants towards the other. In this situation attitudes are formed and modified by the nature of the orientation that each party has towards each other and towards the matter in hand. This may either be competitive, whereby the parties are motivated to defeat or win the other over to their own point of view; this may be individualistic, in which the parties concerned pursue their own self-interests without any regard for the position of the other; or it may be cooperative, whereby each party is concerned about the other as well as its own position. An extreme form of this may be a form of collusion, whereby the parties concerned form a coalition in which they pursue a common purpose possibly to the detriment of other groups within the organization.
- *Staff relations:* the final matter to be considered here is the form of intra-organizational style of staff relations that is concerned to maintain a balance and equilibrium about the organization; and to prevent issues from arising that affect this balance. The main part of this process is to ensure that people understand the true nature and strength of their own position; to ensure that people's expectations are met in such situations; and to ensure that the two are compatible.

Source: Walton and McKersie (1965)

- Serious disputes occur either when one side is determined *not to settle*; or when there is a genuine *misreading* of the signals; or when there is a genuine misunderstanding of the positions.
- Settlements reached are normally couched in *positive terms* in relation to all concerned, to avoid the use of words such as 'loss', 'loser', 'climb-down' and 'defeat', which have negative connotations for anyone associated with them, and tend to store up resentment for the future, and polarize attitudes for the next round of negotiations.

The following standpoints in the bargaining process may usefully be identified:

- It may be necessary to settle with one group or part of the workforce, at the expense of others (distributive).
- It may be possible to resolve problems to the satisfaction of all concerned (integrative).
- It may not be possible to satisfy everyone, or anyone, fully.
- It may be necessary to take a hard initial stance to try and persuade the other party to revise its expectations.

Part of the function of the process is also to structure the attitudes of each party towards the other, and to try and build impressions of honesty, trust, openness, firmness, reasonableness and fairness, as necessary. This can only be done if fundamental credibility and mutuality of interest and understanding is fully established.

Objectives of bargaining systems

Within this context, collective bargaining systems have four specific objectives.

- To provide a means for agreeing the price of labour.
- To provide a means of industrial government, and establishing workplace rules and regulations.
- To provide a means for controlling the stresses and strains inherent in any work situation.
- To provide a means for the conduct and resolution of disputes.

Formal and informal bargaining systems
There are both formal and informal systems to be considered. The former is constituted with agenda, objectives, purposes, outcomes, deadlines and timescales; the latter is the means by which the former is oiled, and consists of corridor meetings, contacts and networks that enable the formal system to function. Public services, municipal and local authorities, and multinational companies tend to have sophisticated formal procedures and highly developed networks, which are extensively used and relied upon to identify the often complex issues which the IR institutions of such organizations have to address.

Figure 4.1

The collective
bargaining process

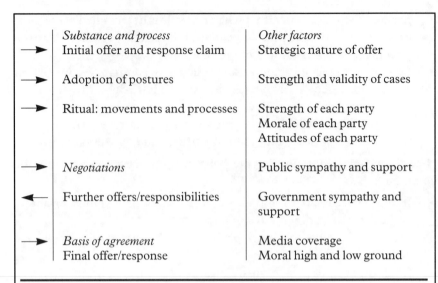

Substance and process	Other factors
Initial offer and response claim	Strategic nature of offer
Adoption of postures	Strength and validity of cases
Ritual: movements and processes	Strength of each party Morale of each party Attitudes of each party
Negotiations	Public sympathy and support
Further offers/responsibilities	Government sympathy and support
Basis of agreement Final offer/response	Media coverage Moral high and low ground

Process

Offer	Area of Agreement	Claim

A	B		C	D
Low				High
				Staff/ union
Management				

The collective bargaining process: offers between A and B rejected by staff; between C and D instantly accepted by staff; claims between A and B instantly accepted by management; between C and D rejected by management; B–C is the basis for negotiated settlement; normal first offer is around A, which leads to instant rejection; normal first claim is around D, but engages the process.

Work organization traditions

Histories and traditions of work organization must be acknowledged. This takes place either through the reformation of bargaining activities, or through the effective management of a wide range of employees' representatives and multi-unionism. All this has its origin in the differentiation of occupations, demarcation, restrictive practices and barriers to occupational entry, devised by groups of workers to protect their trades and give them a measure of exclusivity; and allowed to grow by employers, partly because their need for staff was overwhelming, partly because they had no alternative to offer, and partly because they were unable or unwilling to address the problems that cause this form of industrial organization.

Employee expectations

Employee expectations have either to be met, or to be understood and dealt with. Employees expect an annual percentage pay rise and improvement in conditions. There have also arisen concepts of 'pay leagues', whereby a given occupation would offer terms and conditions of employment in relation to other occupations. To alter these 'leagues' generated resentment on the part of those occupations which perceived themselves to be moving down the 'table'. Closely related to this is the general concept of the 'going rate' for a job – the anticipation that, by joining a particular occupation, a known range of benefits will be forthcoming.

IR AND REALPOLITIK

In IR terms, this is the art of being effective in the total organization in which activities are being carried out. It requires full situational knowledge and understanding. Those concerned have therefore to devise their own means and methods of becoming effective.

They must be able to survive long enough to do this. It follows from this that they must understand and be able to work within the formal and informal systems of the organization and to establish their place in them. Especially in the informal system, they will require to find their own niches, and from there go on and develop networks and support within the organization and its IR mechanisms. Large, complex and sophisticated organizations have many layers of both formal and informal organization, determined by profession, location, status, department and division; and people in such situations must discover those that are suitable, those that are unsuitable, those that are supportive, and those that are antagonistic.

They will therefore develop a keen environmental sense. This comprises the ability to spot 'straws in the wind', gain access to the grapevine, become aware of particular and possible changes, developments, innovations and crises. It requires recognition of the departments, divisions, functions and individuals where actual power and influence truly lie. It also requires access to, and generation of, sources of information from within the complexities of the organization, and away from its formal channels.

Those concerned need to assess their own genuine position in the organizational pecking order; and the extent to which they carry true influence in the process of creating effective IR. They will assess their own strengths and weaknesses, the sources of support, the sources and reasons of antagonism and jealousy, and the capabilities and capacities that are required in order to be effective.

They will identify where inter-group frictions (and sometimes hostilities) lie and assess the reasons for these; and in the same way, identify where inter-group alliances are formed. It is necessary to assess where people's loyalties truly lie; and whether they have their own secondary or hidden agenda. Especially in collective bargaining, and other traditional IR situations in the UK, it may be necessary to form alliances on the basis of '*If you support me in matter x, I will support you in matter y*', and so on.

It should be clear from this that the potential for organizational damage, and damage of relationships between individuals and groups within organizations, is extremely high. Much of the operation of collective bargaining, and the organization realpolitik that goes with it, is extremely negative (see Summary Box 4.3). If it is not conducted as effectively as possible, given the extreme constraints indicated above, it is extremely demoralizing and debilitating, both on the staff, and also therefore on the organizations, customers and clients. Ideally, when organizations recognize the problems and pitfalls inherent in these situations, it is necessary for them to take remedial steps, both in the short term to alleviate immediate problems; and also in the medium to long term, to devise more effective and positive IR strategies.

SUMMARY BOX 4.3

Collective bargaining and the EU

Many opponents of the collective bargaining approach to employee relations also tend to view the EU concept of 'social partners' with deep suspicion. There is a widely held view that the social partner approach is simply collective bargaining under another heading.

There is no need for this to be the case. The EU standpoint, and language used, are both different. The EU cites 'a partnership' – rather than a series of conflicting, divergent and entrenched self-interest groups. It also cites ER as being a key feature of overall organization direction and strategy, and integral to commercial success and well-being, rather than as a separate – and costly – organizational activity.

Moreover, as the EU develops its social policy, the place of organizations within it, and the interests of employees, it is clear that these objectives are not to be achieved by recourse to traditional UK collective bargaining processes. The adversarial perspective is contrary to the view advanced by the EU and its institutions for the development of economic prosperity and social harmony. The partnership of the approach requires openness and mutuality of interest; the collective bargaining approach reinforces the divergence and divisions between the interests of particular groups.

The key to the creation of effective collective bargaining systems is communication. Within this, there is clearly a range of core issues that require full understanding. These are:

- that effective IR is based on agreements which everybody understands and accepts; high quality, continuing and full information; the creation of effective channels of communication;
- recognition of the effect that broader organizational activities have on the development and advancement of IR;
- recognition of the fact that, whatever the overall design of IR, its effective implementation can only be achieved if there is clear direction, and precise principles of design on the part of the organization; and that effective institutions, procedures and practices are then generated so that it can be managed, maintained and improved on an operational basis;
- recognition of the fact that, if collective bargaining is a part of organizational IR, then attention is required for each part of the process so that it works as well as possible;
- recognition of the need to develop the awareness and capability of everyone involved to work within bargaining processes and systems, so that they are operated as effectively as possible;
- understanding the legitimate aspirations of all those involved in the situation, and the reasons why these are held.

Collective bargaining remains in extensive use in UK industry and public services. In recent years, its effectiveness as a means of IR conduct and management has been enhanced where there have been shifts away from aggressive and confrontational attitudes towards a more considered approach. If it is to remain as a legitimate and effective vehicle for the conduct of IR, those involved are going to have to develop a still greater understanding of the context, basis and conduct of this approach.

Chapter 5

Industrial relations without unions

INTRODUCTION   There is no line of corporate, industrial or managerial reasoning which arrives at the logical conclusion that people in organizations need representation. The need for representation grew up and became a part of UK industrial culture because of the shortcomings of employers. These shortcoming concerned all aspects of work organization, and their most universal outputs were – and remain – in staff management, labour relations, fairness and equity of treatment, managerial style, and attitude to staff. This might be said to be everything that contributes to IR.

Those who seek to run IR in their organizations without unions or other formal representation arrangements do so for a variety of reasons which may be grouped under the following headings.

- A matter of corporate policy which may reject trade unions for the most positive of reasons ('there is no need for them'); or the most negative ('we're not having them').
- People culture: in which the overriding mutuality of interest has to be maintained, and which the presence and involvement of trade unions would be perceived to dilute.
- A lack of history and tradition in the sector or locality of trade union activity.
- A bad history or tradition in the sector or locality of trade union activity; or an organizational, managerial or individual history of bad IR involving trade unions, leading to the organizational view – legitimate or otherwise – that their staff relationships were damaged or destroyed in the past through union involvement, and that there must therefore be an alternative to this form of IR.
- Prejudices: of the 'we are not having the monkeys running the zoo' variety; or because of the fact, belief or perception that unions represent particular political or extremist points of view.
- Paternalism: the form of unitarism or conformism that states that in return for doing things in the organization's way, top managers and directors will 'look after the staff' (see Summary Box 5.1).
- Cost: the true cost of involving unions in any way outweighs the benefits and advantages accrued.

Each of these is subjective and prejudicial. A more considered and businesslike approach is likely to take one or more of the following views:

SUMMARY
BOX 5.1

The non-
union
approach:
examples

IR in the 1980s
The UK Conservative government of the 1980s advanced the view that much of the industrial and commercial malaise in the UK could be ascribed to the negative effects and activities of trade unions. The point of view was reinforced by the fact that politicians did nothing to suppress anti-union prejudices. There was also extensive legislation to codify and formalize the ways in which trade unions were allowed to carry out their business in general, and to pursue disputes and grievances in particular.

Successful organizations
It is also true that many of the organizations that are held up as beacons of commercial and managerial successes do not recognize trade unions. Examples are:

- *The Body Shop:* which sets high and distinctive standards of ethics and morality in staff management as well as customer service; and which is highly paternalistic in culture (though it ran into some commercial difficulties in 1999).
- *Marks & Spencer:* held up as a beacon of unrivalled commercial success, based on the fact that as well as being an excellent provider of high quality products and services, it was an excellent employer (though again in 1999, it ran into commercial difficulties).
- *John Lewis Partnership:* in which the staff are treated on the basis of complete openness of information, published bi-monthly in company journals; and which is sustained through continued attention to performance and output figures, the human resource at large, and a paternalistic style of management.

- lack of confidence in the quality or expertise of the local or sectoral union and its officials;
- lack of willingness on the part of the staff to join the local or sectoral union;
- the creation of an in-house alternative which is better able to represent the distinctive point of view, skills and expertise of those working for the organization;

and, most of all:

- creating conditions within the organization that remove all of the reasons why people choose or seek to join a trade union (see Summary Box 5.2).

The reasons why people join trade unions are:

- *Fear:* of job loss; pay and terms and conditions loss, disadvantage or dilution; bullying, harassment, victimization and discrimination.
- *Management style and approach:* closely related to fear.
- *Collective capability:* in which it is perceived that the whole – the ability to act in a group – is greater than the sum of individual efforts.

THE REASONS WHY PEOPLE JOIN TRADE UNIONS

SUMMARY BOX 5.2

Joining a union

> As stated in Chapter 3, anyone may choose to join a trade union; or they may choose not to join.
>
> Equally, employers need not recognize trade unions unless they choose to do so, or unless demanded by a clear majority of the staff.
>
> Where trade unions are not recognized, individuals may nevertheless take up or keep up their membership; and they will be able to call on the services of the union if they subsequently find themselves in serious trouble – e.g. employment tribunal; or involvment in industrial accident, injury or disaster.

- *Psychological distance and barriers:* leading to the fact, belief or perception that some groups of staff are at greater risk of being treated with less favour than others; and that such groups would require expert representation in their dealings with the organization.
- *Employment insurance:* for the present and also for the future – especially if there is some real or perceived disadvantage likely or possible in the future, e.g. privatization of what is at present a public service; merger, takeover or divestment; closure or withdrawal from current areas of activity.
- *Legalization and formalization of contracts of employment:* (and of terms and conditions of employment), gives rise to the fact, belief or perception that it is necessary to have some form of expert representation available as and when required.
- *Occupational insurance:* required by statute in certain occupations or professions, especially the public professions of medicine, nursing, teaching and social work.
- *Member benefits:* that the returns on the subscription are known, believed or perceived to outweigh the subscription outgoings; many unions now offer advantageous Visa cards, car, home and travel insurance, and private health care.
- *Subscription levels:* which are generally a few pounds per month only, and therefore affordable to all.

Any organization seeking to conduct long-term effective, stable, harmonious – and profitable – IR without formal representation has to establish a climate, culture and ethos in which as many of these elements as possible are removed.

TACKLING THE REASONS WHY PEOPLE JOIN TRADE UNIONS

Some of these are clearly more straightforward than others. It is not possible to tackle occupational insurance, though it is clearly not necessary to recognize the particular trade union on an organized or formalized basis (see Summary Box 5.3).

Many industrial concerns employ their own nursing and medical staff. Such companies may or may not recognize the Royal College of Nursing or UNISON as a trade union, whether or not they recognize other unions. Nurses have to belong to the Royal College of Nursing or UNISON in order to gain their professional indemnity insurance.

Similarly, the rush for privatization of care for the elderly, handicapped and disadvantaged has led to a great increase in the number of qualified nurses and social workers employed in the private sector. Many of these organizations are very small and do not recognize any trade unions for any reason.

Professionally qualified staff are eligible to apply for jobs in these sectors and agree their own main terms and conditions of employment with the particular employers. However, their professional training and indemnity, supported by their union membership, means that there are specific aspects of professional and expert practice that they must carry out in certain ways; and that there are certain activities that they may not carry out at all.

Similarly, people may keep up their membership because of the range of material (as distinct from organizational or occupational) benefits on offer. The organization may not insist that an individual ceases to be a member of a trade union as a condition of employment or continued employment, even if the union is not recognized.

The main issues that organizations that need to tackle are fear, management style, collective capability and psychological distance and division.

Fear

There is no such thing as a safe job. In recent years, such diverse organizations as the army and the Church of England have gone through programmes of compulsory redundancy. Even where there are nationally defined shortages of nurses, doctors and teachers, or train and bus drivers, people in these occupations have nevertheless lost their job. It is impossible to guarantee employment. It is, however, possible to ensure that people are kept actively informed of the present and developing stage of the organization, and the implications for employment prospects overall, and IR in particular.

Similarly, it is possible to remove bullying, victimization, harassment and intimidation by dismissing the perpetrators when such cases are found, investigated and proven.

Attention to these is an active managerial and organizational responsibility. Nothing is more certain to drive people to seek the measure of security and insurance that union membership brings them than failing to tackle issues surrounding employment security and these forms of victimization.

Management and supervisory style

There is no reason why at any place of work, in any occupation, industrial, commercial or public service activity, management and supervisory style should be adversarial or negative. It nevertheless remains true that this approach is commonplace in all sectors and in all forms of organization (see Summary Box 5.4).

SUMMARY BOX 5.4

Adversarial management style: examples

- *Local government:* a county council in southern England disciplined a chief officer for financial irregularities. When it became clear that the case was without foundation, the county council found a technicality on which to dismiss the chief officer anyway. At one stage during the proceedings, the person leading the county council's case stated, 'At the end of the day, it is your Visa card against our budget of £135 million.'
- *Industrial production:* at a plastics factory on the outskirts of London, the chief executive gave his own personal view of his approach to industrial relations. This was summarized as 'I have all my staff on a final warning, and if I cannot get them on something legitimate, I will make things up.'
- *Financial services:* a sales manager at a highly prestigious city firm made a point of dismissing his lowest performing sales person every quarter. This, he felt, was the way to keep everybody 'on their toes'.
- *Telecommunications:* at a large telecommunications company, a member of the engineering staff was dismissed by his supervisor. The supervisor was subsequently told by the company's IR director that dismissal could not be carried out until a full investigation had been carried out into the matter. The supervisor's response was 'Well, I sacked him anyway.'
- *Postal services:* in South London, a postman was dismissed for a minor misdemeanour. He appealed, and subsequently won reinstatement. He was then kept suspended on full pay at home while the supervisor who had dismissed him tried to scrape together enough other minor misdemeanours – none supported in writing – to dismiss him anyway

Management style may be allowed to emerge or it may be created and designed.

Emergent management style

This is developed from the sum of the approaches in existence at a given point within the organization. It is affected by a combination of factors as follows.

- Recent history of labour relations at the organization overall; and within particular departments, divisions, occupations and functions.
- What is rewarded and punished within managerial and supervisory ranks (see Summary Box 5.5).
- The extent of influence of the views, attitudes and actions of over-mighty subjects, over-mighty players and over-mighty departments (see Summary Box 5.6).

The most insidious approaches to rewards and punishments are as follows.

- *Problem-solving:* in which individuals, perceiving themselves to be rewarded on the basis of solving problems, either look for problems to solve or else – worst of all – create them.
- *Loyalty:* in which long servers are rewarded ahead of those who are effective and successful at their jobs.
- *Output targets:* at all costs.
- *Forms of words:* in which particular phrases are designed to get individuals off the hook – to ensure that no blame is attached to them for particular misdemeanours or mistakes. This is at its worst when it is known, believed or perceived that this approach applies to top and senior managers, but not to others lower down the organization.
- *Regular and extensive use of ACAS and employment tribunals:* to absolve responsibility for mistakes made.

SUMMARY BOX 5.5

Rewards and punishments

- *Over-mighty subjects:* as we have seen elsewhere, an over-mighty subject is any individual who exerts an undue personal (as distinct from organizational) influence on all organizational activities, including IR. From this point of view, this can be taken to mean anyone who is allowed to contribute to an adversarial or emergent management style by virtue of their personality or prejudices by which they run their particular part of the organization. Some site managers or regional managers, for example, run their locations as kingdoms. Staff are actively discouraged – even bullied or intimidated – from approaching anyone away from the site with problems.
- *Over-mighty divisions and departments:* industrial and commercial legends hold these as maintenance, information and computing functions. They become over-mighty when they are allowed to prioritize or ration their input with, and relationships with, other departments, divisions and functions according to strength of personality rather than operational necessity.

SUMMARY BOX 5.6

Over-mighty subjects, divisions and departments: examples

- Prevailing prejudices – especially negative prejudices – about different groups of staff, especially where these have grown up around legends, preconceived ideas, halo effects and stereotyping; and most insidiously and unacceptably of all, around local, regional, national, racial and gender stereotypes (see Summary Box 5.7).
- Managerial and supervisory structures and reporting relations – especially those that are ineffective or inappropriate, but which are nevertheless the driving force behind managerial progress and priority. These are especially the cases at remote head offices, and reinforce and feed the problems and prejudices indicated in Summary Boxes 5.4, 5.5, 5.6 and 5.7.
- Lack of managerial and supervisory understanding and training – this

**SUMMARY
BOX 5.7**

**Stereotypes
and prejudice:
examples**

- *Frozen food:* in 1988, a major frozen food producer closed its operation in north-western England. The company head office in London had decided that people from that part of the world could not be relied upon to produce any effective work.
- *Local government:* in 1993, a county council in southern England was making a junior managerial appointment. There were two candidates, one male, one female. The female candidate went first. When the male candidate was interviewed, he was asked 'When are you going to give all this up and go and have babies?' The candidate was flabbergasted. It subsequently transpired that the female candidate had been asked this question in this way, and had insisted that the same question was put to the male candidate. The question was asked by a senior officer from the council's Corporate Personnel Team. Knowing that this was both prejudicial and illegal, he had nevertheless decided to go ahead anyway.

is often compounded where the best operational, technical or practitioner staff have been promoted beyond their level of competence, or into an area where they have no previous expertise or experience (see Summary Box 5.8).

**SUMMARY
BOX 5.8**

**The Peter
Principle**

'The Peter Principle' was defined by L. J. Peter (1970) as 'promotion or progression beyond the level of incompetence'. Examples of the effects of 'the Peter Principle' upon university organizational IR are as follows.

- A very prestigious university in London paid out large sums in compensation to teaching and research staff in one of its departments. This was as the result of errors by the head of department. The head of department had been appointed because of his pre-eminence in his academic field. He was given no managerial training, including in the field of industrial relations. Accordingly, he had seen fit to dismiss certain members of staff, because he did not like them.
- In the Education Support Services Department of the same university, a new manager was appointed. At his first management meeting he bemoaned the low quality of his staff. He stated that he could do nothing with his people; he asserted that the staff were a law unto themselves and that they could not be made to do any work at all. There was consequently no effective education support that his department could provide.
- At a university in south-west England, the head of the Education Department made a practice of paying people off with huge sums of money – including greatly enhanced redundancy payments and early retirement options. This was because he would rather spend money this way than face people with shortcomings.

Created and designed

Whether for a new or existing organization, management style has to be created and designed if it is to be effective. This means that the following issues are decided on at corporate level, and then promulgated through the IR instruments, procedures and practices.

- *IR policy and direction:* deciding on the overall approach to be taken; setting standards of attitude, behaviour and performance; and paying especial attention to what will, and will not be, tolerated.

- *IR management practice:* whether remote and distant, or visible and accessible; whether dealt with by all managers or a specialist IR function; the extent of the remit given to managers and supervisors at different levels to resolve IR issues; the nature of support given to managers and supervisors when they do tackle IR issues.

- *Management and supervisory training:* in terms of content, and also of the attitude and standpoint from which it is delivered. Problems always occur when managers and supervisors are taught an open basis on which to tackle such matters, but then have to deliver these in adversarial situations, or with little or no support from their own superiors.

- *Reinforcement with actions:* for example, where examples of discipline, discrimination and harassment do occur the perpetrators are indeed dismissed. If this form of reinforcement is not present, then the words and policy become empty and meaningless. Worse still, if someone then subsequently sets out to change standards, they may come up against the possibility of having to face legal proceedings and tribunal cases from those who were, or are now, disadvantaged as the result (see Summary Box 5.9).

Upward spiral

If the IR approach is created and designed, then everyone involved understands where they stand, and also the totality of the broader situation and environment.

If the conscious decision that IR is to be conducted on an adversarial, punitive and proceduralized basis, then those involved can in turn assess the likely volume of their time and energy that will need to be taken in addressing, institutionalizing and resolving discipline, grievance and dispute matters. Those in charge of resources allocation can apportion amounts of finance and staff time as the result. Everyone therefore goes into the situation knowing the opportunities and consequences of the approach.

If the conscious decision is taken that IR is to be open and conformist, then resources need to be apportioned to allow time for staff meetings, management and supervision by 'walking about', discussion and consultation.

The following examples are illustrations of where serious problems have occurred as the result of absolute standards being varied at some point.

- *Plastics extrusion:* a plastics extrusion production line had to be kept open and running continuously. If it were allowed to switch itself off, or to fail, it cost the company thousands of pounds to clean the machinery and start the process up again. Accordingly, anyone who was late for work without explanation on this process was subject to instant dismissal. Over the period since 1985, 42 members of staff had been dismissed as the result of this practice. On the three occasions when it had been tested at employment tribunal, dismissal was found to be fair. Recently, however, a member of staff was not dismissed for exactly the same misdemeanour – failing to turn up on time without explanation. Refusing to dismiss the individual, the production manager said 'The individual is from an ethnic minority, and I do not want racial trouble.' The company was successfully sued by many of the previous incumbents who had been dismissed.

- *Education:* in the north-west of England, a senior teacher undertook extensive management training, and was appointed to the deputy headship of a comprehensive school. Subsequently, the person, a lady in her late forties, applied for six school headships, and was unsuccessful on each occasion. She asked a chief officer at the education head office why this was so. He replied 'Off the record, it is because of sex discrimination. We are not appointing women to these positions.' The lady was severely traumatized, and lost her career and her livelihood. The official from the Education Department was subsequently promoted twice, and now holds a very senior position elsewhere in the country.

Whichever approach is taken, it, in turn, needs to be reinforced with substantial managerial and supervisory training and staff induction and briefing. The result is therefore to create an upward spiral on which IR principles and practices are developed and enhanced. Whether an adversarial or conformist approach is taken, the instruments and practices by which it is managed become sharper and more effective in operation.

Collective capability

In human terms, people have a strong sense of wishing to conform, belong and be accepted. In general management terms, group cohesion is a key part of seeking positive commitment, interest and enthusiasm for both particular departments and also the organization overall. In IR terms, people band together when they know, believe or perceive that their collective effort is likely to produce greater returns than if they approach the organization as individuals.

If they feel that they need to do so, they will identify a collective or common interest, and use this as the basis on which to lobby or bargain.

The best management response is to understand this. The usual management responses are to try to 'divide and rule', or to pick off individuals who are known, believed or perceived to have influence over the rest of the group.

Neither of these approaches works in the long term. The IR problem may or may not be solved or contained, but there is always a knock-on effect on the quality of work, cohesion, and therefore on work output. Also, because a concern which the group has itself believed to be legitimate has not been treated with the respect it deserved, there is a more widely damaging effect on overall morale. This, moreover, is not confined to the particular group in question. The result of their lobby or approach will be known by the rest of the organization, as will the managerial attitude and approach taken in response. All of this has an adverse effect on IR in particular, and normally also has a negative effect on overall organizational performance.

The only way around this is to ensure that, when an issue is raised in such a way, it is treated with respect. Organizations need to recognize that matters are only raised in such a way if there is sufficient group interest to do so; or else that the particular issue is symptomatic of a more serious problem. In either case, the quicker it is faced openly, the more easily it is resolved (see Summary Box 5.10).

Psychological distance and barriers

The presence of these barriers reinforces organizational divisions in general and IR divisions in particular. The output is to create cohesive, orderly, organized groups that lobby on their own behalf for advantage in pay and terms and conditions of employment, often at the expense of others. The problem is compounded when particular groups have an operational or organizational bargaining chip that enables them to ration, apportion or prioritize the amount of work that they carry out elsewhere in the organization; and this especially applies to maintenance, computing, facilities management and information management functions (see above; and see Summary Box 5.11).

The effect is always to dilute the quality, effectiveness and profitability of output, because a substantial part of time, energy and resource, including corporate finance, is being used by the different protagonists on designing and shoring up their own particular corners and interests. It is a short step from this to creating the fact, belief or perception of infallibility or indispensability. In the long term, both require major corporate confrontation if they are to be resolved.

The problem also occurs when psychological barriers are erected. They become known or believed to be insurmountable. When this happens, both the general operational situation, and the specific IR aspects, remain

SUMMARY BOX 5.10

Divide and rule

Advocates of this approach normally take the view that this form of expediency 'shows the workers who is boss' and is an output of 'the right to manage'. Curiously, nobody ever refers to this as part of 'the capability to manage'.

Manchester United (1970s)

This football club went through many managerial upheavals in the 1970s. Matters came to a head when one of these managers, Tommy Docherty, got rid of one of the star players from a previous generation, Willie Morgan. He gave the player express permission to not take part in a club tour, and then notified the local newspaper that the player had refused to take part in the club tour.

Short-term performance was improved, and the club won the FA Cup in 1978. However, the deeper malaise was not resolved. The club did not win the football championship until 1992. Following the Cup win in 1978, Tommy Docherty was dismissed for having an affair with the wife of another member of staff.

The University of London

In 1995, one of the colleges of the University of London appointed a new head of department to one of its most prestigious institutions. In three years, this head of department reduced student intake from 30 to 8. He removed high quality staff, all with substantial expertise in their field, and replaced these with lesser performers.

When the individual left the institution in 1998, he stated, 'I did not know what I was doing. The staff that I got rid off were brighter and cleverer than me. It seemed sensible therefore, to pick these off one by one and to replace them with people that I knew and understood, and that I could control.'

tenable only as long as the groups behind their psychological barriers operate with full integrity.

In practice, it invariably happens that, when they do need to meet, forms of words are devised that mean that real issues are not tackled; and the forms of words come to reinforce the barriers rather than break them down. In these cases, IR problems become both managerial and operational crises and are sometimes only resolved or even partly addressed as the result of a major scandal (see Summary Box 5.12).

From whichever point of view organizations and their senior managers decide not to recognize trade unions therefore, and there are many responsibilities which have to be recognized and acknowledged so that IR is conducted as effectively as possible, recognition of the need for attention to each of these points is essential. Not recognizing trade unions neither removes IR in general, nor specific problems, disputes or grievances. It simply alters the means by which they are approached and

SUMMARY
BOX 5.11

Psychological
barriers:
group-think
and the bunker
mentality

There is always the potential for the presence of psychological barriers between groups. With high performance groups or those selected on the basis of excellence or high status in some sphere, there is a short step only from members knowing that they are always clever and excellent, to believing that they are always right.

This is reinforced if they know, believe or perceive that they can ration or prioritize their expertise as indicated in the text. This barrier is then further reinforced if it becomes known, believed or perceived throughout the rest of the organization that they are indeed 'a law unto themselves', operating outside the rules, regulations and norms of the rest of the organization.

In extreme circumstances, this becomes developed still further into a 'bunker mentality'. This occurs where the group becomes so divorced from reality that it develops its own view of the world which becomes the basis for its existence, activities and operations. This occurs regardless of the true natural of the wider environment.

The phrase 'bunker mentality' derives from the bunker used by Hitler and other leaders of the Nazis in the last days of World War II. Rather than come to terms with the reality of their impending defeat, they created their own version of the world within their operations room or bunker.

In IR terms, this form of group cohesion is extremely difficult to break down. Many managers – and IR consultants and experts also – take the view that, from a point of view of expediency at least, the organization is likely to need to find alternative ways of delivering the product or service that the group offers, and to dismiss or disband the group. This has often led to serious industrial action in the past, as for example, when the Fleet Street newspaper industry found itself in serious difficulties as the result of the printers that it employed having developed this extreme form of group cohesion.

resolved. It is further necessary to have in place attitudes, values and ethics, and to ensure that these are developed across the entire organization, as these in turn reinforce the lack of need for people to join trade unions. It is also necessary to have in place formal and regularized means of staff consultation and involvement to ensure that regular reviews of practice, morale and well-being, as well as specific IR issues, are raised and carried out.

ATTITUDES, VALUES AND ETHICS

The conception of attitudes, values and ethics in organizations, and their application to staff management and IR, is not new. These have been studied over centuries; and the lessons of both the present and previous ages are always being re-evaluated. There are some extremely useful points to be made, the understanding of which is essential to any organization and its managers wishing to design, create and maintain its own

SUMMARY BOX 5.12

Bristol Royal Infirmary Child Care Unit (1990s)

In 1998, the activities of the Bristol Royal Infirmary Child Care Unit became a major scandal. It became apparent that surgeons had carried out botched and sloppy work. It also became apparent that none of this would have come to light if it had not been for a substantial and sustained campaign conducted by the parents of those children who had been badly injured, and in some cases had died, as the result.

It subsequently came to light that the situation had grown up as the result of inbuilt and absolute professional identity on the part of the surgeons; and this was reinforced by years of antagonism with hospital managers.

Concerns had indeed been raised with managers by junior medical staff; but the managers concerned had declined to tackle the problem. Indeed, the managers had allowed junior staff turnover, and had spent money on agency and temporary staff and overtime – indeed, anything rather than approach and cross the psychological barrier that existed between themselves and the surgeons.

There were no trade unions involved, only psychological barriers. As well as bringing to light a major IR shortcoming, there was also a devastating general effect on hospital morale. This was compounded by a universal loss of confidence on the part of the public in the services provided.

staff management and IR approach without the involvement of unions (see Summary Box 5.13).

There are major fundamental IR lessons to be drawn from each of these examples as follows.

- The need to establish a particular quality of life, and quality of working life.
- The need to engage the interests and commitment of everyone if productive work is to be sustained.
- The need to attend to the place of work in the whole lives of people.
- The need to treat everyone with fundamental decency, humanity, respect and value.
- The need to engage a much broader interest than the pure wage–work bargain.
- The need to sustain any approach, and the attitudes, values and ethics inherent, over long periods of time.

STAFF REPRESENTA-TION

Even where unions are not recognized, it is usual for organizations to create and sustain equivalent bodies for the effective management of IR. Organizations are increasingly going to be required to formalize these in the creation of works councils in any case. Beyond this, and whether a paternalistic, adversarial or open attitude and approach is taken, it is useful to have means and methods by which regular consultation and

The pyramids of ancient Egypt

In the building of the pyramids and other monuments of ancient Egypt, it is true that the movement of the great volume and weight of materials was only possible because large gangs of slave labour were used. It is equally true that the precision of design, finish, décor and permanence could not have been achieved without engaging, within the broad culture of the era, the interest and commitment of those with this expertise.

The conquests of Julius Caesar

Julius Caesar maintained the loyalty of his army because he never asked them to do anything that he himself was not prepared to do. If they walked, so did he; if they slept in the open, so did he. Whatever his soldiers ate, he himself ate. In his triumphal procession into Rome at the end of his campaign of the year 59 BC, he rode among his soldiers, not at the front or the back of the column.

Religion and the rise of capitalism

The nineteenth century chocolate manufacturers of the UK – Cadbury, Terry, Fry and Macintosh – all brought with them a strong moral sense of the ways in which their organizations were to be structured. They took responsibility for food, shelter, housing, accommodation, education, recreation and overall well-being of their people.

This enlightenment came from the view that healthy, secure employees who were well housed, educated and fed were much more likely to produce high volumes of chocolate, over longer periods of time, than those who had none of these things.

Scientific management

Scientific management was devised by Frederick Winslow Taylor at the turn of the twentieth century. He took the view that by breaking all industrial activities down into their smallest component parts, individuals could be trained and made excellent at one or two aspects. Products could then be manufactured to a much greater level of standardization and precision, and much more quickly, than had previously been possible. The people engaged on the work were to be highly trained in their particular aspects, and well rewarded financially – overpaid in fact – in terms of the work that they actually did.

The Hawthorne studies

The General Electric Company of Chicago commissioned Elton Mayo to carry out studies into the effects of lighting on production at their Hawthorne Chicago factory in 1929. Different groups of staff were gathered together and briefed about the experiments. Each time the level of lighting was raised or lowered, production from the groups rose and was sustained at new higher levels. The analysis of results, however, showed that this had very little to do with the lighting levels themselves. The increases in productivity came about overwhelmingly because of the interest taken in the groups by the company, and also by Mayo and his team of researchers.

SUMMARY BOX 5.13

Attitudes, values and ethics: examples

Voluntary Service Overseas (VSO)

Since VSO was started in the UK by the British Council in 1959, it has always had more takers than placements available. In the late 1990s, there has been a surge in demand for VSO places. Three main reasons are cited for this:

- the need on the part of individuals to create and provide something for humanity above and beyond the commercial or public service wage–work bargain;
- the lack of availability of enough 'worthwhile' jobs to go around for everyone who wants or needs to work;
- the sheer misery of working in impersonal, results-driven and remote organizations.

information exchanges take place. In non-unionized IR these are usually akin to the joint consultative council (JCC) approaches described elsewhere. In larger non-unionized organizations it is usual either for each department, division or function to elect or nominate a representative, or for an individual from each to be required to attend particular meetings. In smaller organizations, this will be less formalized; indeed, the meeting may be conducted with the entire staff. All organizations also use briefing groups and staff meetings at which IR matters are dealt with together with other issues; chief executive and other senior managerial meetings; and other professional and occupational cluster groups. These are reinforced by written documentation, briefings, newsletters and news sheets that again will deal with IR matters as well as other aspects of organizational activity.

Staff associations

Many organizations that do not have trade unions create staff associations. These are normally formally constituted, and their IR remit is defined. Staff associations often have general welfare and social remits, as well as handling the staff side of IR concerns. Staff association representatives may also be asked to represent or act as witness for employees when they are facing discipline and grievance cases.

Otherwise, staff association representatives make any formal representations necessary on behalf of the staff, raising both general and specific IR concerns.

Staff association membership is normally automatic, occurring when the individual joins the organization, and enabling them to gain all the benefits available to staff. Staff association membership is usually free. It also gives automatic access to any social and recreational facilities provided by the organization; and, for example, at the Sandwich, Kent plant of Pfizer, the drug and pharmaceutical company, the social club is run by the staff association on behalf of the company.

There are critics of the staff association approach. It is argued that staff associations cannot be fully independent of the companies that establish them, and that any conduct of IR must therefore be tainted by organization interest rather than absolute equity and justice. It is also argued that pressure can be put on an individual, forcing them to choose between acting in their own best interest, following morally correct courses of action, and potentially damaging their long-term employment interest if they do not follow a known, believed or perceived company line (see Summary Box 5.14).

SUMMARY BOX 5.14

Travel services

A multi-branch travel agency disciplined and then dismissed an employee for persistent poor and shoddy work.

At the outset a full disciplinary hearing was undertaken at which the regional manager heard the case. The individual's manager put forward a case that was unsustainable. It was based entirely on prejudice and gossip – and with no evidence to support it. It quickly became apparent that the individual was being dismissed because their manager did not like them.

The individual was represented by a colleague from the company's fully constituted staff association.

The individual, a woman in her thirties, was dismissed and took the company to employment tribunal. She was represented by the staff association representative who had conducted her case before dismissal. The individual won the case, and the employment tribunal severely criticized the company, the regional manager and the individual's manager.

The staff association representative, a woman in her fifties, was offered a substantial severance payment and early retirement package as the result of her successful conduct of this matter. This she accepted.

The role of unions in non-unionized organizations

On the face of it, this appears an irrelevance. Yet circumstances change. Staff in a non-unionized firm may have the opportunity to join a union following merger or takeover. Staff in a unionized firm may have the option to withdraw from membership following merger or takeover by an organization that does not recognize trade unions. Unionized staff may become disappointed or disillusioned with the quality of representation that they are receiving. Non-unionized staff may be attracted to join a particular union (whether or not their organization is prepared to recognize it) as the result of a recruitment drive, dynamic presentation, or demonstrable benefits to be accrued. Organizations may also change their views on whether or not to recognize trade unions.

Recognition

If the staff have been persuaded to join a union for some reason, some organizations will take the view that it is better to recognize the union, and to draw up a set of terms of reference, guidelines, and terms and conditions by which relations with the union are now to be conducted. In other cases, even if large numbers of staff have been persuaded to join a union, the organization may continue to refuse recognition. In the latter case, however, all but the worst organizations will at least question why so many staff have now found it necessary to join and why they would be willing to do so even if recognition and formalization is not forthcoming.

De-recognition

It also happens that unions may come to be known, believed or perceived as no longer to be serving the best interests of those that they purport to represent. There are a variety of reasons for this as follows.

- The replacement of an excellent local union official with a poor one.
- Change in overt political stance of the union at large.
- Merger of the union with another or others, so that the staff no longer believe that it will continue to serve their own best interests.
- Fall off in union membership among the particular workforce to the extent that a particular union is no longer acting on their behalf.
- The union fails to deliver the desired results and benefits for the members.
- The union fails to deliver the desired attitude to organizational IR.
- The organization chooses to de-recognize for its own stated policy or

SUMMARY BOX 5.15

Co-Steel Sheerness Plc

In the 1980s, in terms of output, productivity and income per member of staff, this was the most productive steel company in the European Union. This was achieved on the back of fully flexible working practices, extensive attention to staff, training and development, and the engagement of the Iron and Steel Trades Confederation as social and consultation partners.

Following a change of management and direction, the union was de-recognized in 1994. The view was taken that the union no longer served the best interests of the staff.

This destroyed the mutuality of interest and commitment that had existed for the previous ten years. The company lost its pre-eminence as a steel producer, and instead engaged in long running and sustained disputes with individuals and groups of staff. The Iron and Steel Trades Confederation also appealed against its de-recognition and engaged both a regular picket on the company, and legal proceedings.

Matters came to a head in 1999, when the company was sold on to a Canadian multinational. Because of declines in productivity and performance, extensive redundancies were announced.

direction, whether or not membership or effectiveness has changed or been affected. This often comes about as the result of merger or takeover. It may also come about as the result of changes in senior staff (see Summary Box 5.15).

Whatever the circumstances, wherever de-recognition is being considered, it is essential not to leave behind an IR void. Discipline, grievance and disputes have still to be handled. Pay rises have still to be agreed and arranged. The management and conduct of consultation, participation, information exchange and involvement – to whatever extent each exist – must be maintained. Whatever management style exists has to be supported and sustained. The staff need to know that the support that existed previously through the offices and activities of the union is going to continue. Wherever de-recognition is considered, the overwhelming managerial responsibility is to ensure this continuity. This is only achieved if an IR strategy is in place for the future at the time of de-recognition.

CONCLUSIONS

Clearly, many of these lessons constitute best practice and should be adopted by anyone with any IR responsibility. The most important and valuable lesson that anyone can learn is the extent of this responsibility. Organizations that recognize, consult and negotiate with unions on a regular basis have, at the very least, a body whose remit it is to signal particular issues and problems, and to make representations, proposals and recommendations for their resolution (though whether the organizations in question actually do anything about them is another issue).

Organizations that do not have this representation have to act in effect as their own mirrors and carry this out for themselves.

In future, moreover, those organizations that do not take an active or participative view of IR are going to have to do this, because the EU is at present taking an ever more prescriptive interest in the management and rights – and therefore IR – of people at places of work. This is going to be a culture shock to many organizations and their top and senior managers, that themselves adopt prescriptive, remote or single-directional IR policies at present.

Otherwise, the failure to understand the positive industrial, commercial and public service benefits that accrue from identifying and acting upon these matters is going to be ever harder to sustain in the long term as companies and organizations feel ever greater commercial pressures. Quite apart from anything else, the failure to note these points and to take the necessary action in the IR field as the result, is extremely expensive in terms of time, resources, energy and finance.

Chapter 6

The lessons from Japan

Japanese organizations have been studied, assessed and analysed by all students of management for the past forty years. This is because of the great global, commercial success brought about by these companies over this period, especially in the car, electrical goods components and entertainment industries. Products that were dated, moribund and unreliable when produced elsewhere in the world became revitalized and desirable. Quality and reliability were enhanced and subject to constant improvement in all aspects. The companies were extremely effective and profitable in industrial and commercial sectors that were considered by Western companies to be dying.

The main elements common to these companies were:

- the ability to charge high prices because customers were ready, willing and able to pay for the resultant quality, reliability and durability of products;
- the ability to reduce prices if necessary, and to hold them down if required, because their cost base and national industrial and financial structure allowed them to do so for extensive periods. While it is true that part of this was underwritten by the Japanese government and national banking system, the most substantial element was – and remains – corporate willingness to engage in long-term and substantially higher levels of investment than in equivalent industries elsewhere;
- the ability to take a long-term view of the markets served, together with all that implied – that the creation of satisfied customers depended upon having high quality, effective, motivated and productive staff to keep turning out the products required;

and, in the particular context of IR,

- the recognition that effective, productive and motivated staff only remain so if they work in a high quality environment, supported by good levels of pay and reward, and underpinned by a measure of job security.

In support of all this, Japanese companies bring with them their own distinctive approach to staff management, workforce organization, and IR, the main features of which are now considered. Japanese companies draw a direct relationship between workforce harmony and production output; and attention to the specific aspects of IR is considered vital for this success (see Summary Box 6.1)

SUMMARY BOX 6.1

The output of Japanese companies: car production figures 1998

Manufacturer	Plant	Country	Vehicles per employee
Mitsubishi	Mizushima	Japan	147
Honda	Suzuka	Japan	123
Toyota	Takaoka	Japan	122
Honda	Sayama	Japan	112
Mitsubishi	Okazaki	Japan	111
Daewoo	Kunsan	South Korea	103
Toyota	Tahara	Japan	102
Toyota	Tsutsumi	Japan	101
Daewoo Hi	Changwon	South Korea	99
Nissan	Kyushu	Japan	99
Nissan	Sunderland	UK	98
Kia	Asan Bay	South Korea	98
Nissan	Oppama	Japan	97
Hyundai	Ulsan No 1	South Korea	93
Daewoo	Pupyong	South Korea	92
Toyota/GM	NUMMI	US	87
Honda	East Liberty	US	85
Hyundai	Ulsan No 3	South Korea	85
Toyota	Kyushu	Japan	83
Honda	Marysville	US	82
Toyota	Motomachi	Japan	82
Mazda	Hofu	Japan	79
Ford	Wayne	US	79
Toyota	Georgetown	US	78
GM	Elsenach	Germany	77
Ford	Atlanta	US	75
Mazda	Hiroshima	Japan	75
Kia	Sohari	South Korea	74
Nissan	Smyrna	US	72
Ford	St Louis	US	71
Fiat	Malfi	Italy	70
Volkswagen	Navarra	Spain	70
Ford	Chicago	US	69
SEAT	Martorell	Spain	69
GM	Zaragoza	Spain	67
Honda	Swindon	UK	62
Hyundai	Ulsan No 2	South Korea	62
Ford	Dagenham	UK	62
Mitsubishi	Normal	US	61
Renault	Douai	France	61
Renault	Valladolid	Spain	59
Ford	Saarlouis	Germany	59

Toyota	Burnaston	UK	58
GM	Oshaws (2 plants)	Canada	57
Ford	Valencia	Spain	57
Renault	Flins	France	57
Chrysler	Sterling Heights	US	56
Chrysler	Belvidere	US	56
Fiat	Miraflori	Italy	54
PSA	Aulnay	France	51
GM	Saturn, Spring Hill	US	50
GM	Buick City	US	50
Chrysler	Bramalea	Canada	50

Source: Economist Intelligence Unit

Notes
1. Nissan UK have the highest production rate of any car manufacturer in the world outside Japan and Korea.
2. None of the cheaper brands – e.g. Skoda, Lada – feature anywhere in this list.
3. Nissan, Honda and Toyota all have complaint rates of between one fifth and one tenth the rates of those admitted by Ford and General Motors (Vauxhall).
4. In 1998, major industrial disputes took place at Ford, GM/Vauxhall, Peugeot and SEAT. There were no major industrial disputes at any of the Japanese companies listed.

CORPORATE AND MANAGERIAL ATTITUDE TO IR

In one way, this is quite simple: the staff come first. The relationship between staff, customers, shareholders and backers may be summarized as shown in Figure 6.1.

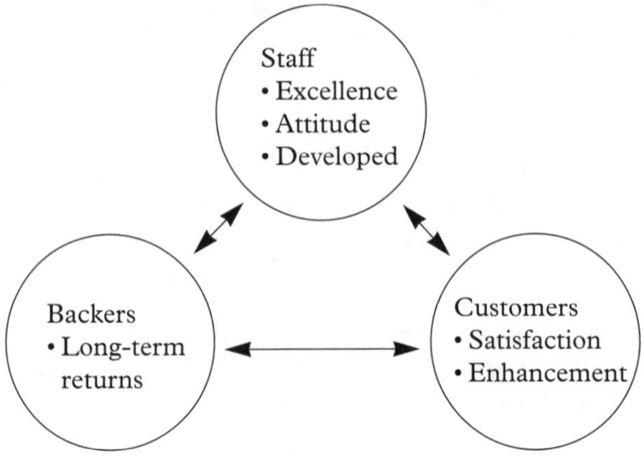

Figure 6.1

The relationship between staff, customers, shareholders and backers: mutuality and interdependency

It signifies that customer satisfaction and therefore sales and profits, and therefore shareholder confidence and continued support, cannot be achieved without excellent high quality, committed and well paid staff. Everything springs from this. Attention is therefore paid in turn, to every aspect of staff management IR to ensure that the decks are kept as clear as possible of all problems and so that effective, profitable and productive work can take place as much of the time as possible.

Beyond this, the corporate and managerial attitude to IR is that a number of issues are always present or potentially present in all organizations. If not addressed properly, these issues cause human, occupational, personal, professional, group and individual problems. If they are addressed properly, these issues and the problems that they cause go away altogether or else are kept to an absolute minimum.

The Art of Japanese Management was written by Richard Tanner Pascale and Anthony Athos, and first published in 1983. It sought to summarize the main factors, elements and features of Japanese management to draw together lessons that could be usefully learned by all students of management, and managerial practitioners (see Figure 6.2). One of the summaries that they produced was the 7S model in which they identified seven distinctive but interlocking elements present in all organizations and to which attention needed to be paid if effective management – and therefore organization performance – was to be contemplated.

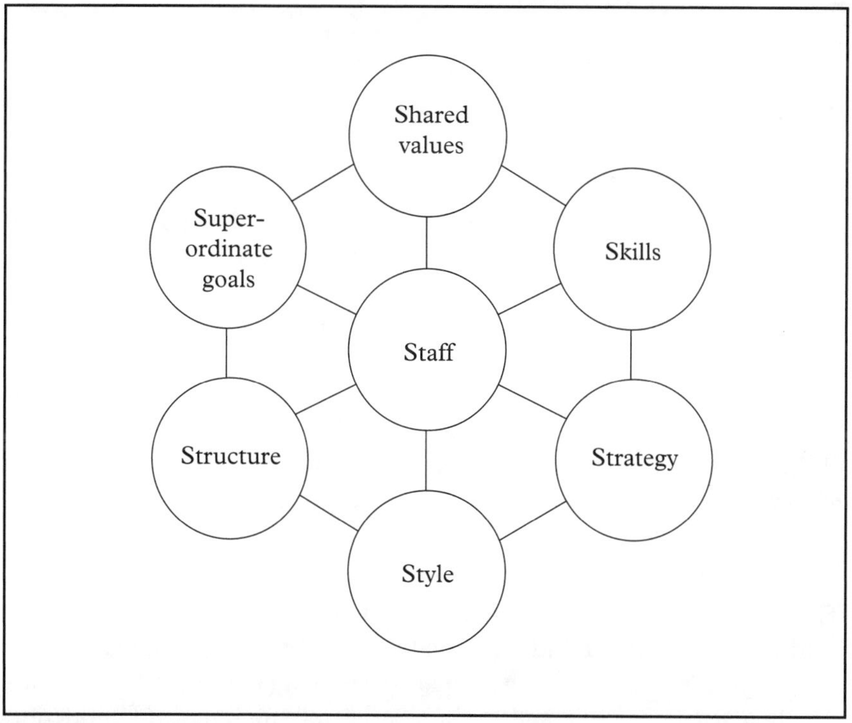

THE ART OF JAPANESE MANAGEMENT

Figure 6.2

A summary approach to Japanese management.

Source: Pascale and Athos (1983)

Of the elements identified, four – skills, style, staff and shared values – applied directly to the human side of enterprise, while the rest – structure, superordinate goals, and strategy, were dependent on human expertise for their creation, sustenance and maintenance. The hypothesis is therefore that it is necessary to concentrate on getting the human conditions right as a prerequisite for effective strategy, direction and operations. IR has therefore a key contribution to make in the effective management of organizations, rather than being a set of procedures and functions for the containment and institutionalization of conflict.

The key features of effective industrial relations in Japanese organizations can be seen in Figure 6.3.

Figure 6.3

Key features of effective industrial relations

- Security of employment
- Initial and continued job training
- Fully flexible working
- Single status
- Union recognition and involvement
- Single form of representation
- IR policy and design
- Pay and rewards
- Openness of information
- Attendance management
- Problem-solving
- Disputes and grievances
- IR procedures

We will now consider each of these in turn.

Security of employment

A major attraction to staff considering working for Japanese companies when they first came to the UK was the promise of security of employment. To begin with, this promise was neither believed in nor valued because many of the people seeking work in these companies had been discarded by great British industries – cars, ships, steel and the coal mines – and had no reason to believe in the promises of outsiders and newcomers. Only when the promise was seen to be fulfilled, and a real commitment made, did people begin to feel fully confident. In any case, the promise itself was, and is, of no value unless other elements are in place to support it.

Initial and continued job training

The Japanese view is that people can only be transformed into effective, productive, motivated and high quality staff if they are trained. All the companies that have established themselves in the UK require those joining them to undertake substantial initial job training and induction periods before they are considered expert enough to begin making products or providing services to customers (see Summary Box 6.2).

> 'I spoke to Lee Iaccoca, who had recently been to visit the Nissan truck plant at Smyrna, Tennessee. He said the technology didn't impress him, that he'd seen better in Detroit, let alone Japan. What did impress him was that fact that Nissan spent $20,000 per employee on job training for all hourly paid staff before they switched the production lines on and began producing trucks.'
>
> Source: Tom Peters, *The World Turned Upside Down*, Channel 4, 1986

For example, in the UK:

* Canon require all their sales staff to undertake a four week residential induction, orientation, product familiarization and customer service course before they start work. This is topped up with regular training days throughout the period of employment, and with two weeks off site and away from the company each year for this purpose. Staff are also required to be familiar with product alterations and innovations, and when these occur, they are again called away from work to ensure that they fully understand them.
* Sony require all their production staff to undertake the same induction and orientation programme as managers, supervisors, research staff and technicians so that everyone understands that they are working for the same organization and that they will be treated with the same levels of humanity, respect and value regardless of occupation.

Fully flexible working

Fully flexible working – the ability to carry out any task required – is a condition of Japanese work organization and staff management. There are no demarcation lines, divisional barriers or restrictive practices among production operative, semi-skilled and unskilled staff. Those joining Japanese companies understand from the outset that they may be required to carry out any job required.

Part of this is cultural. The ideal is for people to be able to say 'I work for Sony/Sanyo/Honda/Sharp' rather than 'I am an assembler/packer/clerk' – because such job titles serve as a point of reference and carry restrictive connotations in industrial and commercial settings throughout the world. Japanese culture also sees the closeness of identity between staff member and organization as a matter of both corporate and personal pride. The organization is supposed to provide both wealth and satisfaction to its employees. Part of the thrust and direction of IR is to ensure that this indeed takes place.

The rest is operational. Fully flexible working is viewed as having the capability to have everyone as productive as possible at all times. This is only achievable as the result of extensive initial and continuous job training and the development of attitudes of willingness to work in these ways.

Single status

All employees have the same basic terms and conditions regardless of length of service, occupation, rank or hours worked. This means that:

- if one person clocks in, everyone does; if one person does not clock in, no-one does;
- if one person is called by first name, so is everyone;
- if one person starts at a particular time, so does everyone;
- there are no personalized car park spaces except on the basis of need;
- everyone eats at a single canteen; there are no executive or differentiated dining rooms;
- everyone abides by the same staff handbook, codes, rules, regulations and procedures;
- if there is one provided, everyone wears the same uniform.

This is because, once employed, everyone is valued, and so is their work. Nobody's contribution is considered more important than that of anyone else – neither may people seek preferential treatment on the basis of their particular position in the hierarchy or order of work at the company.

Union recognition and involvement

Japanese companies normally recognize trade unions for the purposes of consultation, participation, individual and group representation. This is very much akin to the EU concept of social partners. Unions are deemed to be the best way of ensuring that employee rights are maintained and upheld. Indeed, some companies take a purely altruistic view of this – that they are so confident of the quality and excellence of their IR approach and delivery that they are happy to have along anyone from anywhere as an independent monitor, reviewer and evaluator.

Single form of representation

Japanese companies are happy to have their staff represented by a trade union, as stated above. In Japan, companies tend to create their own unions which are funded and then operated as independent bodies to represent the staff interest. In the UK, the approach has been to ask established trade unions to tender for single representation rights for all staff either on a particular location or for the whole organization (see Summary Box 6.3). The union is then given sole rights of representation and consultation in the organization. This is known as single union representation or 'a single union deal'.

In the 1970s, when Japanese companies first started asking UK trade unions to tender for representation rights, there was a lot of resistance. This especially came from the more traditional trade unions, whose view was that those who did tender were being asked to sell the right to genuinely represent the interests of the workforce, in return for easy subscriptions from new members. Companies that were only too pleased to promise full representation and consultation at the outset, would quickly rein in those rights once they had got themselves established. Above all, it was not the British way and people from a variety of walks of life were not used to being represented by certain trade unions.

The Japanese companies also refused to undertake collective bargaining, and this too was an affront to the traditionalists among the trade union movement, many of whom saw this form of activity as the key to their whole existence.

Accordingly, any union that did tender for the rights to represent staff at Japanese companies was contemptuously referred to as 'taking part in a beauty contest'; and the perception was widely held (without any real evidence) that the most supine of unions would always win. Any union that either stood up for itself, asserted its own rights or principles, or tried to reposition the Japanese approach to IR, would not be allowed representation rights.

IR policy and design

As stated above, Japanese companies were not prepared to engage in collective bargaining when they first established themselves in the UK and this largely remains the case.

The company takes full responsibility for the design of all aspects of organizational IR. The union is then invited to participate fully in its operation (see Summary Box 6.4).

The organization therefore takes on a prescriptive rather than an agreed approach to the format and design of IR, and it is true that this brings specific responsibilities. These are incumbent upon the organization and its managers and are as follows.

- To make sure that all procedures are fair and equitable both in content and operation.
- To make sure that everyone does indeed receive the same treatment.
- To make sure that the union makes an effective contribution within the stated boundaries.
- To make sure that everything that is promised is delivered – whether these promises are stated or implied.

Most Japanese companies preface their IR policy and design with a statement to the effect that:

SUMMARY
BOX 6.4

Criticisms of
Japanese IR
policy and
design

Critics of the Japanese approach to IR cite the following.

- Full participation is only allowed on company terms. The union – and any other staff representation – has no influence over the content or context of IR, but only over the operation of a preordained set of rules.
- The single union may not be able to represent adequately the hopes, fears and aspirations of the different staff groups at the place of work; in many cases, the union will have had no particular experience or understanding with certain groups of staff, and may also have no particular affinity with them.
- It is dependent for its effectiveness on the company and its managers continuing to operate from the high standards which they have set themselves; and if they unilaterally fall from these standards, there is no protection for staff.
- The companies are dependent upon their continued dominance and expansion of their markets, and this is impossible to guarantee or predict.
- The companies have relocated from Japan to the UK when it suited them to do so, and they will relocate elsewhere when it suits them in the future. The 'permanence' of employment is therefore an illusion.

The purpose here is to ensure effective production and harmonious working conditions which must exist as a condition, in turn, of effective manufacturing of products and continued high levels of customer service and therefore profitability.

In other words, the IR policy is a business document, exactly the same as all other policies and procedures.

Pay and rewards

Japanese companies pay in the upper quartile of both industrial and local 'going rates' in the UK. Thus for example, Nissan pay approximately 135 per cent of the wages paid by Ford and Vauxhall. They also pay higher for industrial and manufacturing activity than anyone else in their locality. This was a company commitment at the outset of activities and remains so to the present.

Pay levels and increases are not negotiated. They are decided upon by the organization and consulted upon with union and staff representatives; and companies need to be able to justify how they arrived at particular figures and why these are fair and reasonable. There is a great and continuing company responsibility and obligation here, and also a key role for the recognized union, because the staff themselves will be fully aware of what both industrial and local norms are at present. Again, if there ever is knowledge, belief or perception that the company is beginning to take advantage, or not to pay what is understood to be 'a fair rate', the distinctive IR standpoint is lost.

Pay increases are always paid on the due date. They are never backdated or staged. Backdating and staging are aggravating to staff – who are not being paid what they have, after all, been told they were worth; and inefficient for the company, which has then to engage in a series of calculations, diverting staff time and resources away from more productive activities.

Percentage pay rises are normally the same across the board. There are very few exceptions, and these are normally confined to those at the bottom of the pay scale. In this way, the principle of basic equality is reinforced.

Openness of information

The standpoint is that all information is openly and freely available in formats that can easily be understood by everyone. In IR terms, the company is required to make available information on:

- present and future staffing levels, supported by business plans, output requirements, real and assessed market strategies;
- present and future pay and reward levels, so that everyone involved knows what the prognosis is in their own individual cases. Honda (UK) and Toshiba (UK) have both entered into extended pay arrangements by which a pay rise is guaranteed at 3 per cent above the retail prices index (see Summary Box 6.5);

SUMMARY BOX 6.5

Extended pay agreements

- Extended pay agreements are acceptable to all concerned because everyone ostensibly benefits.
- Organizations are able to plan with a fair degree of certainty, knowing more or less what the wage and salary bill is to be for the period of the agreement.
- Staff know that they are able to gain real increases in earnings on an annual basis together with compensation for the effects of inflation.
- Resources are not used – wasted – in expensive and divisive collective bargaining and negotiating exercises in arriving at something that is in any case acceptable all round.

In summary, Japanese companies take the view that their approach to pay removes an extremely unnecessary battlefield from the corporate planet – and again releases time, energy and resources to be getting on with other things. This again, it is argued, demonstrates the direct contribution that IR makes to profitable and effective business activities.

- organizational, divisional, departmental and functional income and expenditure: again, supported by the rationale and basis on which this is calculated and apportioned;
- disciplinary, grievance and dispute rates and activities – their causes and how each is resolved;

- broader issues that impact on corporate IR – including product quality, efficiency and effectiveness; customer complaint rates; reject rates.

The whole is then discussed and evaluated at joint consultative committees. The Sanyo example draws direct attention to each of these elements (Appendix 2, Paragraph 6) and itemizes exactly these matters as a legitimate remit of an IR joint consultative committee.

Attendance management

Japanese companies have the lowest sickness and absenteeism rates in the UK for their sectors (see Summary Box 6.6).

SUMMARY BOX 6.6

Absenteeism 1998: examples

Company	Rate (%)
Sanyo	0.2
Sony	0.5
Nissan	0.5
Honda	0.3
Toshiba	0.2
Canon	0.8

As stated in the main text (see below), this is extensively and positively managed.

- *Toshiba:* in its induction programme, Toshiba (UK) make the following statement: 'We are employing you because we need your work. We value the contribution of everyone. We do not carry extra, spare or unproductive staff. If you need to have time off work, you should ask for it. If you are the sort of person who has a lot of time off work, you should consider whether coming to work for Toshiba (UK) is the right move for you. The company cannot afford to employ staff who are not at work for extensive periods of time. The company also takes the view that it is not fair to expect those colleagues who are present to regularly carry additional workloads because of colleagues who are persistently absent.'
- *Sanyo:* anyone who takes self-certificated absence at the Sanyo (UK) plant at Lowestoft, Suffolk is visited at home by a member of the human resources staff. These staff come round to make sure that there is nothing that the company can do, and to try and find out when the employee will be back at work. They bring with them either a bunch of flowers or a box of chocolates together with a 'get well' card from the company.

Both approaches are contentious in their own way. Both caused a brief stir in the UK IR establishment – especially among traditional trade unions when they were introduced. Some trade union leaders especially called into question the integrity of the approach, stating that it was coercive and punitive to people who had genuine illness. The companies' response was that anyone who had genuine illness had nothing to fear from the approach. Both companies, however, failed to comment on the implications for malingerers.

Self-certificated absenteeism is positively managed. Those who take time off are always interviewed upon their return to work. Repeat patterns of sickness are referred on quickly to company doctors and occupational health functions.

This is supported by a clear organizational responsibility where individuals have occupational or non-occupational serious illness or injury. The view ostensibly is that the company want individuals back at work and that they should take as much time as is necessary to make a full recovery from the particular accident or illness.

Problem-solving

The Japanese view is that problems are there to be solved and that the onus and responsibility for this remains in the hands of managers and supervisors. Disciplinary, grievance and dispute activities are to be kept to an absolute minimum. Managers and supervisors who find themselves handling large or steady volumes of disciplinary, grievance and dispute cases always have their own capabilities questioned. The Japanese approach to IR problems has the following distinctive strands.

- Creating the conditions whereby problems do not arise in the first place. This means establishing and maintaining patterns of work and a supervisory style with which everyone willingly complies. Management and supervisory style is based on openness and approachability. Issues are raised and dealt with early, before they become serious or contentious (see Summary Box 6.7).
- When problems do arise, they are dealt with swiftly and effectively. This reinforces the value and priority that the companies place on training and expertise at all levels. It is underpinned with giving managers and supervisors the authority to resolve issues as they do occur, and in supporting them in the actions that they take.
- Avoiding a culture of blame so that, provided lessons are learned from any issue or incident, nobody is penalized when mistakes are made.
- Underpinning the managerial approach with simple clear procedures applicable to all. These are required to be operated quickly (see Appendix 2, Paragraphs 8 and 9).

Disputes and grievances

The overriding objective of the Japanese approach to IR is to keep disputes to a minimum. When they do arise, however, they are to be resolved as quickly as possible and without recourse to strike or other industrial action. The following processes are used.

- Formal open meetings at which each party presents their case to the other. The matter is then thrashed out at a single meeting until agreement is reached.

SUMMARY BOX 6.7

Sony at Atsugi

The Sony organization had serious IR problems in its early days. The approach taken by the company managing director in 1961 at its Atsugi plant took major steps to resolve the problems and ensure that they never arose again. It also served as a set of principles on which the foundations of company IR would be laid for the future. In the words of the then company managing director, Shigeru Kobayashi:

'It was towards the end of 1961, immediately following my taking over the Atsugi plant that the following incident occurred. In a meeting of plant management, the manager of industrial relations reminded us that there had been considerable dishonesty in the handling of time cards. Such cheating, he maintained, could not be tolerated. Watchmen would have to be placed at the time clocks to control the situation.

'I had already given some thought to this time clock problem, and hearing this proposal was enough to make up my mind once and for all. Let's abolish the time clocks I said. All that they have done is to bring about the war of offence and defence that is now going on between the management and labour.

'Anyway, what in the world is a time clock? It has nothing to do with the existence of this plant. Our plant is one which produces transistors. To put it in a nutshell, we are being used by the time clock.

'So I gathered all the employees together and appealed to them. Obviously, I said, we are here to make transistors. Let us decide that beginning tomorrow we will work according to the time schedule without any clocks. Your own reporting of your absences will be sufficient. The company will trust you.

'My overriding task, as you can see, when I came to work at the plant was to eliminate the complete sense of distrust. This, I saw as the root of all our problems. These people had never experienced the joy of living in a climate of universal trust. When management did demonstrate trust, they responded beautifully. You can imagine how exuberant that made us.

'The establishment of cafeteria service counters without attendants, the improvements made in recreational facilities, the abolition of time clocks, and the ensuing changes in organizational patterns were all implemented in parallel and gained increasingly in sophistication.

'As the negative elements in the environment were eliminated, their removal speeded up the progress we were able to make in encouraging people to develop into positive, determined, creative human beings, untroubled by even the slightest feeling of insignificance.

'Under this kind of system, every employee becomes the master of their job and begins to feel that they are their own president. The only difference between the sweeper and the real company president is that the sweeper sweeps the floors and the president steers the company. The value placed on each activity is the same.'

Source: Shigeru Kobayashi, quoted in R. S. Lessem, *The Global Business*, Prentice Hall International, 1987

- If this does not work, binding pendulum arbitration is invoked. When this is to happen, an arbitrator is agreed upon and appointed. The parties then present their cases fully to the arbitrator.
- The arbitrator hears the arguments and then formally decides entirely in favour of one party or the other. There are no compromises or halfway houses. There are no forms of words used to couch the results. One party is known and seen to win, the other is known and seen to lose (see Summary Box 6.8).

SUMMARY BOX 6.8

Pendulum arbitration: the final solution

'The final solution' is the phrase used by Sanyo (Appendix 2, Paragraph 7) to describe their binding pendulum arbitration arrangement. The same phrase is also used by Nissan and Honda; while Toshiba, Canon, Sharp and Panasonic use the phrase 'in the last resort'. The companies take the view that there are strong positive reasons for the approach and distinctive benefits. These are as follows.

- *Operational:* there are overriding operational reasons for having an ultimate speedy disputes resolution process. Strikes and other forms of industrial action are lengthy to resolve, and also leave lingering bad feelings, and these are damaging both to morale and also to operational performance. Such disputes also seriously disrupt production.
- *Cultural:* there is a strong Japanese national cultural attitude to failure. When entering into a pendulum arbitration case someone is going to fail – and that person had better not be the manager or supervisor. Overwhelming cultural pressure is therefore exerted to avoid the situation in the first place, by finding a positive solution to the problem before it gets to this stage.

IR procedures

Procedures are fully comprehensive and published to all. They are simple, clear and direct and apply to all staff. There are no variations by occupation or status, though they may vary by site.

The standpoint is that any issue is to be resolved early so that problems are nipped in the bud. Recourse to procedures is to be kept to an absolute minimum; and again, the approach and capability of managers resorting to procedures or having a steady stream of staff on warnings or raising grievances is always questioned.

Procedures are designed by the companies, and the union is involved in their operation when required at all stages (see Appendix 2, Paragraphs 8, 9 and 10). The maximum length of time for the operation of any procedure is three weeks from start to finish including appeals. In this way, when problems do arise and become formalized, any taking of sides or lingering ill-feeling is again kept to a minimum.

Managers are trained in the operation of IR procedures as a basic part of their management training. Staff are fully briefed at induction on how to raise grievances and respond to disciplinary issues, and the union is normally involved at this part of the induction process. Again, this is designed to ensure that people know where they stand at the outset of their employment; and again, it supports the point of view that serious problems are to be kept to an absolute minimum (see Summary Box 6.9).

<table>
<tr>
<td>

SUMMARY BOX 6.9

The 'Today' programme: Nissan, Panasonic – and the Home Office

</td>
<td>

It remains true in Japanese companies that serious problems do arise from time to time. In 1997, Nissan was taken to employment tribunal by a former member of their sales staff. The staff member, a lady in her thirties, was an excellent and effective employee who always got good results.

However, she was unable to attend evening functions outside her normal working hours. Matters came to a head when she was unable to attend a departmental evening dinner because she had family responsibilities. She gave the view that, as it was outside her normal working hours, she was in any case not obliged to turn up.

The matter when through company procedures including pendulum arbitration. At each stage, including pendulum arbitration, the finding was in the company's favour and against the individual. She was dismissed and took the matter to employment tribunal.

The employment tribunal found in the employee's favour. The tribunal stated that it was wholly unreasonable to expect the employee to turn out in the evenings and that this was not stated in her contract or other terms and conditions of employment.

Nissan duly paid her substantial compensation. On the basis of this case, there was subsequent media interest in the whole Japanese way of doing things. Nissan pointed out the fact that in their fourteen years of existence in the UK, this was their only employment tribunal defeat, and the company went on to state that they would much rather have their IR record than that of anyone else.

The following week, the local chief executive of Panasonic, questioned about similar matters at his factory in South Wales, also took an upbeat view. This was to the effect that, of course the company made mistakes in all its areas of activity, and this included IR; the important point, however, was to learn from them and to improve as the result.

This feature was followed by an interview with a senior politician at the Home Office – an organization not noted for its enduring, effective or high quality staff management practices and IR. Asked whether mistakes had been made by the Home Office concerning a serious and enduring staff–management dispute in the Prison Service, the politician replied that they had not.

Source: The 'Today' programme, BBC Radio 4

</td>
</tr>
</table>

It is necessary to see the operation of Japanese IR in the broader context of the business principles on which the companies are founded. The basic concept is *gambara*, which means 'don't give up, do your best, be persistent, put in a great effort'. This lies at the core of the Japanese work ethic. The Japanese work for the good of their group and their company above all. The view adopted is that the whole only functions effectively when all its component parts are, in turn, functioning to full effect and capacity.

All Japanese management practices are designed actively to prevent problems from happening. This is distinct from elsewhere in the world where great store is often set by the ability of the manager to resolve problems. The Japanese manager is expected to resolve these as and when they do occur. This, however, should be kept to a minimum; organizational and managerial style reflect this.

The decision-making process is a combination of *nemawashi*, which means 'binding the roots', and has come to mean 'thorough preparation'; and *ringi*, which is the outcome of this. In practice, the process involves full consultation and the engagement and cooperation of all those who are to be affected by a decision before it is taken. Preparation and pre-preparation time and effort is everything; and to those who do not come from within the culture it is said that the process appears inert for a very long period. However once *ringi* is reached, once everyone's support is engaged, the matter in hand proceeds at full speed from that point onwards. In IR terms, this refers especially to the provision of information and full consultation, because this is perceived to be critical to the success of all activities. Because of this, effective communication and consultation systems are essential.

Kaizen

Kaizen refers to the constant progress of humanity and the continuous striving for perfection. In management terms, this has become 'constant continuous improvement' and refers to all aspects of all organizations. In IR and staff management terms, this means:

- continuous staff training and development;
- continuous attention to procedures and administration;
- continuous attention to staff–supervisory–managerial relations;
- continuous attention to the operation of disciplinary, grievance and disputes procedures;
- continuous attention to the lessons to be learned from problems and disputes.

It is reinforced by high levels of expectations placed on staff, the high degree of conformity required, and the high levels of pay offered. It is also reflected in the offer of lifetime employment and all that that implies.

Mu

Related to *kaizen* is complete openness. This the Japanese call *mu*. This constitutes a refusal to be hidebound by policies, constraints, directions and structures. These are there to be used and supported by managers and indeed all staff, rather than the basis for operations and activities. Strictly in IR terms, this is the basis for consultation and the provision of information.

This represents the context in which IR is carried out in Japanese companies; and the above pages have indicated and illustrated the main features of the Japanese corporate approach to IR. Its continued effectiveness is founded on a basic belief that IR is one of the threads of effective business production and service, rather than a separate and specialist function. It is essential to recognize that this can only be sustained if corporate and managerial integrity, continuous investment and conformism are retained.

Corporate and managerial integrity

Everything is dependent upon corporate and managerial willingness to act in accordance with the principles indicated above. Especially, openness of information and avoidance of blame are essential if the total is not to be lost. There is also an absolute managerial responsibility to deliver pay rises, handle discipline and grievances, and maintain full flexibility of working, in the ways indicated.

Continuous investment

Continued high levels of investment are a key feature of all aspects of Japanese business and commercial success. In IR terms, this especially means continued investment in training and performance improvement, in induction, and in the development and operation of procedures. Any loss of this is simply going to lead to increases in the levels of misunderstandings, resulting in turn in increases in disciplinary and grievance activity, together with all the traditional IR strife that these bring.

Conformism

In the archetype terms outlined in Chapter 1, the Japanese adopt a version of the unitary perspective on IR. Having accepted responsibility for the policy, design, standpoint, content and delivery of IR, employees and their representatives are expected to conform. Anyone who does not, or who does not wish to do so, cannot expect to remain in employment. The companies require that, in return for security, good pay levels, flexibility and opportunity, and continuous training and development, employees will work in ways and in activities prescribed by the company. In order for this to be successful, it requires vision and direction from the top of companies that is acceptable to all that come to work in them.

This is believed and perceived by some to be coercive, and intrusive into the other aspects of employees' lives. In the Nissan example above, attendance at evening functions outside normal working hours was clearly not optional. In the same way, genuine employee participation and involvement is limited and delivered on corporate terms only. Similarly, some trade unions have found great difficulty, or even impossibility, in agreeing to represent employees under those conditions.

The Japanese approach to IR brings notable benefits in terms of reduced absenteeism, discipline, grievance and disputes, and high overall levels of motivation and commitment. It also contributes to enduring effective levels of product and service output because of the absence of workforce disruption.

CONCLUSIONS

However, any organization and its managers wishing to learn lessons from the Japanese industrial and commercial experience of IR must note the long-term commitment necessary to ensure its success. Many Japanese companies have located in parts of the UK previously known for bad IR and industrial decline, and have succeeded in establishing their own high levels of positive reputation because of their initial and continuing commitment, and not just because they took work to areas where there was none.

Furthermore, it is only through continued long-term commitment and enduring levels of investment and attention to each aspect, that these and other companies will sustain their hitherto effective and successful IR.

Chapter 7

The excellence view

INTRODUCTION The work that has come to be known as 'The Excellence Studies' was carried out in the USA in 1978 and 1979 by McKinsey, the American management consultancy company. The approach adopted was to study both businesses and managers of high reputation and/or high performance, and to try to isolate those qualities and characteristics that made them so. Those working on the study also identified those attributes that they felt ought to be present in such organizations and persons, and to test them against those studied.

Originally, 62 organizations were studied. They were drawn from all sectors of US industry and commerce and included many global firms (e.g. Boeing, McDonald's, Hewlett Packard, 3M).

'High performing' took on a variety of meanings, including: profitability; a global organization (such as IBM); a strong positive image (e.g. Marks & Spencer); a strong domestic organization (Sainsbury in the UK or 3M in the USA); a strong player in a slumped or declining market (e.g. British Airways). It also related to other aspects such as strong general images; customer confidence; and staff and customer loyalty.

The results were originally written up in the book *In Search of Excellence* by Thomas Peters and Robert H. Waterman, and published in 1980. This was followed up by a variety of other studies (see Summary Box 7.1).

The work may be summarized in three ways.

7S MODEL This is represented in Figure 7.1.

It is a configuration of organization pattern and design that reflects the essential attributes that must be addressed in the establishment and development of excellent management.

It is akin to the model of Japanese management proposed by Pascale and Athos (Figure 6.2). Four of the elements are directly concerned with the human side of enterprise – shared values, skills, staff and style; and the other three – strategy, structure and systems – require excellent and capable people to implement them.

In IR terms, there are specific points to note from each of these.

In Search of Excellence was followed up with a variety of other studies carried out by various authors in different companies in different parts of the world. Examples are:

- *Intrapreneurship* and *The Roots of Excellence* by R. S. Lessem
- *Making It Happen* and *Troubleshooters* by John Harvey-Jones
- *The Art of Japanese Management* by Richard Pascale and Anthony Athos

The common thread between all of these studies is the relationship between characteristics deemed or pre-considered to be excellent, and the presence of these characteristics in the organizations and individuals studied. While some of the studies clearly carried more weight than others, the enduring contribution of the approach to both organizations and management has been to establish:

- the direct relationship between managerial excellence and organization success;
- much greater attention to the human (as distinct from the output and financial) side of enterprise (and therefore, in this particular context, attention to IR);
- much greater attention to the need for management styles that commit people, as well as organizations, to effective performance (and again, in this particular context, there is a direct implication for IR).

It is true to say that in very few cases is IR discussed as a separate function. It is rather included as a part of the total portfolio of general management capabilities and qualities necessary for total effectiveness of performance.

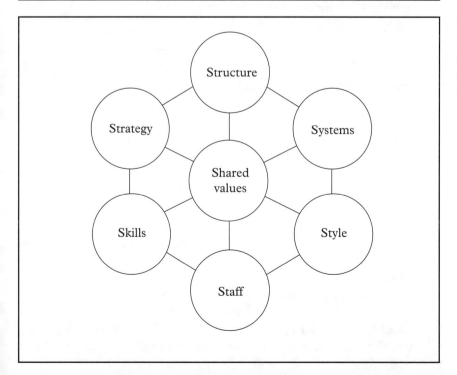

Figure 7.1

The concept of excellence applied to organizations

- The commitment and excellence of staff is recognized as a key element.
- Skills implies the need for continuous training, development and improvement.
- Style requires the application of principles of leadership and appropriateness of delivery for each situation.
- Shared values requires the adoption of a given set of organizational principles with which everyone can identify and comply.

EIGHT CHAR-ACTERISTICS OF EXCELLENT MANAGEMENT PRACTICE

These were summarized by Peters and Waterman as follows.

- *Bias for action:* do it, fix it, try it.
- *Closeness to the customer:* listen intently and regularly to customer needs and provide quality, service and reliability in response.
- *Autonomy and entrepreneurship:* innovation and risk taking as an expected way of doing things, rather than conformity and conservatism.
- *Productivity through people:* employees are seen as the source of quality and productivity.
- *Hands on – value driven:* the basic philosophy of the organization is well defined and articulated.
- *Stick to the knitting:* stay close to what you can do well.
- *Simple form, lean staff:* structural arrangements and systems are simple with small directoral staff.
- *Simultaneous loose–tight properties:* centralized control of values, but operational decentralization and autonomy.

The specific IR implications of this part of the approach are as follows.

- *Bias for action:* creating a climate and working relationships based on operational and managerial integrity. If such an attitude is adopted, mistakes and errors are bound to occur. Some organizations have poor performance criteria as part of their disciplinary procedure; if this is used to penalize genuine mistakes, people will simply withdraw from the required 'bias for action' (see Summary Box 7.2).
- *Closeness to customer:* part of this means identifying the prime importance of customer service and product quality through salary scales and percentages of staff involved in primary activities. Especially convoluted public pay policies that dampen down the salaries of nurses, teachers, social workers, doctors and other front line staff simply indicate a long-term decline in service delivery. This is especially true where support and head office functions are known or believed to benefit at their expense (see Summary Box 7.3).
- *Autonomy and entrepreneurship:* rather than conservatism and conformity. In IR terms, this again refers to what is rewarded and punished. It includes reference to the extent to which people are disciplined for breaches of procedure or protocol; or the extent to

In 1993, a county council Social Services Department, faced with spending restrictions, asked all its staff to review their workload and take a proactive and pioneering approach to their work. The corporate view was that everyone was being buried in ever-increasing caseloads. A proactive approach, with a degree of autonomy and independence, would lead to reductions in the stresses and strains inherent.

Accordingly, the leader of a child protection team in a seaside town in the particular county made time available to carry out research into the true scale of child abuse in his area. From this research, he was able to identify some steps and initiatives, including a model of cooperation with other public agencies and services, that would, he predicted, reduce workloads in terms of both volume and stress in the medium to long term.

He wrote up his research. He supported it with statistics, and presented it to his superiors. While he was waiting for his superiors to consider the work, he presented summaries and opened initial discussions with the police, children's charities, and educational welfare officials in the area. Everyone he spoke to agreed that the work was essential and that he had provided an excellent start.

His superiors hammered the report and his professional and personal integrity. They ordered an immediate stop to these activities, and the liaison with the other bodies. When he pointed out that he was simply taking the county council at its own word, and carrying out what he thought was their express orders, he was dismissed. He was reinstated upon appeal, and relocated to another Social Services office in the county. He was also promoted.

On his old patch in 1999, caseloads for staff are running at 153 per cent of their 1993 levels. No proactive and preventive work has so far been carried out.

Following a major reorganization and a general shift of operational priority towards front line activities in 1994, the company staff anticipated a large pay rise. The company had become much more profitable and streamlined in operation.

Instead the staff involved were invited to either accept a pay freeze; or else, in return for five years' guaranteed job security, a 10 per cent pay cut. At the same time, corporate headquarters staff were awarded a 12 per cent pay rise across all grades; and Cedric Brown, the chief executive, took a 73 per cent pay rise.

This had an extremely destructive effect on staff morale. It made neither for good organizational IR overall, nor did it reinforce the view stated by the company that customer service was now the most important activity.

which they are disciplined for lack of initiative and commitment. This depends on the extent to which conformity and commitment are perceived as being the same thing.

- *Productivity through people:* this refers to the extent to which procedures, practices and style exist to reinforce productivity and output; or the extent to which they reinforce systems and structures, especially if these are known, believed or perceived to be bureaucratic and self-serving. It also is reinforced by the presence or lack of psychological distance and barriers, and the extent to which active steps are taken to acknowledge these and break them down – or to reinforce and build them up.

    Physical distance is also an IR issue here. This occurs in all sectors, in all activities where there is a difference of location between direction and management, and production and/or service output. It becomes a serious problem when IR style and approach, policies and procedures, are designed and implemented by the corporate headquarters without reference to the nature of operations and the structuring of front line work. The Sanyo Model (Appendix 2) is a good example of how such problems are overcome; Sanyo itself is a multi-site, diverse and global organization. The Handbook example given runs to eleven main sections; this can usefully be compared, for example, to the Kent County Council disciplinary procedure for schoolteachers which alone runs to nineteen pages.

- *Hands on – value driven:* in which the basic IR philosophy, climate, ethos and policies of the organization are well defined and articulated. This identifies and defines total overall collective and individual responsibilities, in addition to setting standards of behaviour and performance (see Summary Box 7.4).

- *Sticking to the knitting:* this means ensuring that people do understand the full extent of their IR roles, functions and responsibilities; and ensuring that everyone is trained and briefed in these.

- *Simple form, lean staff:* small hierarchies, extended spans of control, and emphasis on individual and group autonomy have to be reinforced through open and proactive IR approaches and management style. Again, the managing by walking around approach reinforces the capability to identify and address problems early and before they become serious or institutionalized. Where general simple form and lean staff approaches are adopted, serious problems only occur as the result of a genuine misunderstanding being allowed to compound itself; or as the result of a genuine malevolence on the part of someone involved (see Summary Box 7.5).

- *Simultaneous loose–tight properties:* this means drawing a distinction between standards of behaviour (the tight); and establishing an open and positive style of management that encourages initiative, enthusiasm and high levels of motivation (the loose).

The opposite of this is 'hands off' – expediency driven. Whether by accident or design, the effect of undirected, bureaucratic and imprecise IR policies and procedures is to reinforce any knowledge, belief or perception of dishonesty or duplicity that may already exist. Such policies and procedures also dilute and absolve responsibility rather than targeting it. Symptomatic of this dilution of responsibility are:

- extensive and expensive corporate IR functions;
- promulgation of complex and often contradictory procedures (see the Kent County Council example above; Kent County Council has in total 73 different disciplinary procedures);
- extensive reliance on ACAS, employment tribunals, outside bodies; extensive recourse to, and payment of, compensation;
- lack of absolute standards – in which people are treated differently according to their department, division, function or location, or their rank or status or position in the hierarchy; and in which bullying, victimization, harassment and discrimination are rife;
- lack of training in, or corporate support for, absolute standards.

SUMMARY BOX 7.4

Hands on – value driven

In 1996, a special school with responsibility for children with severe behavioural and learning difficulties appointed a care supervisor. The new supervisor, a woman of 32, was responsible for a team of five care workers, and reported directly to the head of the institution. She had no qualifications for the work, but got the job because she had a friend on the institution's governing body who recommended her to the head teacher for the position.

The work was difficult and stressful and she quickly got into difficulties. However, rather than either seeking training or resigning from the post, she systematically victimized each member of her team, several of whom left to take up posts elsewhere. These she replaced either with her own friends, or with persons of lesser character and capability.

The matter came to a head when she alleged that one of the longest serving remaining members of the team had assaulted her. She repeated the allegations to her friend on the governing body. The head conducted an inquiry and a disciplinary case; and the team member, a man in his late thirties, was dismissed.

He took the school to employment tribunal and lost the case. The head and others were persuaded to give evidence against him, and this was fabricated.

The matter was only finally resolved when, following allegations of managerial corruption and mistreatment of the children, a full police and social services inquiry was held. The head resigned. The particular supervisor also resigned, rather than face a further inquiry. The individual received his job back without stain on his character, and with substantial compensation.

SUMMARY BOX 7.5

Children at risk

THE IMPORTANCE OF MACRO-ORGANIZA-TIONAL ANALYSIS

Macro-organizational analysis is dependent upon the strength and style of leadership – the drive, determination, core values and strategic vision necessary to energize and make profitable the organization's activities. In time, this becomes 'the way things are done here'. Managers underpin this through their day-to-day activities – those issues that they concern themselves with, those matters on which they spend resources, those people with whom they spend time. It is therefore a combination of both what they do and how they do it. Messages, signals and cues are given off by this to the rest of the organization. Above all, both the leader of the organization, and those in charge of departments, divisions, functions, teams and groups, between them express the true organizational value through the means by which they conduct themselves in all their activities, including IR.

MACRO-ORGANIZA-TIONAL ANALYSIS AND IR

The IR outputs of effective macro-organizational analysis ought to be the ability to identify the sources and symptoms of good and effective IR and sources and symptoms of bad and ineffective IR.

Symptoms of good and effective IR

Where IR is known, believed or perceived to be good and effective, macro-organizational analysis will identify the following.

- Low levels of absenteeism, coupled with high levels of commitment and output.
- Low (or acceptable or understood) staff turnover, coupled with the ability to find high quality new people when required.
- Few accidents and injuries.
- Few customer complaints which, when they do arise, are successfully dealt with.
- Lack of fear – of anything or anyone.
- Openness of operational discussions, together with understanding of the interaction of each part of organization processes and functions.
- Openness, completeness and clarity of information available to all staff.
- Openness, approachability and visibility of managers and supervisors; supported by a visible and institutionalized style that reflects this.
- Absence of discipline, grievance, disciplinary and dispute activities.
- Absence of recourse to procedures.
- Positive grapevine.

All of this needs to be seen in context as follows.

- Absenteeism rates may be distorted by particular problems in one department, division or function; or with one activity or category of staff; or as the result of previous organizational malfunction or bad management. The results of transition always take time to work through, especially when people are on long-term sickness absence as the result of stress, or industrial or occupational industry.

- Staff turnover is always, to an extent, a function of what an organization can offer. Three points should be noted:
  1. with the best will in the world, some organizations have no trouble in attracting, retaining, motivating and rewarding high quality people for a time, but the limitation of their activities means that people will eventually need to move on
  2. turnover may be caused due to new organizations opening up in the area, and paying over the going rate to instantly attract high quality staff for themselves
  3. low turnover may be caused by: complacency in which staff are over-rewarded for adequate or mediocre performance; stagnation in which they stick with their present jobs because there are no others available; ties, especially applying to those staff who feel bound by chains of gold – e.g. cheap travel in travel companies; hours to suit in retail and public services; cheap personal finance in banking.
- Openness and responsibility is never to be seen as a substitute for tackling real problems. The benefit of a visible style of management is that issues become apparent earlier in their cycle, and can be dealt with more quickly and before they develop into serious problems. When they do arise, they have still to be addressed effectively. In specific IR terms this means having the ability to:
  - deal with requests before they become disputes or grievances;
  - deal with mistakes and misdemeanours before they become disciplinaries;
  - deal with bad practice before it becomes a health and safety or occupational hazard;
  - respond quickly to general requests (e.g. time off, training courses);
  - handle personality clashes before they become claim and counter-claim and before this leads to serious departmental or professional disruption;
  - reinforce company policy, information and direction with clear managerial and supervisory support;
  - use procedures only when all else has failed; and when it is necessary to use them, make sure that this usage is quick and expert.

This reinforces the hypothesis that there is a direct relationship between strong and designed IR policies and procedures, a strong and designed general management style, and a strength of organization performance. The source of good and effective IR is therefore the leadership and direction of the organization itself, and the integration and harmonization of these activities with the rest of the organization.

Sources of bad and ineffective IR

By contrast, these may be identified as follows.

- Lack of corporate realization that this is a potentially valuable and profitable contribution to organization performance.
- Corporate ignorance, fear and prejudice surrounding the realm of IR.
- Corporate belief and perception that this is somehow a separate function, to be conducted as an adjunct to mainstream activities.
- Corporate belief and perception that this is an activity to be managed (as distinct from supported) through extensive written procedures.
- Use of the IR function to get the organization and individual managers off the IR hook when mistakes are made.
- Use of ACAS and the employment tribunal system to absolve corporate responsibility.

Symptoms of bad IR

Fear

The main symptom of bad IR is fear. Any effective macro-organizational analysis must identify this. All managers, whatever their rank, status, occupation or function need to be aware of the extent and prevalence of this within their own ambit. Working back from this, the underlying causes of fear are:

- lack of knowledge;
- lack of relations with other managers;
- lack of relations with other departments;
- and lack of relations with their own staff.

It is essential to understand this. It is a prerequisite to understanding the general levels of morale and motivation, and the likelihood of problems arising. There are also knock-on effects in terms of volume and quality of product and service output. Fear arises from:

- fear of dismissal for trivial reasons, lack of influence, scapegoating, or the personal preference of managers and supervisors;
- fear of discipline for the same reasons;
- fear of bullying, victimization, discrimination or harassment;
- fear of assault or injury from colleagues, customers and clients;
- fear that promises made or inferred will not be kept.

People do not normally consider these fears unless they have positive grounds for doing so. For example, it is very unusual to find people concerned or fearful of harassment where no harassment exists.

More generally, people also fear:

- redundancy, redeployment or forced relocation, as the result of changes in business objectives and business activities; or as the result of merger, takeover, withdrawal or divestment;
- managers and supervisors who are not open, accessible, visible or supportive;
- managers, supervisors and others who need to resort to force of personality to get their own way, when more rational arguments have failed to persuade;
- failure – and this is vastly compounded when people do not know the measures or grounds on which they will be judged for success or failure; the people who are to do the judging; when judgement will be made; how judgement will be made, or what the consequences of that judgement – for good or ill – might be (see Summary Box 7.6).

Other symptoms of which managers need to be aware may be considered from the point of view of being specifically or directly IR-related; and more general, which nevertheless have effects on the prevailing state of organizational IR. The following specific matters should be considered.

Absenteeism
As a specific reflection of IR, this comes in the following forms.

- Self-certificated – there should be cause for concern when this rises above 2 per cent across the workforce; or where the same figure is achieved in individual departments, divisions, locations and functions; or among particular individuals.
- Supported by a doctor's certificate on the specific grounds of stress, breakdown and tension.
- Absenteeism resulting in early retirement on the grounds of ill health.
- Industrial accidents and injuries.

Labour turnover
For reasons other than career advancement or personal and professional relocation. When people state that they do not like their job, this is nearly always not the case. They do in fact usually like the work; what they dislike is normally a combination of their supervisor, management style, work ethics, group interaction – and especially when this leads to feelings of being undervalued or unvalued.

Regular recourse to procedures
Especially grievances and disputes, both collective and individual. There is a resource implication in that managerial time, energy and priority is taken up with resolving such matters, rather than engaging in directly productive and positive activities. This is detrimental to organization, group and individual well-being. It allows the engagement of vested interests and over-mighty subjects – especially staff representatives, IR

SUMMARY BOX 7.6

Fear in financial services

A divisional manager of a large financial services organization operating in the Home Counties of England in the 1990s hotly disputed the validity of concepts of respect and regard in relation to managerial and IR practice. His sole purpose, he declared, was to meet his targets. The way in which this was to be achieved was through instilling fear into the staff who worked for him. They were all, he went on to say, scared stiff of him. They knew that he would discipline or dismiss them if any question arose over the level or quality of their performance. He stated that he would compound this by having days and weeks in which he would make a point of picking on individuals for no better reason than to keep them on their toes. In support of this approach, he went on to declare proudly, his margins were at least as good as anyone else's in the organization. Above all, they were just as good as those who went in for what he called 'soft approaches to management'.

The point came to light during an attitude survey conducted through the organization by a firm of management consultants. Pursuing the points made further, and following up the hypothesis of the particular manager, additional discoveries were made.

- Absenteeism in this department was the highest in the organization at 14 per cent, and seven times the organization average of 2 per cent.
- Attendance levels always rose when the rest of the staff knew that he was going to be away. Checking staff timesheets against the manager's diary movements revealed that self-certificated absence was negligible on those dates when he was booked out of the office. This could be traced back to 1990.
- The department was regarded by everybody else in the organization as a place to be avoided. On the three occasions in one year (1991) when promotions became available, the positions could only be filled by taking external candidates. Neither the staff working in the department, nor potential transferees from elsewhere in the organization, applied for these posts.

Further pursuit of this point – and this manager's hypothesis – led to an analysis of the results achieved by the department. This in turn, demonstrated that the margins in question were being made in spite of this manager and not because of him – that the margins were inbuilt into the particular activities being carried out. While therefore the margin volumes were indeed quite substantial, in percentage terms they were no better than anyone else's. Moreover, the department was undertaking substantial additional cost burdens in order to carry the absenteeism and turnover levels generated by the fear instilled by the particular manager.

specialists and even lawyers – who always have their own agenda. This is especially true where there is a large volume of grievances and disputes, and this always leads to a cumulative negative effect on overall motivation and morale.

Speed of dispute and grievance resolution
The longer it takes to resolve matters successfully and effectively, the worse the state of organizational IR.

Staff withdrawal
The overt or physical form of this is strikes, walk-outs, go-slows and working to rule. Harder to pin down, but ultimately just as destructive, is psychological withdrawal which takes the following forms.

*   *Withdrawal into profession:* in which individuals and groups identify entirely or overwhelmingly with their profession, rather than their organization or employer (see Summary Box 7.7).

Those who manage and direct the organizations and institutions of the UK National Health Service have an extremely strong affinity and identity with the NHS. Those who deliver the front line specialist services – doctors, nurses and other specialist medical professions – do not; they rather identify themselves wholly or overwhelmingly by their profession. Their identity and commitment is primarily and overwhelmingly to their profession, not to the organization for which they work.

SUMMARY BOX 7.7

Withdrawal into profession: health care

---

*   *Withdrawal into work group:* in which the work group becomes the focus of employment life, and members live by its norms and standards, rather than those ostensibly promoted by the organization as a whole (see Summary Box 7.8).

Canteen cultures are informal gatherings of organizational staff which come to develop their own extremely strong and distinctive patterns of behaviour and identity. They set their own norms and values, which everyone accepts, and which become (as stated in the text) a substitute for acceding to those of the organization as a whole.

In 1997, the North Yorkshire police force paid damages of £300,000 and £180,000 to two female police officers after allegations of serious victimization and sexual harassment were proven. This had been carried out by the officers' colleagues and immediate supervisors over a period of several years. The police force had, in its staff handbooks, declared itself to be 'an equal opportunities employer', and had stated elsewhere that no form of victimization would be tolerated, and that anyone found guilty of so doing would be dismissed instantly.

When they received their compensation pay-outs, both officers left the force. Nobody was disciplined or dismissed for their part in the victimization and harassment.

SUMMARY BOX 7.8

Withdrawal into work group: canteen cultures

- *Withdrawal into preferred activities:* in which individuals are employed on a stated job, but actually spend their whole time on preferred activities. Examples are the employee who actually spends the whole of their working life acting as union staff representative or shop steward; someone who is given a project to do as part of their job but spends their whole time doing it; the person who gets themselves appointed to many committees and groups; or the professional traveller – where people are effectively employed to drive around the country. Another example is professional fleecing, in which individuals join organizations for the purpose of professional training, value on their CV, or to gain a foothold in a particular sector, before moving on.

There is no problem with any of this provided it is understood by the organization as a whole. Problems arise when people are known, believed or perceived to benefit as the result of their marginal rather than mainstream activities, to the detriment of those who pursue their stated purpose of employment.

Accidents

Accidents are symptomatic of bad IR when it becomes apparent that the great majority are caused by sloppiness, lack of appropriate supervision, or shortcomings in attitude and value in regard to other people at the organization. This is compounded when people are coerced, threatened or forced into unsafe activities or practices; and are then coerced, threatened or forced into not reporting the accident.

Over-stretching

This occurs when staff shortages are so acute that any further unforeseen absence or sudden vacancy causes serious operational malfunction to the department, division or function, and this in turn leads to staff and managerial stress and malfunction.

More general points that also have a direct effect on the management and effectiveness of IR from time to time are as follows.

Customer and client complaints

These become IR issues where the complaints are about things other than product or service malfunction. These complaints are often about poor or uncooperative staff attitudes; lack of staff responsiveness; concentration by staff on procedures rather than service when handling customer enquiries.

Inability to solve problems

This is symptomatic of a general IR malaise when the approach to operational issues causes negative effects on motivation and morale. It invariably means that those concerned with organizational policy strategy and direction have not thought through the effects of general ways of working on the staff themselves. For example:

- the need to refer simple issues through channels causes frustration and feelings of helplessness or impotence;
- the inability to provide required or acceptable solutions to both customer and internal issues often results in argument, dissatisfaction and further complaint;
- time delays, which are normally frustrating to individuals who want their problems resolved.

These general examples illustrate one part of the direct relationship between operational factors and organizational IR. In many cases, these are overtly easily remedied through attention to the operational end of activities. This does not prevent poor organizations and bad managers trying to resolve matters through the instruments of IR rather than operations.

Culture of blame and scapegoating

This is where organizations and their managers are known, understood, believed or perceived to seek someone to accept full or overwhelming responsibility for organizational activities. The output in all cases is that people seek to avoid responsibility for anything for which they might subsequently be called to account.

Tolerance of unacceptable acts

This falls under three categories:

- Tolerance of bullying, victimization, discrimination, harassment, which are against the law and also morally repugnant.
- Tolerance of blaming junior staff for the shortcomings of the organization or its senior managers.
- Rewarding groups and individuals according to their location, rank and status, rather than according to their output or contribution (see Summary Box 7.9).

Prioritizing adherence to procedures over operational effectiveness

This becomes an IR problem when the effectiveness and output of people is called into question as the result of knowledge, belief or perception that head office values this subservience or use of procedures over their business or service output. This is compounded when those in the field at the front line know, believe or perceive that the fruits of their (so they understand) effective and profitable labours are being squandered on head office luxuries, whims and fancies.

- *Hospital:* in 1997, a nurse was called in at short notice from his day off to cover for a colleague who had gone sick. Unable to park the car, he used the personalized car parking space of one of the surgeons. Later, the surgeon arrived for work. In a towering rage at being unable to park, the surgeon went and found the nurse and ordered him to move his car. The nurse refused, pointing out that he could not leave his ward unattended. At that point, the surgeon hit him. The nurse took out a grievance against the surgeon, and was persuaded to drop it on the grounds that it would ruin his career and not the surgeon's.
- *The Body Shop:* as the result of poor profits in 1997 and 1998, The Body Shop cosmetics company is to 'rationalize' its activities. It is closing and selling off its manufacturing facility, with 260 job losses. The people that will lose their jobs are manufacturing operatives, either semi-skilled or unskilled; nobody at senior levels of the company is envisaged to lose their job.
- *Heat pumps:* in 1997, a company that imported and sold industrial heat pump equipment in the North of England announced record profits. The company chief executive announced that everybody would receive a 10 per cent pay rise; and that sales staff would be included in this. The two sales people working out of the company head office in Leeds duly received their rises. However, the company's regional sales manager, working from a location near Lincoln, and his team, only received a 7 per cent pay rise because they were deemed not to have contributed to the total sales effort of the company. When the sales manager pointed out that he produced a much greater volume of business but that this was mostly for smaller orders from smaller concerns in more rural locations, his requests were ignored. He and his team were subsequently poached by a major rival in the same field; and left taking their existing customer base with them. In 1998, the company in question announced profits down by 78 per cent, in an expanding market.

Macro-organizational analysis draws attention to each of these matters. At the very least, it gives a series of points of initial enquiry into the prevailing state of IR in particular, and also the broader general background of collective and individual motivation and morale. Any manager concerned with the state of organizational and departmental IR should be able to conduct such enquiries; and from this, analyse the results so that some insight can be gained as to why problems are, or are not, arising.

EXCELLENCE AND IR MANAGEMENT

This approach to IR management may be summarized as follows.

- The leadership and management of business and public service organizations requires vision, energy, dynamism and positivism, together with the placing of customers and clients, and their needs, at the centre of activities. IR is interwoven with this and cannot be seen in isolation.

- The closeness of the relationship between the organization and its customers and clients must be maintained. IR and staff management standpoints and practices must be designed so as to enable this to happen.
- Excellent organizations depend on the commitment, motivation, ability, attitudes and expertise of staff. It is therefore extremely bad commercial – as well as IR – practice to design procedures, practices and policies that damage or restrict any of these aspects.
- Supervision levels, hierarchies and establishments are to be kept to a minimum, as these are extremely expensive to sustain and maintain. The purpose of these establishments is to service those who generate the business of the organization, and not to impose unvalued and uncomprehended procedures and practices. Effective IR is therefore a function of this form of supervision; and again, requires skills and expertise in IR on the part of those who are in managerial and supervisory positions.
- From a commercial point of view organizations are dependent upon innovation, improvement and progression; and again, this is dependent upon the excellence, quality, attributes and attitudes of staff. The point is therefore reinforced, that anything that damages or dilutes this, is detrimental to the totality of organization performance.
- Following on from this, if the bias of the organization is supposed to be towards action not procedure, then this too is to be reinforced in the ways in which it structures, manages and develops its IR systems and their operation.
- The culture, values and attitudes – the ways in which activities are carried out in the organization – must be capable of universal acceptance. This is dependent upon the generation of positive attitudes towards the staff; positive beliefs in the quality, excellence and attitudes of the staff; and the role of senior managers in the design and management of the overall culture, style and values (see Summary Box 7.10).

ORGANIZATION DEVELOPMENT AND EXCELLENCE IN IR

Macro-organizational analysis, the 7S approach, and the 'eight' characteristics each require that IR is seen in the context of the progression and development of organizations as a whole, and not in isolation. They also require that equivalent attention is paid to the human side of enterprise, as to outputs, profitability and cost effectiveness.

The organizational development approach requires the following.

- Performance assessment and appraisal; problem raising and acknowledgement; openness, honesty, trust and integrity; access to information, and the capability to analyse and appraise the information.

SUMMARY
BOX 7.10

Criteria for
excellence: the
source of IR
design and
operation

The following criteria for organizational excellence are given by the following authorities.

- Professional organizations are lean and empowered.
- Professional staff require flat structures and autonomy for effective performance.
- Processes and procedures are speedy, simple and effective.

Source: C. B. Handy (1984)

- Excellence is performance thousands and thousands of percentage points over sectoral norms.

Source: T. Peters and N. Austin (1982)

- Innovation and development leading to maximization and optimization of the human resource.
- Innovation in quality of working life.
- Promotion of full and genuine equality of opportunity.
- Models of good practice offer their example to the world and are pleased and proud to be studied.

Source: R. M. Kanter (1985)

In particular, this last set of points draws attention to the direct relationship between organization excellence and IR effectiveness. It also draws broader attention to the human aspect of management, and management style and attitude, that are prerequisites for this success.

- Inter-group activities and cross-fertilization of ideas.
- Organization assessment and evaluation of the development process.

This is dependent upon a corporate commitment to 'doing things this way'. It takes the view that commercial success and service quality advancement are dependent upon the development of staff. It is also aimed at changing, forming and developing culture, values, attitudes and beliefs in positive and constructive ways. In general the key values and qualities reflect a measure of conformity and the willingness of staff to go down the paths indicated; together with an obsession with product or service quality and a strong customer orientation.

Organizations that follow this path gain high levels of commitment, a strong sense of identity and purpose that rise above any divergent individual aims and objectives. Organizations set their own agenda, style and values rather than allowing these to emerge.

This, in turn, is reinforced by a creative and positive environment for the approach to, and solution of, problems and blockages.

It follows from this that IR procedures and practices must be capable of harmonization within this broader approach. Where this form of positive, committed and customer orientated output is genuinely required, it is impossible to have effective IR procedures based on institutionalization and bureaucracy; this is damaging to the output of the organization, as well as providing a counter view in the precise areas of IR activity.

These values become an integral part of the structures and systems of the organization, and these in turn affect every activity. So long as the management style is energetic and positive, this is reflected in the ways in which everyone carries out their work.

Otherwise the specific effects on IR of taking this form of approach to general staff management are:

- reduction in professional, occupational, departmental, divisional and functional barriers, including the psychological barriers behind which people shelter when they are not sure of anything except their own narrow expertise or authority;
- reduction in the need for professional, occupational, departmental, divisional and functional representation in general matters surrounding IR and in the constitution of formal IR instruments and committees;
- increases in mutual confidence which means that issues are raised early and informally rather than being allowed to fester until they become serious problems. If the approach is genuinely adopted, the most likely problem that organizations and their managers are going to have to face is that of frustration, which has come about as the result of the organization not being able to progress at the speed of some of its individuals.

CONCLUSIONS

It needs to be stated that the research carried out, and the standpoint from which it was undertaken, were not clearly rationalized at the outset. It is also easy to form the impression that, because certain organizations work in particular ways, these are therefore the ways forward for everybody.

In specific IR terms, overwhelming attention is paid to management style and the creation of positive and harmonious attitudes and values. It is essential that these are underpinned with qualities and expertise in managers and supervisors who have to deliver this form of organization and the ways of working required. It is also essential that those who work in these situations, and those who aspire to excellent organizational performance, understand the full extent of corporate and senior managerial responsibility in designing, maintaining and developing organizations that can deliver this over long periods of time.

It is also clear that much of this attitude and approach works directly against vested interests and more traditional ways of conducting IR. Staff are not necessarily used to working for organizations that are highly committed to the long-term future; and as illustrated, there are plenty of examples – especially in cases where bad and ineffective IR is apparent – that many organizations fall far short of these standards. What is required in this case is a commitment at first to ensure that these standards are established, and a recognition that there are IR implications as the result. In industries, occupations and locations where there is a long and well-founded history of bad IR, these problems are difficult to address. Wherever organizations have been successful in addressing them, this has only been as the result of the long-term commitment indicated, and the substantial levels of investment in resources, expertise and finance required. Only if this is carried out is there a basis for effective, successful and profitable commercial and public service activities, and the IR that goes with this.

Chapter 8

The managerial view

The effectiveness of IR in the future is dependent on managerial professionalization and capability on the one hand, and on understanding the full implications of the chosen approach to IR on the other. It therefore becomes necessary, in turn, to place the organization in its environment, and IR in the context of organizational and managerial activities as a whole. It is necessary to recognize the main factors that need to be addressed.

This means paying particular attention to those factors that are inside and outside the control of the organization during the course of its existence, and of its conduct of activities. Assessment of the relationship between organizations and their environment are normally carried out as follows.

PEST

This is a corporate brainstorming exercise in which factors inside and outside the control of organizations are parcelled up under the headings of:

- *political factors:* overriding political drives; the influence of political institutions; legal constraints; national, international and governmental policies on interest rates, employment rights, trading conditions, the position of trade unions, and health and safety at work;
- *economic:* with reference again to prevailing financial policies, interest rates, exchange and currency rates; wider conditions of public behaviour, expectation and confidence in the economic state of affairs; whether trading conditions are advantageous or adverse; the precise nature of markets – expanding, static or declining; local and sectoral economic conditions;
- *social:* especially social expectations concerning work, purchasing and buying patterns, and the position of work in society as a whole, and in particular localities; social and cultural expressions – especially the extent to which areas and activities are unionized, regulated, or otherwise limited by social, ethical and religious pressures;
- *technological:* the effect and interrelationship of technology on occupations and work patterns; training for work activities; training

agreements; technological operational agreements; technological output requirements.

Figure 8.1

PEST analysis for IR in a bank branch

POLITICAL	ECONOMIC
• Interest, inflation rates • Minimum wage and salary • Working hours • Technology agreements • Health and safety	• Pay levels • Pay differentials • Differences in terms and conditions • Demands of Head Office
SOCIAL	TECHNOLOGICAL
• Unionization or not • Consultation, recognition • Management of conflict • Working relations • Inter-group relations	• Work patterns and structures • Initial and continuing job training • Unions involved • Occupational mixes

SWOT

The other universal way of analysing the environment, and the position of an organization within it, is to parcel up its attributes under the headings of:

- *strengths:* those factors that enhance organizational performance and reputation;
- *weaknesses:* those factors that diminish organizational performance and reputation;
- *opportunities:* those factors that may become available for exploitation or development;
- *threats:* those factors that may cause the organization to decline or to cease a particular set of activities.

Both PEST and SWOT approaches can be conducted for all organizational activities. The illustrations above serve to demonstrate the position of IR, and clear implications arising, that have to be addressed when considering organizations in their environment. This represents the context in which the managerial view of IR can be taken. Factors for consideration are organizational policy; strategy and direction; managerial fashions and fads; organizational ethics; and human resource management.

STRENGTHS	WEAKNESSES
• Quality of staff • Conduct of IR • Working relations • Pay and reward levels • Other terms and conditions	• Multiplicity of agreements covering different occupations • Potential for disputes in a key area • Differences in status of different occupations
THREATS	OPPORTUNITIES
• Disasters • Disputes with key staff • Loss of public confidence • Inability to maintain high wage levels	• Streamline working arrangements • Enhance consultation and communication • Improve relations with unions and representative bodies

Figure 8.2
SWOT analysis applied to IR at an airline

Most critical of all is to ensure that the approach to IR is compatible with the overall direction of the organization. Useful pointers to the likelihood of this occurring may be considered from the following point of view.

The Porter Model of competitive strategy

Michael E. Porter (1980) identified three effective generic strategic positions as follows.

- *Cost leadership:* cost leadership is where the organization concentrates on being the most effective operator in its sector. In order to be able to do this, it seeks out all sources of cost advantage. All aspects of organization production, marketing and distribution are geared up to this purpose. Organizations that adopt this point of view are likely to offer standard, adequate and medium quality products and services in markets where these are the key characteristics required. The extent of long-term success following this generic strategy depends on the levels of price that can be commanded in pursuit of this in the medium to long term.
- *Focus:* focus is when the organization concentrates on a segment or segments within a sector and seeks to serve them to the exclusion of the rest of the segment. This requires a basic concentration on identifying, anticipating and meeting the needs of the sector and ensuring that this is accurately completed.
- *Differentiation:* differentiation strategies are those which seek a uniqueness or identity for their products in ways that are widely valued by buyers on factors other than price advantage. This involves conducting marketing promotions, public relations and brand

ORGANIZATIONAL POLICY, STRATEGY AND APPROACH

building activities to give the organization and its offerings a distinctive identity.

The following are specific implications for the design, integration and continued effectiveness of IR strategies that arise from these positions.

- *Cost leadership and advantage:* this means concentrating a substantial part of the investment levels and approaches indicated above on staff training and development; procedures and practices; development and redevelopment as a condition of keeping technologically up-to-date and fully productive. It may also require full flexibility of working in order that technological output may be optimized. Where there is extensive unionization, it is essential that this aspect is designed into the procedures under which the IR relationship is to take place (see Summary Box 8.1).

SUMMARY BOX 8.1

Cost leadership and IR: examples

In the UK, Nissan is the cost leader in the car industry, Sony is the cost leader in the electronics industry, and Marks & Spencer is the cost leader in the department store sector. Each company has a high general reputation in its sector and, above all, is widely regarded as a model of good and positive IR practice.

There are caveats, however. Nissan (UK) demonstrated substantial declines in profit in 1999, though the company was quick to point out that this would not affect the fundamental approach to IR. The company recognized the reasons for this as being largely outside its control – especially transfer pricing arrangements between the UK and other states of the EU, the UK and Japan. In any case, the company was sending heavy subsidies back to its loss making activities in Japan.

Marks & Spencer reported substantial declines in profits in both 1998 and 1999. As the result of this, many senior managers were removed. The company appointed a new chief executive, who again expressed his determination to uphold the fundamentally paternalistic and enlightened approach to staff management and IR.

In both cases, it remains a matter of corporate policy that it is not the IR part of the chosen direction that requires reform, but attention to production and service activities – based on the fundamental soundness and integrity of existing IR.

- *Focus:* concentrating a universal product and service delivery to a niche market means high levels of product knowledge and understanding; customer and client familiarity; and an understanding of the wide range of general knowledge among players in the sector. The consequences of bad attitudes for organization representation and therefore performance cannot be overestimated. Once a player in the sector becomes known or perceived to have become uncaring or indifferent in its approach, the word quickly gets around and clients and customers take their business elsewhere. IR concentration is therefore on positive attitudes and approaches; and policies, procedures and practices reinforce these. IR procedures, practices, delivery and style therefore concentrate on quality of performance. All organizations operating in this way need the means to remedy poor performance extremely quickly (see Summary Box 8.2).

SUMMARY BOX 8.2

Subcontracting in the building industry

The UK building and civil engineering industries have a history and tradition of bad IR. At least a part of this is founded on the extensive use of subcontractors; and historically, this has always led to the perception that, because subcontractors were employed, there was very little that the main contractor could do about establishing standards of general behaviour and performance, or specific IR standards, while working on site.

Some of this has been codified in recent years. The main contractor is now required to assume overall responsibility for site health and safety management. Subcontractors that do not comply with this are not normally allowed to work.

Nevertheless, the output of this approach remains very expensive when it does go wrong. Accidents and injuries nearly always become the matter of litigation between subcontractor and main contractor. Overwhelmingly, the subcontractor requires the main contractor to accept responsibility for the injury. Main contractors will normally contest this with the argument that the subcontractor accept responsibility for all aspects of the management of their people while they are on site even though they are working for the main contractor.

In the eyes of the clients, who just want the work done, this is both disruptive and divisive. Clients also do not wish to be tarred or tainted with the fact, belief or perception that their sites are the focus for bad IR in general, and poor health and safety management in particular.

• *Differentiation:* as stated above, differentiation is based on image and impression. IR policy in support of this therefore concentrates on those areas where image and impression are either reinforced or else diluted, damaged and in the worst cases destroyed. IR priorities in this context therefore concentrate on ensuring high standards of individual group and organizational conduct and demeanour; and swift remedial action where this falls short (see Summary Box 8.3).

Reference has already been made elsewhere to the more general point that people prefer not to do business with companies and organizations that have bad IR and will avoid them if possible. It can also be noted that organizations use their own IR as part of their own differentiation processes. Marks & Spencer and The Body Shop for example, have sustained reputations over the past twenty years based on being model employers. A further example of this is Semco, a Brazilian industrial engineering organization (see Summary Box 8.4).

SUMMARY BOX 8.3

The Halifax Bank

The assistant manager of the Halifax Bank in a small seaside town was involved in a night club brawl. News of this reached the local paper; and interest was enhanced when it became apparent that one of the protagonists was quite a senior employee of the Halifax Bank.

The Halifax branch in the particular town was besieged by reporters. Attempts were made to interview both the manager and corporate human resources staff to ascertain what would happen to the individual.

The individual was dismissed. The Halifax stated that it was not prepared to tolerate this form of activity as it was damaging to the overall image of the bank, as well as disruptive to the operations of the particular branch.

The individual took the Halifax to employment tribunal and won the case. The tribunal found that insufficient attention was drawn to the Halifax's own procedures in the relationship between out of hours activities and anything that might be detrimental to the bank's image at large. The company however refused to have the individual back, preferring to pay him substantial damages.

SUMMARY BOX 8.4

Semco

Semco is a Brazilian engineering organization making pumping equipment for the shipping and civil engineering industries.

The company operates a policy of full flexibility of working. It recognizes trade unions, and that they are involved in the company as partners, staff advocates, and for the purposes of pay and terms and conditions negotiations.

The company has a waiting list of 2,500 applicants for employment. In a survey carried out in 1997, 25 per cent of Brazilian university graduates expressed their desire to work for Semco.

The company realizes that any dilution of its approach as a model employer would damage – probably destroy – its perceived reputation as one of the world's leading companies.

The final point to make here is to recognize the opportunities that accrue as the result of integrating IR into whichever strategic position is chosen and the consequences of not doing so. The consequences of not doing so mean that IR is operated as a separate function with all that implies concerning physical and psychological distance, concentration on procedures rather than direction, and the organization expense involved. The failure to integrate IR with overall direction always means that overall performance is damaged or diluted and that long-term effectiveness is only sustainable if the expense and inefficiency incurred as a consequence can be charged to customers and clients in the form of increased prices (see Summary Box 8.5).

This form of compartmentalization emerged in public services in a slightly different way. It is usual for government departments responsible for the overall direction of public services to allocate budgets to particular activities. In the National Health Service, this has had two devastating consequences for the overall effectiveness of IR: the establishment of complex, extensive and expensive IR procedures and practices, committee systems, and negotiating fora, each of which has a budget that it must consume; and the establishment of an agency system whereby those hospitals and health centres that have staff shortages may pay high fees to cover for short, medium and long-term absence. From the point of view of control and command, those in charge of the services know what is available for expenditure on each.

From the point of view of effectiveness of service delivery, and overall morale of those delivering the services at the front line, the effect is devastating. The most minor of problems take months to resolve. Pay rises, changes and improvements in terms and conditions are invariably staggered and concentrate on short-term, expedient and managerial (rather than long-term and operational) priorities. In 1999, in response to a shortage of nursing staff that even the government admitted was critical, and having an extensive adverse effect on service delivery and patient care, the Department for Health offered an increased pay rise for all those nurses entering the profession for the first time. This gained extensive positive media coverage, and there was a perception that 'the government was doing a good job'. However, for those who had been in the profession for any length of time, it was yet again a further mark of disrespect. It was directly damaging to motivation and morale, and the direct consequence was a further loss of experienced, caring and committed staff to other organizations where these qualities would be more highly valued.

Another way of looking at this is through the use of the 'Five Forces Model'.

Five Forces Model

The 'Five Forces Model' of Michael Porter (1980) has the overall purpose of helping organizations and their top managers identify the opportunities, problems, strengths and weaknesses of their operational and competitive position (see Figure 8.3).

There are direct implications for IR.

- *Supply side:* clients may be dissuaded from using suppliers with a bad history of IR problems because of the knowledge, belief or perception of uncertainties in the ability to guarantee supplies. They may be induced to buy up, or buy into, their own suppliers to get over this problem. They may be induced to buy up the supplier with the bad IR history; if this is the case, then investment has to be made in

Figure 8.3

Five Forces Model

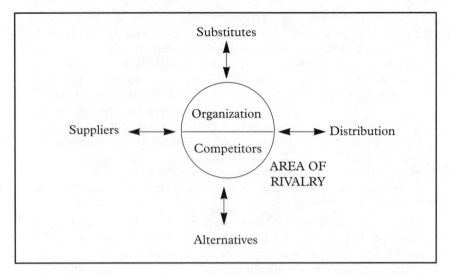

reforming the IR of the acquired company. This is a part that is all too often forgotten (see Summary Box 8.6).

SUMMARY BOX 8.6

Supply side: Supersoft Drinks

Supersoft Drinks Ltd is a producer, manufacturer and distributor of fizzy drinks in the north of England. In 1994, following difficulties on the supply side, the company bought out their main supplier of glass and plastic bottles. For many years, there had been a history of uncertainty of supplies and this was due to the inability of the company that manufactured the containers to get over a long history of IR problems.

Supersoft accordingly went into the venture, believing that, once this had been achieved, all of its problems would be over. However, it was then faced with two problems. First, it had not taken into account the amount of investment, finance, resources and commitment needed to reform IR in the container company. Moreover, when it did try to tackle these problems, it was immediately faced with its own fresh round of disputes, because the container company believed that Supersoft was about to dismiss all of the bottle and plastic manufacturing staff. The second problem that Supersoft had to face was that basic pay, terms and conditions of employment at the manufacturing plant were better than their own. Supersoft were consequently faced with claims for parity in these areas from their own existing staff. The company and its backers and shareholders had failed to take into account any of this when making the bid for the container company. They had only seen the business and strategic opportunity from its most narrow point of view.

- *Distribution:* similar problems occur. Distributors are unwilling to take business from suppliers with a history of bad IR if they can sustain their activities elsewhere. Companies and organizations are similarly unwilling to use distributors with a bad history of IR themselves (see Summary Box 8.7).

Distribution of goods and services by railway is cost effective in terms of moving large volumes around an historically long-established transport infrastructure. However, once at the railway destination, whatever is being transported has to be unloaded and finish its journey by road.

There is therefore an operational problem inherent. This is compounded when the railway distribution system is beset by IR problems. The decline of the distribution of goods and services through the railway network has been accelerated by:

- restrictive practices and demarcation lines, meaning that some groups of staff are allowed to do certain things but not others;
- there is no history of flexible working, nor have the senior managers of railway transport companies taken any real steps in this direction;
- abolition of nationally agreed terms and conditions of employment, allowing local managers to set new lower terms and conditions of employment and wage levels;
- insistence on seven-day working without compensation for the changes in historic work patterns;
- demotion in the status of key staff – especially station and depot managers and train drivers;
- reduction in manning levels on all trains.

Without considering the operational merits and consequences of the overall approach, the railway companies were certain to run into trouble in the operation of their services because of their lack of attention to the process of change and the human elements contained therein. The problem has also been exacerbated by short-term drives and demands from shareholders and backers for asset enhancement and increased share values.

- *Substitutes and new entrants:* if a product or service becomes unavailable because of a strike or dispute, then people will seek satisfaction elsewhere. In some cases, they will return to the original organization when the dispute is over. In some cases, they will have no choice but to do so. In other cases, they will take their business or demand for public services elsewhere if they possibly can. In each of these cases, there is a general residual negative effect on the future relationship.

  In IR terms, substitution may also take place when an organization is able to gain a foothold in a new market as the result of its command of better quality technology, and higher levels of skills and expertise, underpinned by an IR system that enables these to be used to better advantage than those of the existing players (see Summary Box 8.8).

- *Rivalry:* industrial, commercial and public sector activities are dependent to a greater or lesser extent on knowledge, belief or perception that they need 'unique selling points' for their continued success. IR is only a unique selling point in those circumstances where a strike or dispute has caused loss or interruption to suppliers of products and services. However, this may have enduring effects as

SUMMARY BOX 8.8

The entry of Japanese companies into the UK construction industry

Much has been made in recent years of the recession in the construction industry in the UK. While this is undoubtedly true, it also indicates that there are substantial business opportunities for those that are prepared to give priority to the IR and staff management aspects in any sector.

Between 1985 and 1995, the UK construction industry declined in value by one third. During this period, Japanese construction companies gained their first foothold in this market. At a time when there was overwhelming overt pressure on UK companies to secure all the work that they possibly could for the first time, foreign competitors were able to gain a foothold.

Large UK companies went down the route of putting as many activities as possible on a subcontracted – and therefore non-responsible – basis. As a short-term cost cutting method, this was demonstrably efficient, in that reports to shareholders could show that 'attempts were being made' to look at alternative forms of delivery. In terms of management of staff and IR in particular, this resulted in an almost total loss of control, and this was compounded by the knowledge among subcontractors that they were being hired for their cheapness rather than expertise.

The Japanese company Shimizu gained for itself £440 million worth of work in the UK over this period. It was able to do this by offering work quality, delivery, and deadline guarantees. The overwhelming reason for this was the company's attitudes to its staff – everyone was employed on long-term, job-secure contracts, and subcontracting was only carried out for specialist and UK culture-specific activities (mainly concerning the employment of UK lawyers to handle the legal aspects of its contracts). Above all, the company secured full flexibility of working arrangements with its union; and continued to pay wages that were among the highest in the sector.

above. IR often therefore becomes a secondary or subsidiary selling point along the lines of: 'Not only are our products and services as good as any other but we can also guarantee uninterrupted supplies. You will also not be tarred with the brush of dealing with a company that is known or believed to have a history of bad staff management and IR.' This is one of the central themes on which Japanese companies in all sectors have built their long-term commercial success in activities in Western Europe and North America.

Johnson and Scholes

Gerry Johnson and Kevan Scholes (1994) identified eight different points against two variables of price and perceived added value. They identified three strategy types within this (Figure 8.4).

The key IR implications are:

Stategy	Policy	IR
Cost Strategies		
1. Low price/ low added value	Segment-specific	Low wage, low skill High turnover
2. Low price	Price wars, low cost	Low wage, intensive High wage differentials
Differentiation		
3. Hybrid	Low cost base	Flexible work patterns, low wage
4. Differentiation	Perceived added value	Intensive front-line Commercially driven, medium wage
5. Differentiation with premium prices	Added value	Exclusive, medium to high sectoral wages
Failure		
6. Increased price, standard value	Declining market share	Redundancies, recruitment freezes, confrontations
7. High prices, low value	Monopoly	National terms and conditions
8. Low value, standard price	Loss of market	Redundancies

Figure 8.4

The Johnson and Scholes strategic approach

- *Acquisition:* attention to the history and traditions of IR in the organization being acquired, with especial reference to any history of bad IR. Specific work practices, terms and conditions of employment, health and safety issues, and matters concerning trade union recognition, have also to be considered.
- *Divestment:* attention to the enduring nature of IR in the particular aspects of union recognition, staff consultation mechanisms, collective and individual rights. The Transfer of Undertakings Protection of Employment Regulations require that each of these conditions has to be satisfied when divestment is taking place, and that this remains the responsibility of the divesting organization.
- *Harvesting:* in which fully flexible working arrangements are likely to be necessary to ensure maximum quality and volume of output while the particular product or service is so commercially successful; and attention to the staff management and IR implications during the harvest and when the harvest is over. This may include the requirement to transfer staff on to the next round of products and services; and may also include the necessity to pay attention to redundancy and redeployment.

- *Withdrawal:* this comes in two main forms – when an organization stops making a particular product or delivering a particular service; or when it carries on producing the same products or services but uses different methods, technology or work organization (i.e. it withdraws from those ways in which it has hitherto conducted its activities). Various IR approaches are available and need to be considered:
  - redundancy;
  - retraining, redeployment and relocation;
  - job evaluation;
  - staff transformation;
  - workforce expertise, acquisition and divestment.

  Whichever is chosen, there are distinctive implications for the policy and direction of IR (see Summary Box 8.9).

SUMMARY BOX 8.9

The Johnson and Scholes' strategic approach: IR examples

- *South West Trains:* in 1992, South West Trains was acquired by the Stagecoach Company. Following this acquisition, Stagecoach made 30 per cent of the train drivers redundant. These redundancies took effect during 1995 and 1996. In 1997 and 1998 the company became forced to cancel anything up to 40 per cent of its services because of a driver shortage.
- *Mitsubishi:* in 1970, the Mitsubishi Company took the decision to pull out of shipbuilding and to concentrate on car manufacture. It was able to do this without a single job loss, and consequent loss of social and organizational reputation. It engaged in a long-term investment programme designed to transform shipbuilders into car workers.
- *Financial Times/Pearson:* in the same week in September 1981, as the News International Group was having its worst riots outside its new Wapping plant in London as the result of the introduction of new technology and working practices, the *Financial Times*, owned by Pearson, moved its activities to a building adjacent to that of News International. The *Financial Times* required its staff and unions to use new work methods and working practices and technology. It achieved this without any of the troubles that News International incurred. It was able to do this through a commitment to staff management and IR that was integrated with the strategic and organizational drive to change technology and output methods, exactly the same as News International. It managed to do this without a single job loss or dispute. The IR investment at the *Financial Times* was concentrated on gaining the long-term commitment of staff, and their representative unions; while at News International, the dispute was not finally resolved until 1988.

For each there is also an ethical dimension as follows.

Sternberg (1995) argues that an ethical approach to organizational policy and direction must have the aim of securing long-term organizational survival, and that this is only achieved through continuous attention to, and development of, products and services, so that long-term customer and client satisfaction is, in turn, ensured. In this way again, is the long-term confidence and security of owners, shareholders and backers assured, thereby causing them to continue to want the organization to exist.

Sternberg's other premise of an ethical approach is the concept of 'ordinary common decency', which is a summary of the human values required to secure and sustain this. In IR terms, the ethical approach concentrates primarily on ordinary common decency and consists of the following.

- Absolute standards of integrity and probity.
- The quality of hierarchical relationships.
- The quality of relations between individuals, groups, departments, divisions and functions.
- The quality of relationships between the organization and its vested interests – trade unions, employers' associations, professional bodies, the Health and Safety Executive, ACAS, consumer groups, pressure groups, local, regional and national lobbies.
- The standpoint, design and delivery of staff handbooks, procedures and practices.
- The creation and sustenance of the desired style of management.
- Intolerance of activities, attitudes, behaviour and performance that do not conform with the stated organizational standards.

It is also possible to identify:

- *Social ethics:* the norms of the society at large, and the overriding attitudes, values and beliefs that it espouses.
- *Occupational ethics:* reflecting the ways in which particular occupations are to be carried out.
- *Specific ethics:* reflecting the particular demands of, for example, trade unions, membership of professional, occupational or technical bodies.
- *Valued ethics:* reflecting those attitudes and values that organizations require or expect on the part of their staff.
- *Rewarded ethics:* those attitudes, values and beliefs that are rewarded – and by contrast, those that are either not rewarded (reflecting an attitude of corporate indifference), or those that are punished or excluded (see Summary Box 8.10).

SUMMARY BOX 8.10

Ethics and IR

The examples from the previous Summary Box 8.9 can now be developed further.

- *South West Trains:* in the interests of securing a cost advantage through the initial redundancy programme among its train drivers, Stagecoach could be viewed with hindsight as acting in a short-term and expedient – rather than long-term and secure – manner. Further, the specific IR problems that the company had to deal with in recruiting new drivers concerned relationships between the new and existing workforce, terms and conditions of employment and salary levels. The company also had a long-term problem of mutual trust, respect and interest to address.

- *Mitsubishi:* in the transition from shipbuilding to car manufacture, the company was able to reinforce – and demonstrate – its commitment to job and work security. It was also able to use this as an example of where it had been faced with serious business problems, and yet had been able to resolve these without a single job loss or dispute.

- *Financial Times:* the *Financial Times* is a niche newspaper, carrying substantial in-depth reportage on all aspects of business and organization performance. It was able to reinforce this position through its own management of transition and change – with especial reference to the IR and staff management aspects.

**THE PROFES-
SIONALIZATION
OF
MANAGEMENT**

The best managers are highly professional, committed and educated operators, highly trained and with excellent analytical and critical faculties. Beyond this, there is a body of skills and aptitudes, knowledge, attitudes and behaviour which effective managers must have and be able to draw upon.

What is required of effective managers reads, if one is not careful, like a checklist for life. Managers must have strategic, planning and organizational skills necessary to determine and carry out the directive functions required in particular situations. They must understand basic aspects of human behaviour and motivation. They must have a basic grasp of quantitative and analytical methods enabling them to recognize those activities that are truly profitable and effective and those that are not. They must be familiar with information systems and be able to use the information available to them. They must be able to draw accurate conclusions from this. They must be able to ask for information and to present it in ways that the organizations for which they work require. They must be able to manage, maintain, develop and improve the human resource. They must have a good knowledge of all aspects of the law, including IR law. They must understand and be able to apply strategic processes, priorities, schedules, timetables and techniques. They must set standards of performance for themselves, their peers, their subordinates and the organization as a whole, and take early active steps to remedy each of these areas when required.

Related to this, the personal qualities required in managers, and in the management of IR, include vision, ambition, energy, commitment, self-motivation, situational knowledge, drive and enthusiasm, creativity and imagination, a thirst for knowledge, a commitment to improvement, the ability to grow and broaden the outlook and vision of themselves and their organization; together with a positive and dynamic attitude, self-discipline, empathy with the staff, love of the organization and profession, and pride and enthusiasm in the job, its people, its products, its services, its customers and clients. These qualities and attributes provide a springboard for a successful and professional operator.

IR and the professionalization of management

It is now necessary to look at the extent to which this is a genuinely distinctive expertise and profession (see Figure 8.5).

Figure 8.5
Professions

The classical professions are medicine, law, the priesthood and the army. The following properties are normally held to distinguish these from the rest of society.

- *Distinctive expertise:* not available elsewhere in society.
- *Distinctive body of knowledge:* required by all those who aspire to practise in the profession.
- *Entry barriers:* in the form of examinations, time serving and learning from experts.
- *Formal qualifications:* given as the result of acquiring the body of knowledge and clearing the entry barriers.
- *High status:* professions are at the top of the occupational tree.
- *Distinctive morality:* e.g. for medicine, the commitment to keep people alive as long as possible; for law, a commitment to represent the client's best interests; for the Church, a commitment to godliness and to serve the congregation's best interests; for the army, to fight within stated rules of law.
- *High value:* professions make a distinctive and positive contribution both to their organization and to individual members of the society.
- *Self-regulating:* professions set their own rules, codes of conduct, standards of performance and qualification.
- *Self-disciplining:* professions establish their own bodies for dealing with problems, complaints and allegations of malpractice.
- *Unlimited reward levels:* according to preferred levels of charges and the demands of society.
- *Life membership:* dismissal at the behest of the profession; ceasing to work for one employer does not constitute loss of profession.
- *Personal commitment:* to high standards of practice and morality; commitment to deliver the best possible in all circumstances. Commitment to personal standards of behaviour in the pursuit of professional excellence.
- *Continuous development:* of knowledge and skills; a commitment to keep abreast of all developments and initiatives in the field.
- *Governance:* by institutions established by the profession itself.

The professionalization of IR may be seen in terms of comparison with Figure 8.5 as follows.

- *Distinctive expertise:* reflected in a clear understanding of the totality of the situation, as well as the ability to deliver IR skills, qualities, attitudes and expertise.
- *Distinctive body of knowledge:* especially the law; understanding of the organization; understanding of human behaviour and interactions.
- *High status:* someone who is expert in the field enjoys high status in their organization.
- *High value:* someone who is expert in the field makes an enduring positive contribution to their organization.
- *Distinctive morality:* that the IR professional will only be able to sustain a long-term effectiveness in the field if they do not act from the point of view of expediency or partial interest.
- *Personal commitment:* the ability to put one's hand on one's heart in the delivery of the expertise.
- *Continuous development:* and awareness of the different initiatives undertaken by organizations.
- *Governance:* the IR professional is often placed at the mercy of courts and the employment tribunal system, and may have their activities and expertise regulated in this way.

If this approach is taken, the beginnings of a distinctive professional expertise surrounding IR can be observed. This also underlines the long-term commitment necessary to ensure effective organizational IR, and the consequent managerial commitment necessary.

HUMAN RESOURCE MANAGEMENT (HRM)

The other main aspect of the managerial approach to IR is the human resource management (HRM) perspective. The HRM view concerns the integration of all aspects of management that used to be (and in some cases still are) the remit of the personnel function. The coverage is:

- staff planning and forecasting;
- recruitment and selection;
- pay and rewards;
- equal opportunities;
- performance appraisal and measurement;
- training and development;
- career planning;
- health and safety;
- welfare;
- consultation, participation and involvement;
- communication means and methods;

together with the more direct IR concerns of:

- discipline and grievance management;
- dismissal;
- redundancy;
- redeployment and retraining;
- the management of disputes;
- negotiations and collective bargaining.

The HRM view requires direction and integration of all activities, together with an understanding of the combined effects of the inter-actions of each (see Summary Box 8.11).

SUMMARY BOX 8.11

The personnel assistant

A hospital in south-eastern England advertised for a personnel assistant. It promised a starting salary of up to £14,000; it also offered exciting career prospects; and training and development would be available to the right person. The advert was placed in the *Guardian* newspaper together with *People Management*, the journal of the Institute of Personnel and Development.

The hospital received a large number of applicants, and eventually employed a woman in her early twenties, recently graduated from one of the local universities.

Her commencing salary was £9,500. When she questioned this, and especially the disparity between what had been implied in the advertisement and the reality of the starting salary, she was told, 'This salary is *up to* £14,000. Moreover, if you don't like it, you can always leave – we had over 300 applicants.' Non-plussed, she carried on.

During the weeks that followed, her duties consisted of little more than making tea for managers, taking minutes at an interminable round of meetings, and helping the departmental secretary to carry out filing duties.

After six months she was due to be appraised on her initial performance. Her manager kept putting off the appraisal meeting, pleading pressure of work. She finally had her appraisal after eleven months' service. At the appraisal the manager said, 'We never quite knew why we were taking a personnel assistant on. There was no real job for such a position at this hospital. The post was advertised without my knowledge or consent. Furthermore, because of budget constraints in the training and development budget, we are unable to offer you any training or development.'

From that point onwards the personnel assistant concentrated her efforts on getting a new job elsewhere. She relocated to London, and got herself a job at approximately twice the salary as a junior personnel officer for a department store chain.

Some months afterwards, she was sent on a training course at an outward bound centre in north-western England as part of her management development programme. During the period of the course, she became friendly with one of the other tutors, a woman in her early thirties. She was astonished to find that her tutor had been her direct predecessor at the hospital in the south-east of England. On an impulse, the two women decided to telephone the hospital and asked to speak to the personnel assistant. They were told by the hospital switchboard, 'We do not have a personnel assistant at present, though the position is shortly to be advertised. The previous incumbent only lasted six weeks. We have found it impossible to retain personnel assistants. The previous two post holders had clearly got ideas above their station. They were snooty and arrogant and showed no commitment to the hospital, or to the health service. We spend thousands of pounds advertising these posts and go to a lot of trouble to get the selection processes absolutely right. To be quite honest, we are beginning to wonder whether we need personnel assistants at all.'

Specific IR concerns that have to be addressed at the HRM policy stage are:

- Management and supervisory style – because this is what will be implementing and delivering the whole.
- Pay and reward strategies and approaches, and their combined effects.
- The extent to which equality of treatment and opportunity is genuinely delivered.
- The approach and attitude taken to the measurement and appraisal of performance.
- The standpoint adopted towards organizational, occupational and individual health and safety at work.

The delivery of each of these reflects the genuine organizational attitudes held about the staff. Each then either becomes a source of discipline and grievance activity, disputes and dissatisfaction – or does not (see Summary Box 8.12).

SUMMARY BOX 8.12

Watford Football Club 1999

In May 1999, Watford Football Club won promotion from the football league first division to the FA Carling Premiership. The success had been achieved by a group of players who had committed themselves to the good of the club, and to each other.

Immediately the club gained its success – in a play-off final at Wembley Stadium under the rules of the competition – the club's manager, Graham Taylor, was asked by the media at large which new players he would be needing to acquire or purchase, as the present group of players was not of a sufficient quality to sustain life in the higher division.

The manager replied 'I will attend to that when the time comes. At present, you are showing great disrespect for the achievements of a dedicated and committed group of players. For these players, it is the greatest achievement during the course of their careers. Within an hour of this, you are asking me effectively to denigrate them and their achievement. You are also denigrating their achievement yourselves. You should be ashamed of yourselves.'

Each aspect also feeds the others, and the total, either positively or negatively. For example, high levels of concern for health and safety at work are normally reinforced by training and development activities in this area. Performance appraisal that is open and positive normally reinforces a positive and direct form of management. Genuine equality of opportunity is reinforced through the use of open selection methods. Above all, pay structures, scales and increases are reinforced through transparency of the information made available on the financial standing of the organization so that these can be known, as well as believed and perceived, to be fair and equitable.

At its best, the phrase human resource management is used to describe a strategic and contextual approach to the management of people, and to each of the aspects indicated above in organizations, as follows.

- The establishment of a distinctive and designed culture capable of accommodating the different and diverse professions and occupations present.
- Assessment of the opportunities and likely possible and potential threats and consequences present as the result.
- Assessment of the standpoint from which personnel policies are to be drawn up.
- Assessment of the delivery of the personnel function and its component parts (see Summary Box 8.13).

SUMMARY BOX 8.13

Personnel

Historically, two distinctive views have been adopted.

- That it is an expert and distinctive function in its own right delivering high quality specialist expertise separate from the front line and other support activities of the organization (IPD, 1994ff.).
- That it is an integral part of all managerial activities, and that this expertise is therefore required to be present in everyone who aspires to supervisory or managerial occupations; that all managers and supervisors need both full understanding and a large measure of autonomy in the delivery of personnel policies (Peter F. Drucker, 1988).

Two further variations may also be observed.

- The retention of personnel/HR consultancy services which are called upon in support of organizational activities or when there are serious problems to be resolved (Torrington and Hall, 1987).
- The development of strategic personnel cores and nuclei as part of corporate headquarters functions and which work in support of front line delivery of personnel activities and services when required in different departments, divisions, locations and functions (D. W. Griffiths, 1996).

IR aspects of HRM

In this specific context, IR aspects are as follows.

- Assessment of organizational strategy, direction and policy so that the best and most appropriate forms of staff representation, policies, procedures and practices can be determined.
- Assessment of the size, scope, scale, function and delivery of any specialist or distinctive IR input required as a consequence (see Summary Box 8.14).

SUMMARY BOX 8.14

IR aspects of HRM

There are some simple guidelines.

- If unions are to be recognized, then expertise is required in dealing with them.
- If there are highly professional and expert occupations present, then expertise and access is required in dealing with them.
- If there are situational and environmental problems inherently present, then these must be recognized and the means for dealing with them institutionalized.

Tarmac UK Plc

Until the company was broken up in 1999, Tarmac Plc was the UK's largest building and construction company. It also had the worst safety record in terms of fatality, accident and injury rates per member of staff and fatality, accident and injury rates per activity.

In 1994, at a site near Warrington, Cheshire, UK, some men were working in a deep drainage ditch when the earth walls collapsed. One man died. In 1996, at a site at Hebburn, Northumberland, UK, some men were working in a deep drainage ditch when a dumper truck unloaded concrete on top of one of them. He also died.

In each case, the union involved was the Union of Construction and Allied Trades and Technicians (UCATT). UCATT fought for, and won, compensation for each of the bereaved families. In each case also, both UCATT and the Health and Safety Executive heavily criticized the company's attitude to staff safety. The view taken by UCATT was summarized as follows: 'All building and construction sites are inherently unsafe, so organizations and their site managers should take steps to ensure that they are made as safe as possible. Both of these fatalities would have been avoided if simple procedures had been established and followed – and valued by the company.'

The company paid out large sums in damages to the families of both the deceased. Between 1996 and 1999, the company had twelve further fatalities on its sites. At the time the company was broken up and sold off, it had none of the following:

- an institutional approach to its dealings with UCATT;
- an institutional approach to health and safety on site;
- an institutional approach to site supervision.

There was also no formal or informal mechanism for participation, involvement or consultation on these or any other IR matters. The company's market, activities, and income from work declined to the point at which no financial stakeholder viewed it with enough confidence to prevent it being broken up and sold on as a series of assets. The company's attitude to IR simply reflected and accelerated this decline.

- Assessment of specific IR problems present and potential.
- Providing the means, through either managerial, supervisory and staff training, or the retention of experts, for dealing with this.
- Assessing the costs incurred as the result (see Summary Box 8.15).

SUMMARY BOX 8.15

The costs of IR

The costs of IR are as follows.

- *Fixed costs:* incurred in designing, delivering and establishing the policies, procedures and mechanisms for the conduct of IR; these are a condition of organizational establishment and existence, and therefore fixed.
- *Derived costs:* in terms of lost orders, deliveries, contracts, customers and clients as the consequence of bad IR.
- *Hidden costs:* management, staff and representative time spent in meetings and producing the outputs of those meetings.
- *Crisis costs:* the need to be able to command, deliver and prioritize resources to cope with genuinely unforeseen circumstances.

These costs may then, if so desired, be apportioned as follows.

- *Steady-state:* the proportion of total fixed cost or investment required to deliver the IR strategy, policy, direction and activities, and the mechanisms necessary as the result.
- *Innovation and pioneering:* the IR costs associated with changing technology, work location, work practices, hours of work, pay rates and other terms and conditions of employment.
- *Crises and IR:* as indicated in the main text.

- Assessing the bills incurred as the result and their cost effectiveness. These bills are pay rates, pay rises, benefits, perks and other factors built into terms and conditions of employment (see Summary Box 8.16).

SUMMARY BOX 8.16

Barclays Bank

In 1999, Barclays Bank announced what they described as 'a ground breaking pay and partnership deal geared towards improving its troubled relationship with unions and helping it to meet promises made to City of London authorities about controlling its costs'.

At its core was a three year pay and benefits deal, which was generated by a desire to reform the performance-related pay system which it had in place, and which had sparked a series of one day strikes in 1997 and 1998.

The company gave itself three years to phase the new scheme in. Beyond that, the company's main goal in negotiating with unions had been to establish a partnership approach to industrial relations to supersede the previous adversarial relationship.

At the same time, the company also needed to handle 1100 proposed job cuts at its Barclaycard Division. Under the previous relationship, the trade unions would simply have been told that the jobs were going. Under the proposed partnership, ways were established by which people could opt for retraining and relocation. There was a redundancy package also offered, but this was entirely voluntary; there were no compulsory redundancies.

The partnership arrangement also entailed setting up working parties to look at the relationship between IR, organizational and individual performance, and the long-term effects on the bank's range of businesses. The bank also offered NVQ accredited training schemes for trade union and staff representatives.

The approach illustrates a broad and fully operational perspective on the costs of IR; and the contextual point that IR practices contribute positively or negatively to staff motivation and morale – for which there is also a cost.

- Assessing the total costs, benefits and value added or subtracted as the result.

CONCLUSIONS The managerial perspective on IR allows for organization direction, operations, primary and support activities to be seen (Figure 8.6).

The great weakness of all managerial approaches to IR is the overwhelming propensity to see the staff and their expertise as commodities. In some cases, this is overt (see Summary Box 8.17).

In other cases this attitude is less apparent. The worst IR problems occur when people come to know, believe or perceive that they are disposable at the whim of a particular manager, or as the result of physically and psychologically remote decisions taken by senior managers and directors. This feeling is compounded when these senior managers and directors are known, believed or perceived to be acting on the direction of shareholders.

Figure 8.6

The managerial perspective on IR

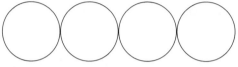

Direction   Operations

Primary   Support

Ideally, there is a large measure of integration between each.

Adoption of this approach is also likely to prove useful in identifying sources of actual or potential dysfunction. For example:

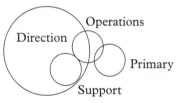

Direction Operations Support Primary

where everything operates on its own;

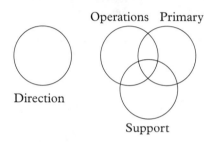

Operations Primary

Direction

Support

where policy and direction is out of synchronization with the rest, and insufficient attention is given to full integration. This could occur, for example, as the result of preferred or ordered change in direction and strategy;

Operations

Direction

Primary

Support

where the organization has adopted a faddish or sales package approach piecemeal without regard to the management of IR.

In each case, the sources of dysfunction and potential conflict are apparent, and the likely nature, scale and extent of IR problems can then be assessed.

The unitary or pluralist approach identified in Chapter 1 still holds good. The main lesson from the managerial approach to IR is to design and integrate the approach with the rest of organization activities. It leads to a better understanding of why particular points of view and perspectives are adopted and what it is expected to contribute to IR as well as to the organization as a whole. It gives particular insight into the likelihood and extent of contribution to profitability and effectiveness of the IR approach adopted. Above all, the managerial approach to IR underlines the need for a long-term perspective rather than conducting matters on a short-term or expedient basis.

SUMMARY BOX 8.17

Staff as commodities: examples

- *Football:* all football clubs maintain a watching brief in the asset value of their players. In some cases, this creates a relationship bordering on contempt – one of the world's top players by reputation is paid a basic salary of £70,000 per week by one of the world's top clubs (also by reputation); the result is a mutually non-productive and adversarial relationship. Mutually bound by contract, neither can get rid of the other, except by transfer, for the next two and a half years.
- *Journalism:* many newspapers operate under the knowledge, belief or perception that they require to overpay for 'star columnists'. These are perceived by mainstream journalists to be divisive and disruptive in terms of the advantageous salaries, terms and conditions of employment that they are able to negotiate for themselves. In many cases also, the star columnists have been hired as the result of their expertise or reputation in other areas (e.g. cookery, sport, music).
- *Subcontracting in building and construction work:* many construction and civil engineering companies view this as a purchase arrangement in which they are able to absolve themselves of any responsibility for standards of behaviour or practice on projects and sites.

Chapter 9

The organization culture view of IR

Attention to organization culture is a key aspects of macro-organizational analysis from the point of view of any aspect of management. Especially when considering staff management and IR, it is essential to understand the desired and prevailing attitudes, values, beliefs and patterns of behaviour.

A simple definition of organization culture is '*the ways in which things are done here*'. For example, during officer training, recruits are taught 'the army way'; and similarly, during induction programmes, recruits to commercial organizations are taught 'the Body Shop way', 'the Marks & Spencer way', or 'the Canon way'.

A more extensive definition of organizational culture is given by Schein (1992):

> a pattern of basic assumptions – invented, discovered or developed by a given group as it learns to cope with its problems of external adaptation and internal integration – that has worked well enough to be considered valuable and therefore to be taught to new members as the correct way to perceive, think and feel in relation to those problems.

Luthans (1994) identifies six characteristics of organization culture, each of which has extensive implications for the style, standpoint, quality and delivery of IR.

- *Observed behavioural regularities:* when organizational participants interact with one another they use common language, terminology and rituals.
- *Norms:* standards of behaviour including guidelines on how much work to do, how to carry it out, how to establish and maintain inter-group and superior–subordinate relations.
- *Dominant values:* akin to shared values, these are the major values that the organization advocates and expects its staff to share.
- *Philosophy:* policies that set forth the organization's standards and beliefs and demands about how employees are to be treated.
- *Rules:* strict prescribed guidelines underpinning standards of behaviour; and unwritten rules related to getting along in the organization. Luthans calls this 'learning the ropes'.

- *Organizational climate:* an overall feeling conveyed by the physical lay-out, interaction of staff, departments, divisions, groups and functions, and the ways in which people conduct themselves away from the organization.

It is also useful to distinguish the following.

- *Dominant culture:* a set of core values, attitudes, patterns of behaviour and ways of working shared and subscribed to by a majority of the organization's members; and which are underpinned by IR and staff management policies and procedures in their delivery.
- *Subcultures:* sets of values, attitudes, patterns of behaviour and ways of working shared by minorities of the organization's members; the extent and prevalence of subcultures needs to be recognized by all those with IR responsibilities, especially in large, diverse, multi-site and complex organizations. Subcultures typically are a result of autonomous work patterns; autonomy of site, departmental or functional supervision; and group members who have strong professional or occupational mutual identity. This identity may be in addition to, or in place of, organizational identity.
- *Strength and weakness:* some organizational cultures may be defined as strong, others weak. Cultural strength is a reflection of the extent to which the desired attitudes, values and beliefs are capable of assimilation by all members of staff; the degree of identity with the organization; and the nature of relationships between the organization and its staff, and between different staff members and groups. Where there are no standards or cohesion, and where people tend to set their own standards and values, and where these are accepted rather than modified by the organization, the totality of the organizational culture is weak.
- *Designed cultures:* this means that the culture is shaped by those responsible for organizational direction, behaviour and results; and it is created in the pursuit of this. This involves establishing the standards of attitudes, values and behaviour that everyone is required to subscribe to as a condition of joining the organization.
- *Emergent cultures:* this is where the culture is formed by the staff and staff groups rather than directed by the organization. The result is that people think, believe and act according to the pressures and priorities of their peers and groups (including vested interests) to which they belong. This in turn leads to the staff setting their own informal procedures and sanctions, or operating formally in ways that suit their own purposes rather than those of the organization.
- *Informal cultures:* these relate to membership of different groups:
  - *the canteen culture:* whereby the shared values adopted are those of groups that gather away from work situations but elsewhere on the premises;

- *elites and cliques:* whereby strength and primacy is present in some groups at the expense of others: this normally leads to over-mightiness;
- *work regulation cultures:* whereby the volume and quality of work is regulated by the group for its own ends rather than those of the organization;
- *informal norming:* whereby individuals are pressurized to adopt the attitudes and values of those around them rather than those of the organization.

Cultural pressures vary between organizations. The main factors that need to be considered are as follows.

CULTURAL PRESSURES

- *History and traditions:* the origins of the organization; its initial aims, objectives, philosophy and values; the regard in which these are currently held; the ways in which they have been developed.
- *Nature of activities:* historical and traditional, and also current and envisaged.
- *Technology:* the relationship between technology, the workforce, work design, work patterns, organization and structure; alienative factors and steps taken to get over these; levels of technology, stability and change; levels of expertise, stability and change.
- *Past, present and future:* the importance of the past in relation to current and proposed activities; special pressures (especially mythology struggles and glories) of the past; the extent to which the organization is living in the past, present or future.
- *Purposes, priorities and attention:* with a special reference to the position of staff, the genuine respect, value and esteem in which different staff groups are held by the organization.
- *Size:* and complexity, expertise mix, and organization structure.
- *Location:* geographical location including reference to local, national and sectoral traditions and values.
- *Management style:* the stance adopted by the organization in managing and supervising its people; the stance required by the organization of its managers and supervisors; the general state of relationships between people and the organization; the general nature of the relationship between superiors and subordinates.

Each of these areas either has a direct impact, or else places limitations, on the characteristics of organizational culture. There are direct implications for the management of all organizations in general, and for the standpoint and conduct of IR in particular. Especially organizations that are operating in areas that have a long history and tradition of trade unionism, normally need to make reference to those traditions when establishing IR policies. Extensive use of specialist technology or personal and professional expertise normally means that the staff groups involved seek for themselves special marks of respect, esteem and value. Persons with a high degree of personal, professional or technological expertise normally expect to be treated with compliance and respect, rather than confrontation and hostility.

Attention to each aspect shapes and develops the behaviour of the organization at large, and gives a precise definition for the standpoint and delivery of IR in particular; and this happens in all cases, whether by accident or design. For example, weak, fragmented and uneven IR is invariably a by-product of weak and emergent organization cultures, where no commonality of purpose or clear values exist.

OTHER CULTURAL AND BEHAVIOURAL ASPECTS

It is also necessary to recognize the influence of the following.

- *Relationships with the environment:* including the ways in which the organization copes with uncertainty and turbulence; the ways in which the organization seeks to influence the environment.
- *The internal relationship balance:* the mixture and effectiveness of power, status, hierarchy, authority, responsibility, individualism, group cohesion; general relationship mixtures related to task/social/organization development.
- *Rites and rituals:* these are the punctuation marks of organization operations. These include: pay negotiations; internal and external job application means and methods; disciplinary, grievance and dismissal procedures and handling; pay and rewards; individual, group, departmental and divisional publicity; training and development activities; parties and celebrations; key appointments and dismissals; socialization and integration of people into new roles, activities and responsibilities.
- *Routines and habits:* these are the formal, semi-formal and informal ways of working and interaction that people generate for themselves or which the organization generates for them. These make comfortable the non-operational aspects of working life. They develop around absolutes – especially attendance times, deadlines, work requirements, authority and reporting relationships; and include also regular meetings, regular tasks and routines, forms of address between members of the organization and groups. There are also key personal routines to be considered, especially pay days, holidays and some development activities.
- *Badges and status symbols:* these are the marks of esteem conferred by organizations on their people. They are a combination of location (near to or away from the corridors of power for example); possessions (cars, technology, personal departments); job titles (reflecting a combination of ability, influence and occupation); and position in the hierarchy pecking order.

Especially the effects of rites, rituals, routines, habits, badges and status symbols all lie in the value that the organization places on them. They have a direct influence on the conduct of IR by all participants. Trade unions seek to gain for their members those benefits that are of material value to their members, and that are also respected – and therefore limited in their issuing – by the organization.

Similarly, staff expect their representatives to go through forms of ritual in order to secure for themselves the best possible pay, rewards and terms and conditions that are available in the circumstances. As discussed, especially in the sections on collective bargaining (Chapter 4), it is essential that the behavioural side of agreements is satisfied, as well as the capability to deliver acceptable, substantial gains and improvements; in other words, staff need to believe that they have received substantial gains and improvements as well as having the bare facts set out before them.

These characteristics, influences and other factors shape and direct the state of, and development of, organization culture. It is now necessary to consider the culture and behaviour of organizations in IR terms from the point of view of:

* leadership;
* motivation;
* power;
* conflict;
* realpolitik.

It is first useful to define leadership. **LEADERSHIP**

* '*A leader is someone who exercises influence over other people*' (Huczynski and Buchanan, 1993).
* A leader is: '*Cheerleader, enthusiast, nurturer of champions, hero finder, wanderer, dramatist, coach, facilitator and builder*' (Peters and Austin, 1985).
* '*The leader must have infectious optimism. The final test of a leader is the feeling you have when you leave their presence after a conference. Have you a feeling of uplift and confidence?*' (Field Marshal Bernard Montgomery).
* '*Leadership is creating a vision to which others can aspire and energising them to work towards this vision*' (Anita Roddick, founder of The Body Shop).

All organizations need to establish their own clarity of leadership, both overall and for each function, division and department. From this emerges the real nature of total organizational leadership. This in turn emphasizes the leadership/directional expertise and standpoint required. Each of the definitions given above refers to the relationship between the leader and their people. There are therefore direct implications for the style and standpoint of IR, and staff management in general. Another view of this is given by Luthans (1994), Summary Box 9.1.

SUMMARY BOX 9.1

Luthans (1994)

- A single person or founder has an idea for a new enterprise.
- The founder brings in one or more other key people and creates a core group that shares a common vision with the founder.
- The founding core begins to act in concert to create an organization by raising funds and resources, and organizing work.
- At this point others are brought into the organization and a common history and tradition begins to be built.

Some more general priorities may also be established:

- getting optimum performance from those carrying out the work;
- ensuring continuity, development and improvement in those carrying out the work; monitoring and evaluating both the work and those involved; and taking remedial action where necessary;
- relating the skills and capacities of those involved in the work to the work itself;
- seeking continuous improvement in all aspects of the work environment; and providing opportunities for continuous development and advancement for those in the organization and its departments, divisions and functions;
- motivating and encouraging the staff, and promoting positive, harmonious and productive working relations.

Leadership is therefore a key feature of organizational behaviour and organization culture for these reasons. By implication it has therefore a major impact on the style, standpoint and effectiveness of IR.

The relationship between organization effectiveness and leadership has been studied for a long time, and from many different points of view. The following are universally acknowledged; and each has direct implications for the conduct of organizational IR.

Trait theories

Attempts to identify the traits and characteristics present in successful leaders are largely inconclusive, in that none identify all the attributes necessary to lead; nor do they provide a universal body of traits that are common to all successful leaders (by whatever criteria 'success' is judged). However, the following are found to be applicable to most situations.

- The ability to communicate effectively.
- Decision-making capability.
- Commitment to all aspects of the organization.
- Concern for staff, including respecting and trusting them; valuing their contribution; understanding them, and their aspirations, and reconciling these with those of the organization.
- Commitment to quality.
- A given set of values with which others will identify, and to which they will commit themselves.
- Personal integrity, including vision, enthusiasm, strength of character, commitment, energy and interest; and including the establishment and determination of high absolute standards of moral and ethical probity.
- Positive attitudes – held by the leader and transmitted to staff.
- Mutuality and dependency of the leader with their staff; successful leaders know their own weaknesses and the importance and value of the people with whom they work; above all, they know what they cannot do and where and when to go for help and support in these areas.

Leadership types

The following different types of leader may be distinguished.

- The traditional leader whose position is assured by birth or heredity; or in organizations by virtue of their position as founder, or founding family.
- The known leader whose position is secured by the fact that everybody understands this. This is closely akin to the functional or expert leader, whose position is secured by virtue of expertise.
- The appointed leader, whose position is legitimized by virtue of the fact that he or she has gone through a selection assessment and appointment process in accordance with the rules, wishes and demands of the organization.
- The bureaucratic leader, whose position is legitimized by the rank held.
- The charismatic leader, whose position is secured by the sheer force of personality.
- The informal leader, whose function is carried out by virtue of personality or charisma, but whose position is not formally legitimized by rank, appointment or tradition.

Leadership styles

The rationale for studying management styles is that employees work better for managers who use particular styles of leadership than they will for others who employ different styles. However, it is essential to recognize that any management style must be supported by mutual trust, respect and confidence existing between manager and subordinates. If these factors are not present then no style is effective. There must also be a clarity of purpose and direction and this normally comes from the leader.

The initial implication for IR is the foundation of trust and integrity; and again, if this is not present, then no organizational IR will be truly effective. Whether on an individual or collective basis, all aspects of IR are conducted on the basis of mistrust and conflict. Even if an organizational, departmental, divisional or functional leader chooses an adversarial approach to their staff, this must be presented honestly if there is to be any effective IR even in that context.

It is usual to classify leadership styles on an authoritarian–democratic continuum. There is a body of evidence that relates high levels of success of business and work, job satisfaction and employee motivation, and fewer disputes and grievances, to the participative and consultative end of the continuum (see Figure 9.1).

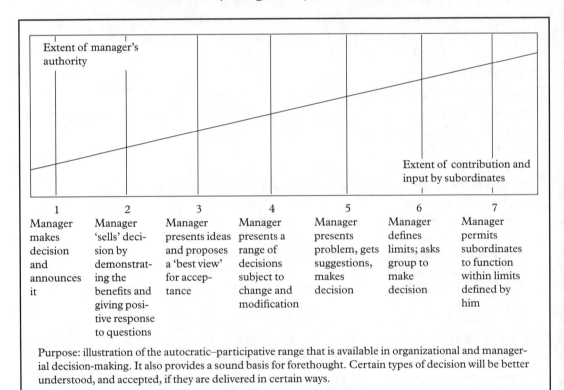

1	2	3	4	5	6	7
Manager makes decision and announces it	Manager 'sells' decision by demonstrating the benefits and giving positive response to questions	Manager presents ideas and proposes a 'best view' for acceptance	Manager presents a range of decisions subject to change and modification	Manager presents problem, gets suggestions, makes decision	Manager defines limits; asks group to make decision	Manager permits subordinates to function within limits defined by him

Purpose: illustration of the autocratic–participative range that is available in organizational and managerial decision-making. It also provides a sound basis for forethought. Certain types of decision will be better understood, and accepted, if they are delivered in certain ways.

Figure 9.1

Leadership continuum.

Source: Tannenbaum and Schmidt (1958)

From this, it is possible to tabulate more specifically certain leadership and management styles (see Figure 9.2).

Autocratic (benevolent or tyrannical)	Consultative/participative	Democratic/participative
1. Leader makes all decisions for the group 2. Close supervision 3. Individual members' interests subordinate to those of the organization 4. Subordinates treated without regard for their views 5. Great demands placed on staff 6. Questioning discouraged 7. Conformist/coercive environment	1. Leader makes decisions after consultation with group 2. Total communication between leader and members 3. Leader is supportive 4. Leader is accessible and discursive 5. Questioning approach encouraged 6. Ways of working largely unspecified 7. Leader retains responsibility and accountability for results	1. Decisions made by the group – by consultation or vote 2. Simple majority rules 3. All members bound by the group decision and support it 4. All members contribute to discussion 5. Development of coalitions and cliques 6. Leadership role is assumed not specified 7. Leadership may vary (e.g. by function, 'buggins turn')

Figure 9.2

Leadership and management styles

Contingency approaches to leadership

Contingency theories of leadership take account of the interaction and interrelation between the organization and its environment, and between work groups within the organization as they pursue their own activities in their own part of their environment.

F. E. Fiedler (1960)

The concept of contingency approaches to leadership was first developed by F. E. Fiedler in the 1960s. The work identified situations where both directive and participative styles of management worked effectively. The directive style was found to work well at the extremes, where the situation was either very favourable to the leader, or else very unfavourable.

Favourable was defined as a combination of circumstances where: the leader was liked and trusted by the staff; the task was clearly understood, easy to follow and well defined; the leader had a high degree of respect within the group; the leader had a high degree of influence over the group members in terms of reward and punishment; the leader enjoyed unqualified backing from the organization; and the leader enjoyed unqualified support from the staff.

Unfavourable was defined as the converse of this. It also referred to where the task was not clearly defined, or where the work was to be carried out in an extreme environment (e.g. discomfort, or working away from home).

In the former case, the group would accept it because of the high general level of regard; in the latter, it brought at least a measure of order and clarity. Indeed, to be too participative in the latter extreme may be regarded by the staff as compounding the uncertainty, and therefore as a perceived sign of weakness and ineffectiveness on the part of the leader.

Between the two extremes, the work of Fiedler found that the participative approach worked much better in the long term. While it was possible to gain short-term positive results and advantages through directive or coercive styles in the short term, these could not be sustained over longer periods of time (this finding is supported by Rensis Likert (1961) – see below).

Best fit
The theory of 'best fit' was developed by C. B. Handy (1986) and adopts the view that all leadership theories have a contribution to make, but that none by itself is the right or complete answer. Handy describes this as consisting of:

- support behaviour that enhances group members' feelings of personal worth;
- interaction facilitation which encourages members to develop mutually satisfying and supportive relationships;
- goal emphasis which is behaviour that stimulates desire and drives for excellent operational performance;
- work facilitation, reflecting the classical management activities of scheduling, coordination and control.

This recognizes the need to translate qualities and attributes into situational applications; and that these qualities and attributes may need different translation or different emphasis according to the changing nature of situations.

Whichever approach to leadership is adopted, there are clear implications for the design, ordering and management of IR. It is clearly implied that many of the enduring problems of IR, whether structural or individual, can be addressed at an early stage if organizations pay attention to the quality of leadership – both overall, and in terms of the qualities that are sought when appointing people to positions of departmental, divisional or functional management or supervision. At the core, however, remains the need for a fundamental integrity of approach, whichever standpoint and perspective is adopted.

MOTIVATION   There is a direct correlation between the amount of trouble taken to motivate staff and profitable and effective organizational performance. The ability to motivate staff in the workplace stems from understanding the following.

- A general appreciation of how human beings think and behave in particular situations, and in response to their needs to satisfy and fulfil basic drives, instincts, needs and wants.
- An understanding of the nature of the work that must be carried out, and the effects that this will have, or is likely to have on those who are to do it. This concerns especially the extent of intrinsic satisfaction and fulfilment that is present in the work; the interface between staff and technology; and the style of management and supervision adopted.
- The wider standards and expectations of the relationship between people at the workplace. The background and climate for this is created by management and infuses everyone, either positively or negatively, at the workplace. At its best, it contains a variety of elements including: enthusiasm and commitment on the part of everyone to the organization and its products, services and customers; a corporate belief in the organization and all its works; a clearly understood and established set of principles and operational standards by which the organization functions; adequate, effective and relevant communication processes and methods; and preventative approaches to problems, and commitment to resolve these quickly when they arise.
- Conversely, it is necessary to recognize that where these elements are not present, or where they are diluted, not believed in or not valued, there will be a tendency towards demotivation and alienation.
- Organizations cannot be all things to all people. They can only accommodate a range of divergent interests and aspirations insofar as these can be made to harmonize with the overall direction and values. Dysfunctions arise from these divergencies; and conflicts of interest, the proliferation of disciplinary and grievance issues, are most common in multinational hierarchies and public and health services, where the organization style and structure is either inefficient or irrelevant to the true purpose of the organization itself.

It is necessary to consider briefly the major theories of motivation.

Rensis Likert: System 4

Likert's contribution to the theories of workplace motivation arose from his work with high performing managers – managers and supervisors who achieved high levels of productivity, low levels of cost, and high levels of employee motivation, participation and involvement at their places of work. Groups that achieved high levels of economic output, and wage and salary levels, were also heavily involved in group maintenance activities and the design and definition of work patterns. This was underpinned by a supportive style of supervision, and a generation of a sense of personal as well as occupational worth.

Likert identified four styles or systems of management.

- *System 1*
  exploitative authoritative: where power and direction come from the top downwards and where there is no participation, consultation or involvement on the part of the workforce. Workforce compliance is thus based on fear. Unfavourable attitudes are generated, there is little confidence and trust, and there exist low levels of motivation to cooperate or generate output above the absolute minimum.
- *System 2*
  benevolent authoritative: similar to System 1 but allowing for some upward opportunity for consultation and participation in some areas. Again, attitudes tend to be unfavourable; confidence, trust and communication are also at low levels.

In both Systems 1 and 2 productivity may be high over the short run when targets can be achieved by a combination of coercion and bonus and overtime payments. However, both productivity and earnings are demonstrably low in the long run; and there is also high absenteeism and labour turnover, together with proliferation of disputes and grievances.

- *System 3*
  consultative: where aims and objectives are set after discussion and consultation with subordinates; where communication is two-way, and where teamwork is encouraged. Attitudes towards both superiors and the organization tend to be favourable especially when the organization is working steadily. Productivity tends to be higher, absenteeism and turnover lower. There is also a demonstrable reduction in disputes and grievances, improvement in working relationships, reduction in operational costs, and higher levels of earnings on the part of the workforce.
- *System 4*
  participative: in which three basic concepts have a very important effect on performance – the use by the manager of the principle of supportive relationships throughout the work group; the use of group decision-making and group methods of supervision; and the setting of high performance and very ambitious goals both for departments and also for the organization overall. This was Likert's preferred System (see Figure 9.3).

Abraham Maslow: a hierarchy of needs

The 'hierarchy of needs' is normally depicted as a pyramid. The 'hierarchy of needs' works from the bottom of the pyramid upwards. It shows the most basic needs and motivations at the lowest levels; and only when these are satisfied are other needs addressed.

Maslow identified five key needs.

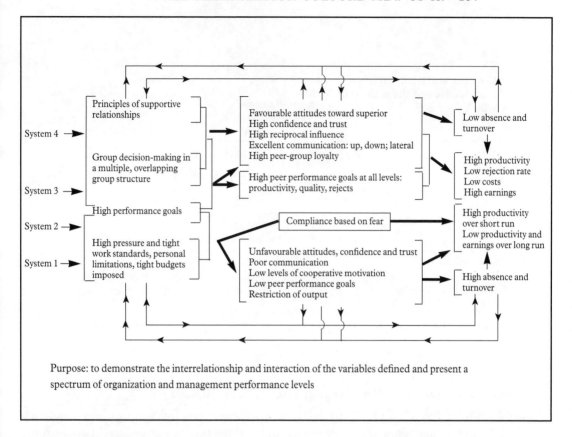

Purpose: to demonstrate the interrelationship and interaction of the variables defined and present a spectrum of organization and management performance levels

- *Physiological:* the need for food, drink, air, warmth, sleep and shelter.
- *Safety and security:* protection from danger, threats or deprivation, and the need for stability.
- *Social:* the sense of belonging to a society and its groups; for example, the family, the organization, the work group; basic status needs within these groups, and the need to participate in human activities.
- *Esteem needs:* self-respect, self-esteem, appreciation, value, recognition and worth.
- *Self-actualization:* the need for self-fulfilment, self-realization, personal development and accomplishment; the need to progress as far as possible in whatever terms the individual chooses to measure this.

Figure 9.3

Rensis Likert: System 4

Maslow reinforced this by stating that people tended to satisfy their needs systematically. Until one particular group of needs was satisfied a person's behaviour would be dominated by them. Maslow also made the point that people's motives were constantly being modified as their situation changed, and in relation to their levels of adaptation (see Figure 9.4).

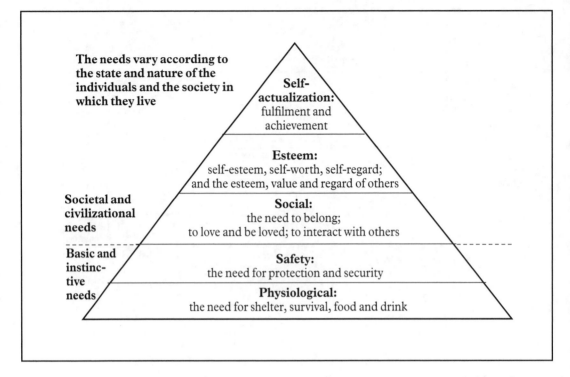

Figure 9.4   Douglas MacGregor: Theory X and Theory Y

Abraham Maslow:
a hierarchy of
needs

MacGregor identified two distinctive sets of assumptions made by managers about employees; and from this, he articulated two extreme attitudes or views and called them Theory X and Theory Y.

Theory X

This is based on the following:

- people dislike work and will avoid it if they can. They would rather be directed than accept responsibility. They have no creativity except when it comes to getting around the rules and procedures of the organization; above all, they will not use their creativity or talents in the pursuit of the job or the interests of the organization;
- they must be forced or bribed to put out the right effort. They are motivated mainly by money and this remains the overriding reason why they go to work;
- their main anxiety concerns their own personal security which is alleviated by earning money;
- they are inherently lazy, requiring high degrees of supervision, coercion and control in order to produce adequate output.

Theory Y

This is based on the following:

- people wished only to be interested in their work and under the right conditions, they will enjoy it. They gain intrinsic fulfilment from it; they are motivated by the desire to realize their own potential, to work to the best of their capabilities, and to employ the creativity and ingenuity with which they are endowed in the pursuit of this;
- they will direct themselves towards given, accepted and understood targets; they will seek and accept responsibility and authority; they will accept the discipline of the organization in the pursuit of this;
- people will also impose self-discipline on themselves and their activities in order to get work done to the best of their ability.

Frederick Herzberg: Two Factor Theory

Herzberg's research established two sets of factors as follows.

- Those factors that led to extreme dissatisfaction with the job, the environment and the workplace.
- Those factors that led to extreme satisfaction with the job, the environment and the workplace.

The factors giving rise to satisfaction Herzberg called motivators. Those giving rise to dissatisfaction he called hygiene factors or demotivators.

The motivators that emerged were: achievement, recognition, the nature and content of work, levels of responsibility, prospects for advancement and opportunities for personal growth and development.

The dissatisfiers that emerged were: company policy and administration; supervision and management style; levels of pay and salary; relationships with peers; relationships with subordinates; status; and security. These are factors which, where they were good or adequate, would not in themselves make people satisfied; by ensuring that they were indeed adequate, dissatisfaction was removed but satisfaction was not in itself generated. On the other hand, where these aspects were bad, extreme dissatisfaction was experienced by all those whom Herzberg studied, and led to the proliferation of disputes, grievances, high levels of conflict, absenteeism and labour turnover, and low generaal morale (see Figure 9.5).

Victor Vroom: expectancy theories of motivation

The expectancy approach to motivation draws a relationship between:

- the expectations that people have in work situations;
- the efforts that they put in to meet these expectations;
- the rewards offered for successful efforts.

It therefore becomes necessary to recognize the need to balance expectation, effort and reward. If expectations are raised and then not fulfilled,

Figure 9.5

Frederick
Herzberg:
Two Factor
Theory

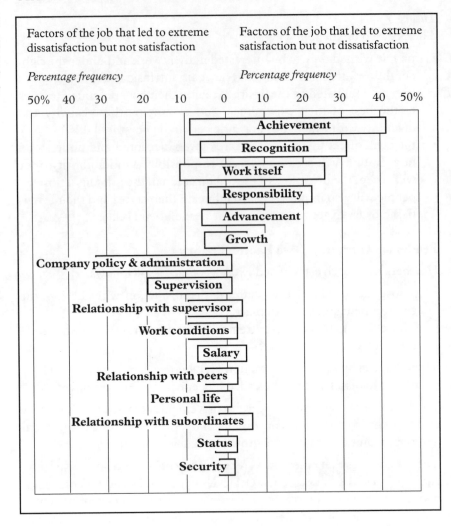

effort declines. If high levels of effort turn out to be unproductive, expectations are repositioned downwards. If the anticipated rewards are not forthcoming, effort declines. The effect of each is always to demotivate and demoralize where one or more of these factors is out of balance with the others. Motivation is adversely affected when efforts do not bring the anticipated rewards; when the expectation of rewards is not fulfilled; and when efforts in the pursuit of expectations and rewards turn out to be far higher than anticipated (see Figure 9.6).

Motivation and IR

There are a number of common threads that run through each of the theories. Motivation is, above all, a joint venture – organizations are entitled to expect motivation on the part of their people and, in turn, they must ensure that motivation is provided for the people who come to work for them.

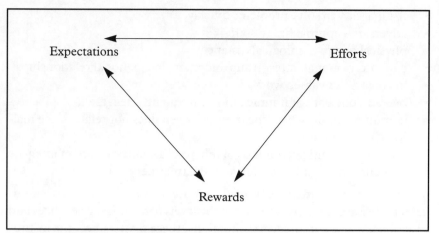

Figure 9.6

A simple expectancy approach to motivation

High levels of work motivation are based on:

- demanding, interesting, varied and valuable work that people are capable of carrying out;
- recognizing and rewarding achievements;
- taking early remedial action when standards fall;
- treating everyone equally and with respect; creating workplace relationships based on trust, honesty, openness and integrity;
- creating a unity of purpose and mutual interest between organization and staff;
- developing positive work, professional and personal relationships within and between groups;
- giving everyone the opportunity to progress and develop as far as they possibly can whatever their occupation, salary level or personal aspirations;
- attending to individual needs, wants, drives, hopes, fears and aspirations;
- high, regular and increasing levels of pay in return for high quality work.

If all of this is in place, organizations are entitled to expect high quality, high value work, and a commensurate reduction in IR problems. Creating these conditions is the organization's responsibility. The potential for this is enhanced where it is known that the organization is relatively secure in its activities both at present and into the future; and where it is known, believed and understood that, should conditions change, the organization will take whatever steps necessary to ensure that personal and occupational disruption are kept to a minimum; and that work security is assured as far as possible.

Motivation is adversely affected by:

- management style, especially the invisibility of managers and supervisors;

- the inability to solve problems quickly;
- adversarial approaches to staff;
- physical and psychological distance;
- bad interpersonal, inter-group and inter-occupational relationships;
- boring and unvalued work;
- bad and unclear communications infrequently delivered;
- communications where the message given does not relate to the reality of the situation;
- facts, beliefs and perceptions of inherent dishonesty, lack of integrity and unfairness and unevenness in the treatment of people.

Where insufficient attention is paid to those factors that tend to demotivate, there is a commensurate rise in the levels of disputes, grievances and disciplinary cases. In the worst situations, these matters become institutionalized and much time, money and other organizational resources are consumed in resolving them. In the worst cases indeed, it becomes a part of the reason for the organization's existence, to resolve such disputes and grievances.

Acceptance of the relationship between motivation and performance is one of the major steps that can be taken by organizations, their managers and their supervisors towards the improvement of IR. It is then possible to look more deeply at the conflicts, disputes and grievances that do occur, in order to assess the reasons for these, and to begin to be able to take effective remedial action.

CONFLICT

It is first necessary to recognize different levels of conflict.

- Argument and competition, which may be either healthy and positive or unhealthy and negative.
- Warfare, which is always negative.

In this context, IR is concerned with creating the conditions for productive and positive argument, discussion and debate; the management of warfare; and in the long term, the abolition of warfare.

Productive and positive argument is only possible if the following are in place.

- Mutual interest of all concerned in the solution of the matter in hand.
- Commitment to the matter in hand.
- Honesty and openness so that differing views may become public and be heard without prejudice or penalty.
- A structure that addresses issues, facts, feelings, values, perceptions and beliefs.
- Mutual trust and confidence in the personalities and expertise of those involved.
- Respect for all points of view.

It is therefore possible to discuss both the positive and negative aspects of the argument without prejudice. This is likely to indicate in turn, where more serious differences may lie, especially if these indicate persistent professional or individual clashes; where alliances start to form; and where people adopt contrary positions based on countering the views of someone else in the group.

This is of particular importance when establishing joint negotiating committees, joint consultative committees, health and safety committees, and works councils. At the core is the creation of a forum where a positive and effective debate and discussion can take place, and where all matters concerning the management of IR can be addressed (see Summary Box 9.2).

SUMMARY BOX 9.2

The nature of argument and competition

In terms of the organization and management of IR this may be:

- closed or distributive, where one party wins at the expense of others;
- open or integrative, where there is scope for everyone to succeed;
- collaborative, where the boundaries of operations of each party can be set to ensure that everyone has their fair share of whatever is under discussion.

In both organizational behaviour and IR terms, argument and competition are both likely to be more fruitful and productive if they are open and if the rewards for those involved are available across the board. This normally degenerates into conflict where, for example, competition for resources or accommodation, pay or rewards, is closed and one party succeeds at the expense of others (especially where the same party is known, believed or perceived to succeed at the expense of others all of the time).

Warfare and IR

Warfare exists where personal, professional or inter-group relations have been allowed to get out of hand. It may also be a common or key feature of superior–subordinate relationships. In these cases, the main aims and objectives of activities have been lost, and priority is given by all concerned to 'winning the war'.

For those concerned with the management and effectiveness of IR, the following causes and symptoms of conflict and warfare should be assessed.

- The extent and prevalence of 'divide and rule' managerial approaches.
- Poor communications between groups, individuals and the organization and its managers.
- Poor inter-group relationships, especially those based on envy and jealousy.

- Deterioration of personal and professional relationships.
- Increases in absenteeism, sickness, labour turnover, timekeeping problems and accidents.
- Proliferation of non-productive, ineffective and untargeted papers and reports.
- Proliferation of rules and regulations.
- Escalation of disputes and grievances arising out of frustration and anger.
- Proliferation of control functions at the expense of front line functions.
- Proliferation of the formal use of discipline, grievance and disputes procedures.
- Increase in influence of informal corridor and washroom gatherings that persistently discuss wrongs, and situational and organizational decline.
- The growth of the use of arbitration: that is, the handing up of organization disagreements to higher (and sometimes external) authorities for resolution.
- Disregard and disrespect for persons in other parts of the organization.

It is also necessary to enquire in detail into the following.

- Differences between corporate, group and individual aims and objectives.
- Interdepartmental and inter-group wrangles, especially those concerned with territory or prestige; or especially when some groups and departments are known, believed or perceived to have been accorded greater status than others.
- Lack of clarity of reporting relationships.
- Lack of confidence between seniors and subordinates; lack of productive relationships between seniors and subordinates.

Most IR procedures are designed so that these matters can be addressed when they arise. They become symptomatic of much more serious IR problems when they become a dominant or driving priority for the organization; and this again means that resources are inevitably directed away from productive purposes and into the management of conflict. This in turn tends to reinforce the position of lobbies and vested interest groups, including trade unions, as key influential, even over-mighty, players in particular organizations.

POWER AND INFLUENCE

Influence, power and authority are present in all organizations, and within their component groups, departments, divisions and functions.

Influence is where a person, group or organization changes the attitudes, values, behaviour, priorities and activities of others.

Power is the capability to exercise influence in these ways.

Authority is the legitimization of the capability to exercise influence and the relationship by which this is exercised. Authority therefore legitimizes the use of power and influence in organizations. This may be overt or covert – if subordinates believe and accept that they are in junior positions, they legitimize the power and authority of the superiors; if an organization believes it is heavily influenced by its trade unions and their activities, it legitimizes this position in its own way.

Sources of power in organizations

These are as follows.

- *Physical power:* the power exerted by individuals by reasons of their bodily shape, size and strength; or strength of personality (this includes charismatic power).
- *Traditional power:* the ability to command influence derives from accepted customs, norms and structures.
- *Expert power:* based on the expertise held by an individual or group and the demand for this from other parts of the organization.
- *Reward power:* the ability to influence behaviour and activities by holding out and offering rewards for compliance and acceptance.
- *Punishment power:* the power to adversely influence, or to withhold rewards.
- *Coercive power:* especially the ability to bully or threaten people into doing something that they would not otherwise do.
- *Legal rational power:* the limitation, ordering and direction of power and influence based on the establishment of rules, procedures, regulations and norms acceptable to all.

Power also exists to a greater or lesser extent in particular locations in organizations:

- managers and supervisors; hierarchies; functional expertise; professional and technical expertise; resource command and utilization; and status;
- pressure groups and lobbies, cluster groups of managers, supervisors, technical and professional experts, specialist groups, trade unions and professional bodies all exert power and influence in their own way;
- over-mighty subjects and over-mighty departments wield levels of influence and autonomy in certain conditions.

The source and use of power and influence must be dependent upon a fundamental integrity. Power and influence may therefore be used in both positive and negative ways (see Summary Box 9.3).

SUMMARY BOX 9.3

———

Misuses of power and influence

According to ACAS, the extent to which power and influence is misused in the UK by people in organizations has never been greater. The main features are listed below.

- *Favouritism:* the ability to influence an individual's career prospects and advancement by virtue of a personal liking.
- *Victimization:* the blocking or reduction of career prospects and advancement.
- *Lack of manners and respect:* treating subordinates with contempt, giving individuals dressings-down in public; conducting discipline in public.
- *Bullying and harassment:* overwhelmingly by superiors of subordinates. This is usually found in the following forms: racial prejudice; sexual harassment (overwhelmingly of female staff by males); bullying of the disabled by the able-bodied; bullying of juniors by seniors; personal likes and dislikes, especially where the dislike is based on a perceived threat to the security of the senior's position; scapegoating; inequality of opportunity.

ACAS reported that some cases are so acute that people are being driven to despair, nervous breakdown or even suicide by the activities of managers.

Source: *ACAS Annual Report*, HMSO, 1994.

Influence, power and authority are all themselves limited by organizational structures and methods of behaviour. Authority is normally given out for a limited range of activities or people only, and the extent of influence and the ability to wield power are therefore also limited. Those concerned with the management of IR need to take an active interest in ensuring that authority is always legitimized, rather than being allowed to emerge and gain life through negligence, custom or practice. This is especially true where written rules and procedures state that matters are to be conducted in one way, but where they are conducted in other ways, or rules and regulations flouted, because of the informal but acquired authority, power and influence of participants.

Where power and influence are known, believed or perceived to be misused by individuals, groups, departments or vested interests action is required to ensure that this ceases. It is also important to note that each of the elements referred to by ACAS (see Summary Box 9.3) can be carried out on an institutional or group, as well as individual, basis.

CONCLUSIONS

The cultural and behavioural perspective on IR indicates some major points of enquiry, at both macro and micro levels.

On the standards of organization behaviour overall, attention needs to be paid to the extent to which this is desired or devised by the organization, and the extent to which it is created by staff, staff groups and vested interests. From this, it is possible to identify staff management blockages and barriers as well as those aspects that are working in the ways desired by the organization and the reasons for these.

It is possible to assess behaviour regulation from an ethical perspective – the extent to which people are behaving in ways which they know to be right or wrong, as distinct from complying with either formal or informal requirements.

Following this, it is possible to assess the extent to which the dominant or prevailing norms are genuinely those of the organization. It is often very easy to take the 'hygiene' view that unless something is malfunctioning, it is working perfectly. From this, it is a short step to benign neglect, and then managerial remoteness. More directly still, attention needs to be paid to the standards of behaviour imposed, required and requested by trade unions and other staff representative bodies, professional associations, inernal IR institutions, and also the design and operation of procedures. It may also be necessary to attend to specific aspects of group-think, cohesion and identity, especially where these are negative or divisive.

It may be necessary to look at the totality of the philosophy, ethos and dominant values of the organization. This concerns the extent to which those prescribed by the organization are translated into reality. Serious problems occur if the reality is either that these are not reflected by groups and individuals; and such problems become more serious still when groups, departments, divisions and functions set their own dominant values in spite of those prescribed by the organization. IR problems also occur where overall policies are not precisely defined or not delivered as stated; or where the overall policies give no genuine respect or esteem to the efforts of the staff.

From the cultural and behavioural point of view, it is finally necessary to consider the general organizational IR climate. Points that need to be addressed concern the overall feelings of well being and quality of working life. More specifically, this is also the source of such phrases as 'a culture of fear', 'a culture of coercion', and 'a culture of remoteness. Especially, a bad or negative organizational IR climate is apparent when all major dealings are conducted from a formal proceduralized and ritualized standpoint; and this is also apparent in the extent and prevalence of written rules and guidelines and the ways in which these are used. In these ways IR is assessed from a behavioural point of view.

Chapter 10

Organizational priorities in IR

INTRODUCTION   Whatever their size, good organizations strive constantly for greater achievements in all areas, and the best organizations include the design and management of IR in their deliberations. They recognize that operational positions of market dominance, being a key public service, cost or brand leader, are entirely dependent on the continued efforts of high quality, motivated and effective staff – and that insufficient attention to IR policies and practices dilutes motivation and therefore damages, and ultimately destroys, their overall effectiveness. IR is therefore a key feature of strategic, operational and functional management and makes a major contribution – positive or negative – to overall performance (see Summary Box 10.1).

SUMMARY BOX 10.1

The football World Cup in France 1998

'I knew I was wrong to kick Simeone [the Argentine midfield player]. When I was sent off I felt as if I had let everybody down. I knew I would get the blame from the supporters. After the game, Tony Adams, the captain, came and sat with me. He put his arm round me, and tried to comfort me, for about twenty minutes. The manager [Glenn Hoddle] never spoke to me at all – in fact he has not spoken to me since.'

These words were spoken by David Beckham at the end of the England–Argentina football match in the World Cup in France in 1998. Beckham had been sent off for kicking an opponent, Diego Simeone, in an off-the-ball incident.

Everyone makes mistakes. Some of these are more serious than others. However, blame is only to be used where the mistakes were the result of malice or negligence; and even then it is the actions and behaviour that are at issue, not the character of the individual. It is therefore damaging and destructive – and wrong – to consider the character rather than the behaviour in such circumstances.

In general terms (and leaving aside the vagaries of the football industry) it is clear from such an example that the particular manager had no expertise in the area of staff management; and from this, in turn, it is a short step only to losing the confidence of both superiors and subordinates.

It is therefore necessary to consider the full integration of IR with the overall drive for the professionalization of management, and the search for managerial excellence. The following aspects must therefore be addressed.

- The organizational outputs of IR.
- Collective bargaining and collective agreements.
- The management of vested interests.
- Managerial priorities for the twenty-first century.

The issue facing all organizations and managers lies in the matter of determining what these key outputs are to be, how they are interrelated with other organizational activities, and how they are to be delivered.

THE ORGANIZA-TIONAL OUTPUTS OF IR

The most important matter is to determine the desired relationship with the staff – whether unitary or pluralist; consensus, conformist, participative, cooperative or adversarial. As stated above, there is nothing inherently wrong with any of these approaches provided that, whichever is chosen, it is:

- designed and predetermined rather than allowed to emerge;
- understood that there are consequences and commitments required in their effective delivery;
- developed and managed effectively (see Summary Box 10.2).

At first, there appears little to recommend adversarial IR as a designed and approved course of action; and it remains true that this brings with it a greater propensity for general damage to staff morale and organization performance.

However, practical arguments for this approach nevertheless remain. There may be a history of strong trade union (including multi-union) identity in the industry, sector or locality which is very difficult to address in the short term except in a form of incrementalist approach. Such an approach would include moves towards single status, single terms and conditions of employment, streamlined procedures and unity of managerial approach. Multi-locational organizations take the view that they will have localized semi-autonomous IR practices. Or one of their activities may be located in an area of skills or labour shortage, and they may have no choice but to overpay or over-compensate in relation to those carrying out the same or similar work elsewhere in the organization. In each of these cases, while it may ideally be desirable to adopt a more altruistic approach, it may not be instantly possible.

Some staff groups may not consent to be represented by a unitary body or single-union agreement. This is compounded where:

- works councils are constituted in such a way as to actively seek representation from professional, occupation and expertise groups;

SUMMARY BOX 10.2

The future of adversarial IR

- membership of a particular union or professional association is required for professional indemnity insurance (e.g. nursing);
- there are general problems of confidence with alternatives which the particular organization does not feel able or willing to tackle;
- it has been very difficult to convince the staff of the need to change.

Especially where a form of consensus has emerged, or where there is in practice an overtly positive coexistence, organizations may simply take the view that reform in this area is not a priority. Provided that this is the result of genuine managerial consideration and not a form of benign neglect, there is no reason why this cannot be completely legitimate in some circumstances.

In any case, those who take this view are still going to have to design and institute works councils and other representation formats in order to comply with continuing EU legislation.

For this to succeed organizations and their managers need to take a much more comprehensive view of where their workforce fit into the overall picture. Whichever approach is taken, IR policies and practices need to be designed in order to ensure the best possible outcome. One way of looking at this is to use the alienation–internalization spectrum as follows (see Figure 10.1).

Figure 10.1

Alienation–
internalization
spectrum

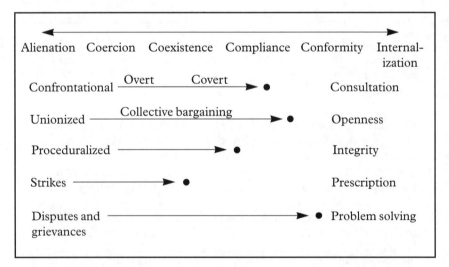

Alienation

This is where the lack of mutual interest is recognized and accepted together with the high potential for conflict. Formalized policies, procedures and mechanisms need to be established that can be operated as quickly and effectively as possible, recognizing that they are going to be in frequent use. There is therefore a clear derived need for extensive IR training for managers and supervisors and briefing for staff. There is a clear need to ensure that sufficient time is in-built into the workload of managers and supervisors to deal with IR problems. If this is accepted the management of conflict inherent in the situation is made as effective as possible.

Coercion

This is where extensive wider personnel and HR effort is required as well as attention to specific IR issues. Labour turnover and absenteeism is likely to be high, so access to a steady and extensive supply of labour is required. This means in turn, that the employment relationship can be made productive – or not – through the nature and extent of induction and job training activities.

It then becomes important to recognize why staff would want to work in such circumstances. The reasons are invariably financial, a lack of choice of alternative employers, or an introduction to the type of work in order to get a track record and experience. So the key managerial obligations are to ensure that the financial side is delivered; and to recognize that there will be labour drift away from the organization as soon as alternative work becomes available.

Once this is recognized and accepted a form of positive coexistence, consensus even, can be achieved because everyone knows where they stand. Moreover, coercive organizations gain reputations for being so in the localities in which they exist, so that people who go to work for them do so with a measure of understanding of what they can expect.

Coexistence

This is where groups of staff, departments, divisions, functions and occupations are overtly employed on different terms and conditions, status levels, and with different managerial approaches. Here the IR effort is as follows.

- To concentrate on maintaining a measure of harmony so that productive effort can be achieved for most of the time.
- To recognize the propensity for interdepartmental, divisional and functional strife and to design policies and procedures for its containment; and when it does occur, to recognize the long-term propensity for damage to the organization as a whole. This is a direct consequence of either actively encouraging internal political systems, or else using them on a basis of expediency once they have emerged.
- To ensure that within defined boundaries a fundamental equality of treatment takes place.
- To recognize that the priority of each group is to its own people, and not to the organization as a whole. This is especially true for profes-

sional and expert occupations; and it is true also for any organization group that finds itself having to lobby on its own behalf because of some fact, belief or perception of organization neglect.

In coexistent IR a measure of harmony can be created provided that the work outputs of each group, department, division and function can be coordinated successfully, and provided that the groups are given no reason to fight with each other. The IR effort therefore needs to be directed at each of these factors.

Compliance

The main issue here is to recognize the multiplicity of interests that exist and that people only go along with the organization direction so long as their own interests coincide. These interests operate at two levels:

- professional or occupational, in which individuals work in the organization's ways so long as their own professional or occupational aspirations can be accommodated. This form of compliance is extremely prevalent in organizations in the medical, social services, education, engineering, finance and consultancy sectors;
- personal, in which individuals work in the organization's ways so long as these allow them to pursue their own priorities away from work. This means recognizing that those in this form of compliance are unlikely to want to put their lives on hold just because the organization finds itself in some form of crisis, or has a sudden rush of orders, or other work overload.

The IR priority in compliance situations is to recognize these needs. Failure to do so normally results in problems of discipline and grievance. Any organization that seeks or wishes to upset or disrupt the compliance must build in managerial and supervisory time to accommodate this.

Conformism

The main IR issues here are to ensure that people can conform personally, professionally and socially with what is required of them; and that this is maintained and developed as a key organizational priority (see Figure 10.2).

Disruption to a fully harmonious conformist approach can occur at any stage in an organization's existence or development and is caused by:

- changes in top management;
- merger, takeover, withdrawal or divestment;
- changes in influence of key lobbies and vested interests;
- changes in trade union or professional body recognition or influence;
- changes in work patterns, work and organization structures and technology and occupations.

Figure 10.2
IR and
conformism

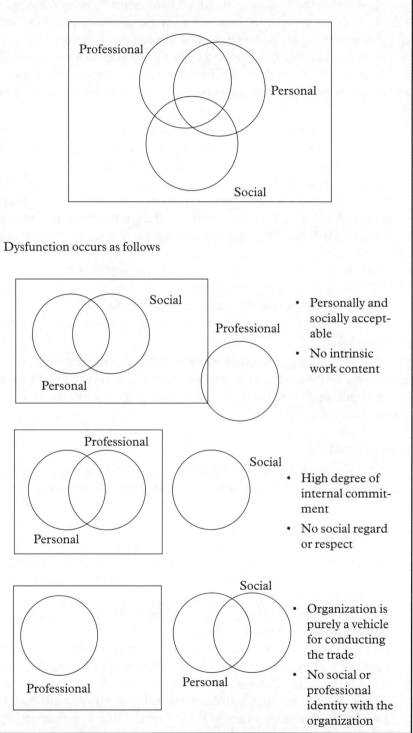

Some, if not all, of these are certain to take place at some point. The particular issue is therefore to ensure that the changes and developments are managed within the principles by which conformism has been achieved. These principles are only to be broken up if the conclusion is deliberately arrived at that they are no longer worthy or relevant; and steps then need to be taken immediately to replace them rather than to leave a void. IR problems arising when a conformist situation is broken up are two-fold, and again organizations and their senior management need to be aware of these.

- Sudden overall loss of motivation and morale which occurs as the result of people having had their certainties and assurances removed. This results in loss of production and output and a rise in labour turnover. It also causes individual, group and occupational stress (one of the main reasons why so many people in public professions have suffered from such high levels of stress in recent years is that the basis and values of the organizations for which they work are changing so often).
- Increases in real and perceived grievances, both group and individual. These occur as a behavioural response to uncertainty and are used to try to get real information about the future which has suddenly become the unknown rather than the perceived, certain and predictable.

If IR is to be properly managed when this does occur, priority must be given to the communication effort, and this needs in turn to be supported by a commitment to attending to the specific needs of groups and individuals affected.

Internalization

In IR, human resource and staff management terms the main issue is to recognize where the forms of internalization exist. These may be as follows.

- *Work and life:* in which the individual commits to the organization for life. In return for this, their personal, professional, occupational and social lifestyle is supported for life both financially and psychologically.
- *Work:* in which the individual joins what is often a chosen organization in order to be able to pursue their career at 'the best' (e.g. academic work at Oxford or Cambridge) or 'the most certain' (e.g. industrial work at Nissan or Sony).
- *Life:* in which the life of the individual is totally entwined with their organization (e.g. Richard Branson at Virgin; Ted Knights at Nike; Mick Jagger at the Rolling Stones).
- *Environmental:* in which individuals working in other situations have internalized these as a fact of their working life. For example, the 'Affluent Worker' studies identified high degrees of alienation and

coercion in the companies studied; however, they also identified a belief of absolute guarantees of jobs for life.

IR problems occur in each case where the situation is disrupted. They occur both individually and collectively. Part of this concerns the broader moral obligation to employees. Internalization is akin to belief and faith, and it is always traumatic when these are destroyed or damaged, whether at work or anywhere else. If an internalized situation is to be broken up, counselling for individual and group leadership needs to be made available if common humanity as well as effective work are to be preserved (see Summary Box 10.3).

Some specific examples and implications for those in internalized organizations and occupations, together with the effects on IR, are as follows.

- *Nursing:* nursing in the UK was always perceived (by society at least) as a vocation, and for many years those who went into it committed themselves utterly to patient care and absolute standards of professional practice. In recent years, this has been badly damaged by declining salaries and other terms and conditions of employment. It has also been seriously damaged by substantial changes to the occupation in practice. This above all concerns moving nurses away from caring for patients into the management of wards and other occupations and reconciling the demands of patient care with political and managerial pressures.
- *Virgin and Nike:* business and sectoral analysts have already identified problems for these organizations when the founding parent either dies or moves out. Organizations such as these are bound together by the distinctive personality of the leader as well as their professional business expertise. Problems have already started to occur with Nike because the company has seen fit to locate some of its production work in Third World countries, where it is able to pay minimum wages for maximum output.
- *Vauxhall:* since the 'Affluent Worker' studies, the fact of job security for life has become an illusion. However, despite exhortations to 'work harder' to ensure as much certainty as possible, Vauxhall's production, market share, income and profits have all declined over the past forty years in the UK – exactly at the time when consumer demand for cars was rising steeply. Part of this is explained in the globalization of competition and the resultant increase in consumer choice. However, the company needed to pay much greater attention to the specific IR concerns of alienation on the one hand, and the internalization of this on the other. It only began to do so in the early 1990s, by offering extended pay and job security deals to the workforce in return for greater flexibility in working practices. For the first time in forty years, the company addressed the needs of the workforce from their own point of view. As the result, output per member of staff rose in 1998 for the first time.

SUMMARY BOX 10.3

Internalization and IR

COLLECTIVE AGREEMENTS AND COLLECTIVE BARGAINING

Collective agreements and collective bargaining are both expensive and unwieldy if they are not actively and purposefully designed and managed. On the other hand, they are culturally and behaviourally enshrined in much of UK industry, public service, transport, energy and distribution sectors. The approach is therefore certain to continue in some areas for the foreseeable future. Indeed, many extremely effective collective agreements are being made and implemented as the result of a traditional but targeted approach. Some lessons may be drawn as follows.

Collective agreements

The Sanyo example (Appendix 2) is a form of collective agreement. It is precise, targeted and streamlined. As a consequence, it is easily understood by the parties to the agreement, and easily explained to those who are covered by it.

There are clear lessons here. The most important is to simplify matters rather than complicate them. This does not mean that the coverage must be vague, sloppy or imprecise. However, attempting to cover every aspect of human behaviour and performance necessarily results in failure because no two incidents are ever exactly the same, nor can the ways in which they are to occur be precisely predicted.

There is a joint responsibility here. If matters are to be clear and straightforward, this can only be achieved on the basis of mutual identity of positive interest between the organization and unions involved. There is no basis for effective or productive agreements unless this is first recognized. Key questions have therefore to be asked.

- Why are we entering, or seeking to enter into, this agreement?
- What do we want out of it? What do they want out of it?
- What do we want from them? What do they want from us?
- Is this reasonable? Is this compatible?
- What contribution does the approach make to effective performance? What are the problems and pitfalls inherent?

Genuine effectiveness of collective agreements depends on genuine answers to these questions. It may depend on accurate identification of secondary, hidden or duplicitous motives on the part of anyone or everyone involved. It may also depend on attitudes, values and prejudices changing, and if these cannot be at least understood, then the effectiveness of the agreement is certain to be diminished.

It is also necessary to identify and define the coverage of the agreement. This is normally now the organization's responsibility and prerogative. Part of this will concentrate on what is not to be covered, the reasons for this, and the ways in which these exclusions are explained to the unions and staff representatives involved. Each aspect of IR coverage requires full support and justification; and if this is not forthcoming, then the organization will be perceived to be fundamentally dishonest.

It is then necessary to establish whether the agreement is to be:

- integrative, by which all those covered receive the same fundamental treatment, recourse to procedures, terms and conditions of employment and opportunities for pay and reward enhancements;
- distributive, by which different groups of staff receive different treatment and are engaged to work on different terms and conditions of employment, procedures, and opportunities for pay and reward enhancements.

While the moral and ethical case can be argued much more strongly for the former, in practice, there is very often nothing wrong with the latter *provided that* its delivery is open and honest. Serious problems occur when what is stated is integrative, but what is delivered is known, believed or perceived to be distributive.

In future all collective agreements will need to address the real and actual concerns of people at work, or else provide overwhelming evidence of why these should not be addressed. These are:

- job security, and work security where there is any chance that work methods, practices and technology will develop, rendering some occupations obsolete, while creating staff shortages and vacancies in others;
- redundancy because it has affected everyone in all occupations;
- redeployment and transferability because of the great increases in the numbers of company mergers and takeovers, withdrawals and divestments; and because of privatization and changes in status and delivery of public services. Certain measures of employment protection are given by the Transfer of Undertakings Protection of Employment Regulations and underpinned by the European Union Social Charter; again covering these from the employer's particular standpoint reinforces the overall integrity of the agreement;
- initial and continued job training – in support of the drive for job and work security, as well as professional, technological and occupational advancement;
- wages and salaries – wage and salary scales are normally at least referred to in collective agreements even if the responsibility for their design rests with the organization. It is normally necessary to publish criteria by which pay increases will be achieved and with special reference to profit and performance-related pay (see Summary Box 10.4);

SUMMARY BOX 10.4

Collective agreements and pay

Pay and rewards remain one of the key areas for an effective and positive contribution from collective agreements.

Very high on the list of everything that is damaging to individual and group motivation, commitment, morale and therefore output is the fact, belief or perception that people are being under-rewarded and therefore undervalued for their efforts. The best collective agreements ensure that this issue is addressed through the publication of pay scales, rules for the award of bonuses, and other aspects of the total package. The rules for this are as follows.

- Pay and reward packages must be written in clear and unambiguous terms.
- They must promise only what they can deliver.
- They must be available to all concerned.
- When people meet the criteria by which bonuses are to be awarded, these must be paid.
- The fairest way of rewarding people for performance is to pay everyone the same percentage of their salary, above and beyond their salary. This payment is either in the form of money or shares. Thus, for example, a bonus of 10 per cent of salary might be arrived at as the performance or profit-related element; if this is the case, someone on £10,000 a year would receive a bonus of £1,000, while someone on £30,000 would receive a bonus of £3,000, and so on. This reinforces the message that everyone's contribution to the organization is vital, rather than that some people are more important than others (which is what happens if discretionary or differentiated bonus rates are awarded).

In public service terms, the same rules should apply. Performance bonuses should be awarded across the entire service or not at all, and on the same equitable basis. Without exception other approaches are divisive and demotivating.

- specific operational aspects – these cover the rules and principles by which shift premiums, travel and other expenses, overtime, and disturbance allowances are to be paid, and the amounts of money involved;
- core and flexible benefits – this covers the nature of benefits involved, and the extent and principles by which they are made available. These normally include canteen, refreshments, pensions, car parking, travel, crèche and nursery, parental leave, personal emergencies, uniforms and protective clothing. Some organizations also include flexitime and the ability to work from home;
- share ownership schemes – this covers the ways in which the schemes are operated, and the rules by which people are eligible to join;
- crisis management – this covers the rules and principles by which IR makes its contribution to the management, organization and performance crises and emergencies. Normal coverage includes reference

to the conditions under which short-time working, lay-offs, garden leave, pay reductions, and redundancy and redeployment, are to be consulted on, negotiated and agreed; and the best agreements cover what is to happen when the crisis is passed;

- IR and staff management principles and procedures: covering discipline, grievance, dismissal and disputes;
- genuine occupational qualifications: in which specific conditions applying to particular categories of staff are clearly spelled out. Such coverage includes, for example, the rights of sales people and others to work off site or from home; and the extent of the rights of autonomous work groups to organize their workload as they see fit. It should also be noted that genuine occupational qualification is the sole ground on which racial or gender discrimination may take place;
- representation rights – including a statement of which trade unions are recognized, and the extent of this recognition – whether they are to be involved in each of the areas indicated, or whether they are to be included in some areas but not others;
- collective bargaining – in which those matters on which genuine negotiations take place are clearly delineated and defined.

Collective bargaining

As stated above (in Chapter 4), collective bargaining has importance in the development and effectiveness of UK IR for a variety of reasons.

- It is a perceived trade union traditional core function.
- It is the most widely understood means of arriving at perceived, fair and just agreements.
- It is a means of reconciling the basis of conflict and mistrust that exists throughout much of UK industry, and some public services.
- It deals with the perceptual and psychological needs of those involved, as well as the substance.

Indeed, most of the process of collective bargaining is behavioural. The central problem is therefore to reconcile the behavioural needs of everyone involved with organizational effectiveness implications that are dependent on the speed with which they can be delivered to the satisfaction of all concerned. From this arises the concern to speed up the process without detracting from universal feelings of satisfaction.

In situations where there is a long history of bad IR and extensive negotiations on all aspects of working life this is often very difficult to achieve; and many organizations have taken the view that it is better to destroy the existing situation and rebuild from its ashes rather than to try to reform.

Nevertheless, improvements can be made provided that organizations accept that:

a) theirs is the key responsibility for designing and delivering effective IR mechanisms and practices;

b) unions and staff representatives have a primary duty to represent the best interests of their members in every situation in which they are given bargaining or consultation rights;

c) all effective IR – adversarial or cooperative, unitary or pluralist – is ultimately dependent on the nature, quality and volume of information available and the ways in which this is delivered;

d) everyone involved is going to want something positive out of any negotiation, something that they can take back to their people that is known, believed or perceived to be a success (in whatever terms their people are going to gauge it). If this principle is adopted then the integrative approach is clearly signalled. If a particular benefit is given to one group but not others, or given at the expense of others, then ideally something positive has to be found for the others if overall harmony is to be maintained (see Summary Box 10.5);

SUMMARY BOX 10.5

IR in the future: the view of the General Municipal and Boilermakers Union

Speaking in June 1999, John Edmonds, the General Secretary of the General Municipal and Boilermakers Union, warned that the demise and decline of 'old style' IR was in danger of leaving a vacuum. Partnership agreements would go some way towards filling the void, he said, but if those agreements had neither substance nor strength in delivery then there would be a drift back to the worst aspects of collective bargaining.

He went on to say:

'We have a great opportunity to deliver a new system of IR but we have to accept that what is needed in this country is a massive cultural change. We accept that the only way we can deliver our members' aspirations is by working with employers in partnership. In that partnership agenda, we can also deliver what management wants most: flexibility and commitment. However, our training standards are at best patchy, and at worst appallingly low. And working people in Britain remain more suspicious of the motives of their managers than those in almost any European country.'

Source: John Edmonds, speaking at the British Chambers of Commerce Annual Conference, 1999

e) consequent recognition of mutual active responsibility to ensure that this approach is used to help deliver long-term effectiveness and viability. Collective bargaining activities have therefore to be conducted within the context of the organization's total range of activities, rather than away from them, or as an adjunct;

f) the use of the institutions and mechanisms of collective bargaining as a vehicle for organization development – and this includes entering into training and employment security arrangements and agreements, as well as developing general mutuality of interest and cooperative attitudes and approaches (see Summary Box 10.6);

The International Labour Organization was born out of the economic and social chaos at the end of World War I. It was based on the view that a lasting peace would only be achieved if there was also social justice. A part of its constitution states, 'The failure of any nation to adopt human conditions of labour is an obstacle in the way of other nations that desire to improve the conditions in their own countries.'

In 1999, following the appointment of the Chilean trade-unionist Juan Somavia, to the post of Director General, the organization published a report, *Decent Work*. In this, it called for four strategic objectives to be pursued:

- fundamental principles and human rights at work;
- 'decent' employment for all men and women;
- improved social protection and social security;
- and a commitment to social dialogue.

Within this the organization went on to ask for these matters to be delivered as part of the recognition of 'the social and ethical dimensions of business, rather than a return to high degrees of regulation'. A key to the delivery lies in effective forms of staff representation and strong trade unions working in partnership with socially aware and responsible employers, underpinned by positive and enabling regulation and legal bases produced by governments.

SUMMARY BOX 10.6

The future of IR: the International Labour Organization view

There is nothing radical about this. However, the key to speeding up the processes, especially the behavioural aspects of collective bargaining, lies in the creation of mechanisms and institutions that can demonstrate a mutuality of approach. If this can be achieved then collective bargaining will become more productive and effective both in the narrow matter of attention to specific IR issues, and in the broader aspects of enhancing staff motivation and commitment, and a positive contributor to organization effectiveness and success.

A part of the development of the traditional or collective approach to IR must concern itself with the future management of vested interests. These include trade unions; lobbies and pressure groups; key departments, divisions and functions; key expertise groups; and statutory bodies.

THE MANAGEMENT OF VESTED INTERESTS

Trade unions

Much of the approach necessary in the future effective management of trade unions is covered in the section above. It is also necessary to consider the background managerial effort required, however. This is overwhelmingly concerned with the production of high quality, relevant and comprehensive information delivered in ways easily received and understood by all. This in turn requires supporting through the use of all channels and media of communication.

Under no circumstances should trade unions be used as the only vehicle or conduit. In the past this has been attractive to managers especially on an expedient basis when needing to leak bad news or negative information; and unions were never slow to accept this because it was understood that it strengthened their overall position. However, the approach is ultimately destructive.

All forms of communication are to be used; and this, in turn, means management training in communication. While it has long been accepted in academic and research circles that communication is a key management skill, the practice of management in many organizations has still to recognize this and the benefits that accrue as the result. Good and effective communication feeds the measures of trust and integrity necessary if any form of IR is to succeed; and bad and ineffective communication reinforces both mistrust and any perceived lack of integrity, as well as reinforcing psychological barriers and the propensity for conflict.

Lobbies and pressure groups

Lobbies and pressure groups arise on the basis of legitimate concerns; or else those perceived to be legitimate. They also arise as the result of illegitimate concerns and the ability to gain real or perceived advantages in organizational political systems.

Legitimate

Legitimate or perceived legitimate concerns have always to be addressed. They should be dealt with openly and as quickly as possible. They are likely to arise as the result of the findings of cluster, managerial and professional groups, and quality circles and quality improvement groups. These will be as the result of having identified:

- specific IR concerns – for example, health and safety issues or the extent and prevalence of particular forms of discipline, grievance, absence and sickness; or
- derived IR concerns such as the effects of prevailing work patterns or managerial style on motivation, morale and commitment; or
- operational concerns that may at some point affect the state of IR – for example, labour turnover, customer relations and complaints.

This again reinforces the point that IR is integrated with, rather than separate from, the rest of organization activities, and that it makes a direct and positive contribution. Above all, if it is then possible to address the concerns positively, it removes the substantial need to become involved in extensive attention to individual and group problems, use of procedures and dealing with a trade union and professional representatives.

Illegitimate and non-legitimate
This form of lobbying is symptomatic of a deeper organization malaise, especially where it is widespread and where it is widely known, believed or perceived that it can be effective. It is compounded when it is actively encouraged under forms of 'divide and rule'.

It is extremely destructive and is therefore to be addressed and nipped in the bud as soon as it becomes apparent. However, it will only be addressed fully when the total managerial attitude is changed so that this form of approach is recognized as being wrong and unacceptable from every point of view.

Key functions

The problem here is to ensure that those departments, divisions, functions and groups and individuals that command key or primary resources, skills, knowledge or expertise do not use these to gain personal advantage. When it is present, it is universally acknowledged and recognized at least at the informal level.

Such matters are addressed by:

- opening up formal communication and meeting groups at which the key player or department is required to be present;
- where necessary, confronting the extent of rationing or prioritizing the particular activities using real, supported and documented examples;
- engaging those involved in simple direct agreements not to do this in future; and where necessary, this should be written down.

This can then be reinforced by communicating the result to the rest of the organization. There is no need for this to be punitive, at least at first. Indeed, it is likely to have arisen and become influential because it has been allowed to do so. Again, therefore, alongside the operational drive is the need to address the behavioural aspects. The overall drive needs to be broad and operational, rather than narrow and compartmentalized into an IR or collective bargaining situation.

Statutory bodies

Dealings with statutory bodies may be active or passive. Those with particular concerns in IR include the Health and Safety Executive, employment tribunals, workplace and occupational regulators, relevant professional bodies, and ACAS. Dealing with these bodies is normally carried out by organizations from the following points of view: contempt, rejection and ignorance; expediency; or enlightenment and acceptance.

Contempt, rejection and ignorance
There is no doubt that it is possible to take this attitude and to get away
with it for extensive periods of time. However, the message to the organization at large is of a lack of basic integrity, and this influences wider
organization, professional and occupational relationships as well as the
precise conduct of IR.

Expediency
Many organizations use the findings, orders and recommendations of
statutory bodies to implement initiatives that would otherwise not be
possible (or not perceived to be so). For example, orders made by the
Health and Safety Executive may be used to drive extensive improvements in this aspect of work, or to gain resources for these activities that
would otherwise not be made available.

Others use it to get themselves of a particular hook. For example, there
are many instances of organizations defending employment tribunal
claims knowing that they have no grounds for doing so; and then when
the case comes to tribunal and is lost, the tribunal (rather than the organization and its staff) can be blamed for the result.

Each of these is certain to become more expensive in the future. Employment protection now exists up to one year's continuous employment
regardless of hours worked for all staff; and maximum compensation for
unfair dismissal has been raised to £50,000 in 1999. Moreover, there is
an ever-greater concentration on the fundamentals of human treatment
and the need to follow procedures and establish minimum standards (see
Summary Box 10.7).

Acceptance
The very best organizations and their managers use expert guidance as a
check against their own high standards. Others assess the publications,
guidance, inspections, reports and recommendations and provide positive and considered responses whether or not they are to implement the
particular matters.

The main issue is to recognize the point of view from which the work of
the statutory body is coming. There is no point in slavishly adhering to
advice or in seeking statutory body guidance over every last issue because
this destroys the expertise and confidence which already exists in the
organization. Moreover, if it becomes widely known that organizations
will blindly follow external experts' advice, this acts as a spur for anyone
to pursue any matter through these bodies rather than internal mechanisms. It also means that trade unions, staff groups and professional
bodies will gain advice from these bodies when advancing their own interests, in the knowledge that they will thereby gain credence.

SUMMARY BOX 10.7

The perils of an expedient approach

Raspin: the United News Shops Ltd

Raspin was dismissed on suspicion of theft. However, the employer failed to follow its contractual disciplinary procedure and Raspin made a claim for breach of contract.

The employment tribunal held that Raspin's dismissal was in breach of contract and awarded her three weeks' pay – the time that the procedure would have taken had it been followed in full. Raspin also argued that, had she been employed for a further three weeks, she would have achieved the two years' continuity of service which at the time was needed to bring a claim of unfair dismissal. She said that she should be awarded further damages to reflect her loss of opportunity to bring such a claim.

Raspin took the case to employment tribunal where she won; and when the employer appealed to employment appeal tribunal, Raspin won again.

This indicates the complexity of the law, and the perils of taking an expedient approach to employees. Now that the qualifying period for unfair dismissal has been reduced to one year, and the compensation limit raised to £50,000, organizations need to ensure that they have a good disciplinary procedure in place and that managers are adequately trained to operate it. While in the past, recourse to tribunal has been viewed as 'a price easily paid', this example should serve to illustrate that this may not always be the case in the future.

IR MANAGE-MENT IN CONTEXT

The key issue is to ensure that the policies and practices of IR in organizations support, encourage and facilitate the ability to produce high quality products and services, and deliver these to customers and clients. The materials so far discussed in this chapter have concentrated on three priorities that are of particular interest and value to those working in organizations in the UK. However, the general principles hold good universally. From this, it is necessary finally to consider the broad context of IR, and the organization and managerial implications that underpin this (see Summary Box 10.8).

SUMMARY BOX 10.8

The US car industry

'Everybody in the United States knows that the Japanese automobile makers acquired 30% of the US car market in ten short years from the mid 70s to the mid 80s. But few realize that none of this gain was at the expense of America's two top manufacturers Ford and Chrysler – on the contrary – both actually gained market share. One third of the Japanese gain was at the expense of Volkswagen; two thirds of the Japanese gain was General Motors' loss; its market share slumped from 50% to 30%.

'For 15 years, General Motors did nothing except fiddle with prices and discounts – none to any effect. Then finally, in the late 1980s, it decided to counter-attack with a new car called the *Saturn*. The *Saturn* is a little, but slightly more costly, imitation of the Japanese in its styling, its manufacturing and marketing, its service and its labour relations. And GM badly bungled its market introduction. Still, it was a smash hit since a great many people in the United States were hungry for an American made car of the new kind.

'But as almost everyone outside GM immediately realized *Saturn* did not compete with the Japanese makes. All its sales came at the expense of declining – if not dying – GM brands such as Oldsmobile and Buick. And then GM – and even more so GM's labour union, The United Automobile Workers – began to throttle the *Saturn*. The car was denied money for expansion – that money went instead into futile attempts to modernise Oldsmobile and Buick plants. It was denied money to develop new models – again, that money went into Oldsmobile and Buick redesigns. And the Union of Automobile Workers began to whittle away at the *Saturn*'s new and successful labour relations for fear that *Saturn*'s example in building management–labour partnerships might spread to other plants operated by GM.

'So neither Oldsmobile nor Buick has benefited. Both are still going down-hill. But the *Saturn* has been all but destroyed. And both GM and the United Automobile Workers have continued their decline.'

Source: P. F. Drucker, *Management Challenges for the 21st Century*, Harper Business, 1999.

This means that there is a prime responsibility on the part of all IR players, stakeholders, and vested interests, to accept responsibility for their future involvement and influence. While it is true that it remains possible in the short term to preserve a degree of autonomy, Summary Box 10.8 is a useful illustration of the long-term decline resulting from persisting with such an approach.

Organizations require strategic and operational definition. This means attention to everything that contributes to, or detracts from, the effectiveness of activities. Because there exist legal, social and ethical restraints everywhere, effective organization (and therefore IR) strategies are established within these boundaries, in order to make operations effective – rather than being diverted every time there is a particular issue to be faced. Standards of behaviour and performance have to be established that transcend these constraints, rather than being restricted by them (see Summary Box 10.9).

In operational terms, every activity needs assessment in terms of its contribution to the total performance of the organization. Long-term enduring organizational performance is dependent on ensuring long-term customer and client satisfaction, and therefore all managerial activities – including IR and staff management – require assessment with the view to analysing their contribution to this. Any IR policy, practice or procedure that dilutes,

In 1999, the managers of a home catering for the severely mentally and physically handicapped children in Norwich, Norfolk, UK dismissed a female member of staff for being pregnant. The particular member of staff had worked for the organization for eight months, and had become pregnant three months into her employment. The managers of the home consistently refused the member of staff time off for antenatal care. When one day she collapsed at work and went home, she was dismissed.

The member of staff made a claim to industrial tribunal for unfair dismissal, claiming that she had been victimized on the grounds of her pregnancy. At first, the institution rejected her claim; but subsequently settled. The institution's defence was that, as the senior managers were from the USA, they could not be expected to know, or to comply with, the myriad of rules and regulations in this area promulgated by the UK and EU.

As the result of failing to pay attention to this aspect of IR management, the institution lost two major public service contracts.

reduces or in any way calls into question the ultimate quality of customer and client satisfaction, requires review and change.

In practice, this is not always going to be easy to achieve. Many IR functions, and the individuals working within them, have made extensive and successful careers, even if this has been alongside the long-term decline of their organizations. Nevertheless it is essential that structure, design and delivery of IR is assessed from a business or operational point of view, and changes made where necessary, if it is to contribute positively to enduring organization effectiveness and existence.

This in turn means concentrating on either:

* designing and implementing a style and approach to staff management IR that is appropriate for the human aspects of management, as well as ensuring operational effectiveness;
* making as effective as possible those institutions, mechanisms, policies and practices that are in existence, that cannot easily be changed.

While ideally the former may be desired, in practice in many cases, only the latter will be feasible. Where this is so, a substantial investment in time, energy and resources, and also in organization priority, is required; and a direct relationship between the operation of IR and organizational effectiveness is required when changes to the policies and practices present are envisaged. Where adversarial situations exist, and where these are not easily remedied, the strategic and operational focus needs to be on reducing the overall propensity for conflict; taking steps to resolve it as quickly as possible when it does arise; and ensuring that the means and methods adopted contribute to organizational effectiveness rather than reinforcing the perceived problem-solving expertise of those involved in the particular dispute.

For large organizations this is complicated further by the globalization of activities. In IR terms again, this means producing policies and approaches that transcend national boundaries, laws and customs; and providing ways of working, and styles of management, that are both universally and locally acceptable. They keys here are:

- organization transparency – based on a universal availability of information; a universal equality of treatment of staff; and universal value on all activities wherever their location;
- unity of authority and direction – again, based on standards that transcend the different areas of operation, staff groups and locations;
- integrity – based on high levels of ethical self-belief, that are capable of both internal and external scrutiny, whether this scrutiny is to come from the functions and institutions and vested interests of IR, or a broader social and ethical basis; and above all, that these standards are capable of being tested legally, socially and ethically wherever in the world such questions may arise.

CONCLUSIONS The purpose of this chapter has been to illustrate the specific interventions that are required in existing IR practice; and to indicate the increasing requirement for integration with all organizational activities.

At the core of this lies the requirement for expertise and professionalization of all aspects of management. IR as an area of functional expertise will exist to provide expert advice and, where necessary, executive or consultancy services. However, the day-to-day delivery of IR must be based on effective integration into organization strategies and operations that are concerned at their core with delivering effective and enduring products and services; and on a style of management that is compatible with ensuring that the productive efforts of people, and their expertise and knowledge, are positively engaged in the directions required.

Chapter 11

Conclusions

Most people enter trades, professions and occupations in order to pursue a career, vocation or calling. Very few people consider this from the point of view of having to manage people, at least when they first start work. However, it is almost inevitable that at some point they will be called upon to implement IR in some form or another; and those who gain managerial responsibilities will be required to take an ever more active role in this.

INTRODUCTION

The purpose of this last short chapter is therefore to draw out and summarize the main points of which everyone needs to be aware, if they are to stand any chance at all of conducting effective IR in the future. These threads are summarized under the headings of:

*   the value of macro-organizational analysis;
*   influence;
*   and keys to the effective management of IR in the future.

Each of Chapters 2–6 indicated a basis on which macro-organizational analysis may be carried out. While each of the approaches suit themselves better to some situations than others, it is essential that this is addressed everywhere.

THE VALUE OF MACRO-ORGANIZA-TIONAL ANALYSIS

Whichever standpoint is used, the IR outputs are:

*   attention to the state of organization culture;
*   attention to effectiveness of management style, perspective and attitudes;
*   attention to the effectiveness of IR policies, practices, procedures and implementation;
*   attention to the relationship between staff management and organization performance.

Specific points of enquiry may then be chosen as follows.

*   *Excellence:* in terms of the sector, required return on investment, profitability, stakeholders' demands, assessing the position of the organization. It is then possible to assess the actual contribution, and desired contribution, that IR and staff management makes to this, and where the reasons for any discrepancies lie.
*   *Japan:* assessing the lessons that are available from the success of

Japanese manufacturing and construction organizations in the UK; and from this, determining the extent to which these can and should be applied to other organizations.

- *Strategy:* in some cases, this will mean reference to the very existence of IR strategies (many organizations do not have them); and where IR and staff management fit into overall organizational strategy, policy and direction. Again, it is then possible to assess the contribution – positive or negative – that is made. This can then be developed further, in order to assess whether the IR approach speeds up operational matters or slows them down; and whichever is the case, whether or not this is for the good of the organization.

- *Culture:* overtly this is straightforward – is the culture strong, positive and unified, or weak, divided and emergent? From this, it is possible to ascertain the existence, prevalence and strengths of subcultures and canteen cultures; the extent to which people tend to go their own way, and the reasons for this. Where culture is weak, steps can be identified to improve, develop and enhance it; and where it is strong, steps can be identified to ensure that it remains so (see Summary Box 11.1).

SUMMARY BOX 11.1

Organization culture and IR

'The medical and social service professions are among the most intrinsically satisfying in the world. There can be no higher calling or vocation than to serve those most in need, at their time of need.'

These words were spoken by Aneurin Bevan in 1945, to mark the launch of the then proposed National Health Service.

In the UK at the turn of the twenty-first century many public service jobs are almost impossible to fill. The reasons for this are, in order of importance:

- lack of value, respect and esteem;
- style of management and remoteness of management;
- non-professional priorities of the services (especially concerning budget restrictions and political interference);
- undirected change and the rate of change;
- personal stresses and pressures;
- overall quality of working life, above all that brought about by having control neither over resources nor work and operational schedules.

There has never been greater demand for this work, and this is certain to continue. Those who work in some parts of public services can literally choose their own working hours. However, the ways in which things are done – the culture – is simply not acceptable to professional and trained people, and it is becoming increasingly tiresome to ancillary staff.

Source: *The Professional Manager,* May 1999; *British Medical Journal,* May 1999

- *Union:* the union perspective requires organizations to take an active view of whether or not to recognize trade unions, for what reasons, and on what issues. Again, the focus needs to be on the contribution to the activities of the organization as a whole. An active view also needs to be taken as to why people join (or do not join) unions in the particular organization, and in its divisions, departments, locations and functions (see Summary Box 11.2).

SUMMARY BOX 11.2

UK trade unions at the turn of the twenty-first century

In 1999, the Trades Union Congress reported an increase in membership of 110,000 of those belonging to trade unions affiliated to the TUC. Two reasons for this were given: attempts to recruit female members were at last beginning to be successful; and people were starting to take out trade union membership as a form of employment protection insurance.

An example of the outputs of both of these points occurred in July 1999, when Beverley Lancaster, a former housing officer with Birmingham City Council, was awarded £67,000 compensation for work related stress. She worked an 18 hour week on a salary of £7,000 per annum. She had joined the Council in 1971, and in 1993 she was ordered into a new post.

The case was fought with the full support of UNISON, the public services union. In 1997, the union had also secured £175,000 damages award for John Walker, a social worker, who had succumbed to an impossible work-load and suffered a serious nervous breakdown. The employer, Northumberland County Council, was deemed to be responsible for this, by failing to provide extra staff despite repeated requests.

In 1997, Pembrokeshire County Council paid out £100,000 to a school-teacher, Anthony Ratcliffe, after he had had two nervous breakdowns following repeated bullying by the head teacher for whom he worked.

These examples demonstrate the full range of the employment insurance benefit available as the result of joining a recognized trade union. It also demonstrates that employers are going to be required to take a much broader responsibility for the health, safety and well-being of their staff; and that this applies to all members of staff, regardless of length of service or hours worked. The case of Beverley Lancaster also reflects the fact that this concern is extended to all members of staff, and not just those who work in occupations more widely acknowledged to be stressful.

From this arises the need to manage the instruments, mechanisms and procedures of IR. This starts with an active consideration of the issues for which they are designed. Commitment then needs to be given to ensure that the relationship is maintained and developed rather than being allowed to stagnate. It also means taking a much broader general view of the relationship if cases such as those illustrated in Summary Box 11.2 are to be avoided.

- *The non-union view:* if the decision is taken to manage IR without unions, then the reasons why people join need to be addressed. Above all, it is essential that IR policies and management style are such that the need for formalized institutionalized representation is removed. If this is not done, people will join unions anyway; and while there is as yet no legal pressure on organizations to recognize them, anyone who takes a case as far as employment tribunal is entitled to call on their union to represent them at each stage (see Summary Box 11.3).

<table>
<tr><td>

SUMMARY BOX 11.3

Trade unions and the City of London

</td><td>

In the summer of 1999, the Manufacturing, Science and Finance Union (MSF) launched a recruitment drive in the institutions of the City of London.

MSF represents skilled and professional people in a variety of sectors. Many of their members are white collar workers earning an average of £25,000 per year. It is also the representative body for Members of Parliament, and has close links with the Professional Football Manager's Association.

There is no particular history of high density of union membership in the City of London. However, the union has overhauled its approach in order to bring the kind of benefits and support that members working in such institutions require. These include assistance to individual members when workplace rights or benefits are under threat, and advice, support and legal representation to all members.

The union is extensively represented in banking, insurance, finance, stockbroking and research sectors. One financial services company regards the arrangement as sealing a partnership as follows:

'We regard our partnership agreement with MSF as a foundation stone for ensuring good employee relations. The partnership means making for a common goal and it will help us to avoid misunderstandings which have so often characterized labour relations in the past.'

In selling itself, MSF regards its concentration on individual members, and their protection from bad practice, as of paramount importance. It also seeks to enhance and reinforce good human resources relationships.

</td></tr>
</table>

- *Communications:* effective macro-organizational analysis is certain to identify where communication systems, processes and practices are at their most and least effective. Again, the extent to which they contribute to, or hinder, the effective management of staff, becomes apparent; and this will be underlined by the presence or absence of disciplinary, grievance and dispute proceedings brought about as the result of misunderstandings, bad or toxic communications, or hidden or secondary agendas.

Partly because of macro-organizational analysis, and also as the result of a greater expert (rather than prejudicial) understanding of IR, comes the ability to understand where influence in the organization truly lies, and its extent and impact on operations and activities in general, as well as all aspects of staff management in particular. This especially refers to the following.

INFLUENCE

Legal aspects

The source of much legislation is now the EU and is certain to remain so for as long as the UK continues to be a Member State. Statutory rights are at present certain to be extended into the areas of union membership, health and safety, wage levels, pensions, collective representation on works councils, and continued efforts to ensure individual rights. It is also certain that the EU will legislate to tighten up employers' obligations when mergers and takeovers take place. The best organizations will accept the facts of these legal obligations and use them to their own advantage.

In the UK the funnel for this is certain to be ACAS. Its advisory remit is being extended continuously; and it produces an ever-wider range of publications. While it may make charges for some of its publications, the advice nevertheless remains impartial and independent. ACAS has a continuing statutory duty to mediate, and to become involved in all cases that are referred for consideration by employment tribunal.

Individual rights

It is also incumbent upon organizations to recognize and acknowledge individual rights, especially those that relate to the provisions of the European Union Social Charter; the provisions of specific directives; the outputs of other EU statutory influence and advice; and with specific reference to the rights of women, the elderly, children and the disabled in employment.

Moreover, the employment security of whistle blowers – those who speak out against bad organization or managerial practice – is now enshrined in UK law (Employment Relations Act 1999).

Collective rights

This refers to the influence of the staff as a vested interest of the same standing as shareholders. This is, however, clearly a different type of influence, because there exists no UK legislation so far that enables employees to block a merger, takeover, withdrawal or divestment, though there are enduring employment obligations in the Transfer of Undertakings Regulations.

Shareholders

The extent of influence of shareholders and the Stock Exchange, on IR, employment practice and staff management, is nearly always neglected. It is also true that most shareholders and share dealers take no account of the effect on staff of mergers, takeovers, withdrawals and divestments (see Summary Box 11.4).

SUMMARY BOX 11.4

Mergers and takeovers

Surveys conducted by the Institute of Management and the Industrial Society in 1996 and 1997 found that 87 per cent of corporate investment, mergers and takeovers, withdrawals and divestments, failed to achieve their stated business objectives.

The reason for this is because at the point when such activities take place, the overwhelming concentration is on shareholder interest. Stock markets have a specific influence here – any sale or acquisition of companies tends to move the share price up, and this also is excellent in the short term for the controlling interest.

However, once the company has been acquired or divested, productive activities have then to take place into the future. This means a special reference to the compatibility of existing activities with the new or desired management style; and specific reference to the principles, practices, collective and individual rights that have been acquired or divested.

The problem is often compounded when the shareholder or Stock Exchange influence uses phrases such as 'synergies' or 'leanness and meanness' or 'extra competitiveness' without actually going on to justify why such a phrase is appropriate, or what it means in the particular set of circumstances.

Source: Institute of Management, 1996; Industrial Society, 1997

Power bases

It is essential that these are established (however unacceptable this may be to organizational management and directors), if particular forms of power and influence are to be assessed and analysed. It is normally necessary to consider the following.

- *The IR industry:* the key players in the IR industry enjoy their own influence; and for the future, this needs much greater assessment. Of especial concern are IR experts, departments, divisions and functions which have grown their influence on the basis of solving problems; each therefore needs problems to solve to preserve its own reason for existence. This is certain to remain an issue wherever IR is seen as an adjunct to activities rather than being fully integrated. This also applies when considering the design, composition, remit and terms of reference of IR and staff management committees.
- *The power to block:* wherever present, this is negative and divisive; and

this also applies where resistance is being applied for the most altruistic of reasons, because it means that the particular matter in hand has not been explained properly.

The need is to consider where and why IR blockages occur, and to take steps to manage them away. It is only achieved through effective communication and consultation leading to the maximum level of staff insight possible.

Over-mighty subjects, departments, divisions and functions

These occur as the result of weak, negative and divided cultures, and are reinforced through the diversity of operations and locations, and psychological distance and alienation. The first steps towards resolving the problems that these bring is to acknowledge their potential for existence, and from this, to analyse the source and extent of influence that has been allowed to grow.

From this, steps can then be taken to ensure that they gain neither life nor influence for the future.

Prejudices and nostrums

The starting point for all IR prejudices is either political persuasion or received wisdom. At the core of this is the phrase 'the right to manage'.

In absolute terms, nobody has the right to manage unless they also have the capability and expertise. There is no substitute for this. Indeed, one of the main lessons of any detailed study of every aspect of management is the need to get over the preconceptions and prejudices that people so often bring with them (see Summary Box 11.5).

SUMMARY BOX 11.5

Prejudices and nostrums

IR prejudices and nostrums fall under the following headings:

- the truly meaningless, which usually involves references to staff in annual reports as being 'the organization's greatest asset', or 'the dedication and loyalty of all our staff';
- bland phrases such as 'negotiations/consultations are ongoing';
- the insidious, in which the above phrases are used at the same time as extensive restructuring and redundancies are going on. This is also reinforced with phrases such as 'macho management', or 'good guy, bad guy'. Other prevailing insidious attitudes are expressed in phrases such as 'fighting fire with fire', or 'we'll safety ourselves out of business';
- real warfare, which is apparent when more attention is paid to the forms of words used in collective agreements and the resolution of individual problems, than to the substance and delivery of those agreements. This is at its worst where it is known, believed or perceived that 'the workers want to screw us' (management), or 'the management want to screw us' (workers).

Other prejudices and preconceptions include the unwillingness of functional managers to acknowledge or recognize the need for attention to their own contribution to IR in their own sphere. This is often reinforced by views expressed along the lines of 'We had none of this soft stuff in my day,' or 'My people always know that they are doing a good job if they don't hear from me otherwise.' Both are untrue – in the first case, whole industries were destroyed in the UK because insufficient attention was paid to the human side of management; while in the second, people understand all too well, not that they are doing a good job, but rather that they are purely a function or resource, or asset, to be used or disposed of at any time.

It nevertheless remains true that each of these 'approaches' still holds considerable credence and influence, and they are only to be shaken out of organizations if an active corporate will to do so exists.

Trade unions, professional bodies, employers' associations and federations

For each of these bodies national, social and political influence has declined. This also applies to the Trade Union Congress (TUC) and Confederation of British Industry (CBI). For these bodies, however, two forms of influence may be noted for the future:

- sources of expert advice, guidance and representation in response to member demand, and offered as part of a range of member services and available to an ever-increasing audience. For example, some trade unions now offer their services to non members at organizations at which they are recognized;
- promulgation of best practice and new initiatives through media coverage and the trade press. This consists of ensuring that good and bad IR stories gain the maximum possible national and sectoral coverage, together with carefully appraised and analysed lessons and consequences to be drawn from the particular matter in hand.

Other vested interests

The management of the influence of vested interests in IR is a potentially serious problem, as discussed in Chapter 6. At this stage, it is necessary to draw attention to the following.

Financial interests

As stated above, the diversions of stockmarket and staff interests, especially in relation to the acquisition and sale of companies and organizations as commodities in themselves, has to be considered. It is also necessary to fully assess the enduring influence of financial considerations on long-term IR and staff management, and therefore productive capability. The following aspects especially must receive attention:

- the financial interest is satisfied whenever a company is bought or sold, and is therefore of no enduring interest to the financial markets, unless someone makes it so;
- managers are left to ensure that the staff and IR side of mergers and acquisitions, withdrawals and divestments are made to work, very often with little support and no institutional forethought;
- the financial interests of the acquiring organization never consider the staff management aspects or IR policies and practices that they have bought when they take over a particular organization;
- staff groups and their representatives assume that their interests will not be looked after in what is invariably a transition driven by short-term financial gain rather than long-term operational effectiveness;
- the management of promises and commitments made to staff and their representatives under the previous regime are often either not considered fully, or not considered at all or, worst of all, wilfully ignored (see Summary Box 11.6).

SUMMARY BOX 11.6

IR and the financial interests: privatization of county council social services in the 1990s

The privatization of social services care in the Home Counties of the UK in the early 1990s was carried out because of political and short-term financial imperatives, and without adequate reference to staff interests in general, or IR in particular. Two examples of the results of this were as follows.

- *Kent:* following the privatization of part of the residential provision for care for the elderly, the county council was faced with subsequent grievances and actions from those who had been transferred over to the new private institution, on the grounds that their individual and collective representation rights, pension rights and career prospects had not been sufficiently considered.
- *Surrey:* one organization, which bought a part of Surrey County Council's residential accommodation for caring for the elderly and disabled, was then taken over by another company; and the provision was then subsequently sold on to a third party. At no stage were the staff ever fully informed of their rights to continuity or protection of employment; nor were they consulted on the steps taken to ensure that their career prospects, pension rights and salary protection, enjoyed under local government terms and conditions, would apply, or what would be put in their place.

Both cases therefore ensured that extensive managerial and IR expert time and resources – and large amounts of money – were spent subsequently on resolving these issues.

Management consultants

Many consultancy arrangements and agreements fail to take sufficient account of the effects on IR of proposals for change, business development, restructuring, de-layering and outsourcing (see Summary Box 11.7).

Faddish approaches to management have been common since the early 1980s; and it is true to say that they greatly increased following the publication of *In Search of Excellence* (T. Peters and R. Waterman, Harper & Row, 1980). It remains a useful way of describing directive and prescriptive approaches to management issues and problems, especially those proposed by large firms of management consultants. Examples are as follows:

- *Job evaluation:* the analysis of job and work activities according to preset criteria in order to rank them in importance, status, value and place on the pay scale.
- *Business process re-engineering (BPR):* attention to administration, supervision and procedures for the purpose of simplifying, clarifying and speeding up their operation.
- *Total quality management (TQM):* attention to every aspect of organizational practice in pursuit of continuous improvement, the highest possible standards of practice, products, services and customer service.
- *Benchmarking:* in which standards of activity are set against that with which other activities can be compared and rated.
- *Virtual organization:* organization structures based on technology rather than physical presence.
- *De-layering, downsizing, rightsizing:* in which ranks, titles, functions and layers of management, supervision and operational activity are removed from the organization structure in the belief that costs are being cut.

Each of these approaches has the staff at its core, and it is the staff that have to bear the brunt of these prescriptive approaches to change. In most cases, staff are never consulted when these approaches are engaged. Schedules and timetables are established without adequate recourse to consultation or involvement. In particular, organization directors and senior managers buy in the services of consultants offering these ways forward in order to avoid direct responsibility for the staff management aspects because they consider it possible to absolve themselves of responsibilities, because they are then only carrying out the instructions given to them by the particular firm of consultants.

The problem is compounded when, following the engagement of a particular initiative, IR and staff management problems do indeed become apparent; and there has existed no part of the consultancy agreement that requires the consultants to address and resolve the problems that have arisen.

In general, there is great psychological pressure placed on those who commission projects and engage consultants to carry out work, especially when there are high fee levels involved, or when the organization is doing its best to face up to serious operational problems. However, anyone engaging this form of approach, or external consultants or advisors, needs always to ensure that the IR and staff management question is addressed. Failure to do so is the greatest single cause of such projects and initiatives not delivering the required results.

- Understanding the complexities that have to be addressed, which means, above all, recognizing the importance of IR as a field of managerial expertise and responsibility in its own right. Of all aspects of management, IR is the one which is accompanied by the greatest volume of preconception and prejudice. This needs to be acknowledged so that steps can be taken to replace this with real knowledge, expertise and understanding.
- Understanding that active and expert management in this area is critical to the long-term performance of organizations. There is a direct relationship between bad IR, and organization, industrial and sectoral decline.

In this context, therefore, managerial expertise means actively designing, implementing, monitoring, evaluating and developing IR policies, procedures, practices and mechanisms that contribute to the particular organization in its own environment. This means drawing on lessons from elsewhere, and adapting the underlying principles to suit the given set of circumstances; and when these circumstances develop, so again will the overall IR approach.

It is also necessary to accept the responsibilities inherent. It is certain to mean attention to staff, supervisory and management briefing and training. In many cases, it will also mean lobbying those who either do not have stated HR or IR remits, or else who do not understand these fully. It may also mean attempting to ensure that other interests – especially those concerning finance and problem-solving – accept the contribution made by IR to business ventures in the long term; and especially where insufficient attention is paid, the negative and destructive effects on those ventures overall.

It is necessary to understand that effective IR transcends industrial, commercial and public service sectors, and different and divergent work patterns and locations. Whatever the activities of the organization, or patterns of work involved, the principles of good IR need application universally.

It is necessary to manage the realm of vested interest and influence that together comprises the 'IR industry'. This also means active managerial involvement in deciding whether particular vested interests are to be involved and recognized, and the extent to which this is to occur. This means having, or acquiring, the managerial expertise necessary to analyse and evaluate the contribution required from each in order to improve and maintain IR and staff management, as well as overall organizational performance. This, in turn, reinforces the standpoint that IR is an integral part of effective organization performance, rather than an adjunct or side show.

Finally, IR is about regulating the behaviour and performance of people in places of work. In the past, in many organizations too much attention has been given to the regulation, and not enough to the people. In future, the overwhelming need is to be able to understand what makes people behave in particular ways, and to relate this to organization requirements for performance, and to improve or amend this when it is found to be necessary. This is the core issue that needs to be addressed if effective IR is to be maintained and developed for the future.

Appendix 1

Employment and IR law in the UK

It is necessary to understand the legal framework in which IR takes place. This is founded in a combination of UK and EU legislation, and its application through the tribunal, court and justice system.

In the UK, the sources of employment law are the same as all other legal areas.

- *Statute law:* defined by acts of parliament.
- *Criminal law:* consisting of offences against the nation or the Crown.
- *Civil law:* allowing for the resolution of disputes between individuals.
- *Precedent:* in which a judgment on one case is held to apply to others of a similar nature.
- *Custom and practice:* in which legal status is accorded to something that has gone on for a period of time.
- *European law:* the ultimate point of reference for any UK citizen on any legal matter including employment.

Recourse to the law for alleged breaches is the same as all other legal areas – the courts, Court of Appeal, House of Lords, and the European Court of Justice. Employment matters may also be taken to Employment Tribunal. UK employment law also specifies the following factors that must be taken into account when considering workplace situations and issues:

- fairness and reasonableness;
- natural justice;
- best practice;
- precedent.

Fairness and reasonableness

All organizations are unique and because they vary so greatly the test of what is fair and reasonable in particular sets of circumstances is always applied. Fairness and reasonableness is based on a combination of:

- the size of the organization, the resources at its command and disposal;
- the nature of business and activities, the technology and equipment used, commercial and operational pressures;

- the nature of people employed, their skills, knowledge, qualities and expertise;
- ways of working, including interpersonal relationships;
- respect, value and esteem for staff and customers, honesty and integrity, and ordinary common decency;
- specific legal standards (e.g. health and safety, product quality and description, trading standards).

Fairness and reasonableness applies to conduct, behaviour and performance; and to both employers and employees.

Natural justice

Quite apart from any legal obligation, natural justice demands that people are treated equally and fairly and with respect and honesty in all walks of life; and work (or indeed lack of it) plays a significant part in everyone's life.

Best practice

Standards of staff and human resource management set by ACAS, the Department for Education and Employment and expert bodies such as the Institute of Management and the Institute of Personnel and Development establish what is known as *best practice*. Best practice is a combination of fairness and reasonableness, honesty and integrity and natural justice, together with the operational ways of organizing and directing people in order to optimize organizational performance.

Precedent

Workplace and employment tribunal cases are treated as distinctive and individual, and therefore on their own merits. Tribunal judgments do not set precedent. Precedent is only set in employment law cases where these are referred on or pursued beyond the Employment Appeal Tribunal and into the mainstream judicial system.

AREAS COVERED BY EMPLOYMENT LAW

Contract of employment

This is the basis of the relationship between employer and employee. Not later than eight weeks after starting work, any employee who works more than eight hours per week must receive a written statement giving:

- the name of the employer and the employee;
- the date when the employment began, taking account of any period of employment with a previous employer which counts as continuous with the present;
- pay or the method of calculating it, and payment interval;
- terms and conditions relating to hours of work, holiday entitlement,

other time off including public holidays and holiday pay;
- job title or brief description of job;
- place of work or places along with the employer's address;
- any other specific or stated terms of employment.

This is the principle statement and must be contained in one document. In addition, the following information must also be given or be reasonably accessible to the employee:

- health and safety matters reflecting the employer's duty of care;
- terms and conditions relating to sickness, injury and sick pay;
- any pension arrangements;
- the length of notice the employee must give and receive;
- the period of employment, if it is temporary or fixed term;
- particulars of any collective agreements by which the employee is to be bound;
- any specific conditions that apply when the employee is to work outside the UK for more than one month;
- any disciplinary rules applicable to the employee, and the person to whom employees can apply if dissatisfied with a disciplinary decision or if they have a grievance about their employment and the procedure to be followed;
- any implied terms of employment, and employee obligations.

Information given in job advertisements, job descriptions or other company information may also constitute part of the contract of employment.

Any change to the written particulars must be consulted on and agreed, and notified in writing to employees individually within one month of the change. If there is any dispute about the written statement, either the employer or the employee may refer the matter to an employment tribunal.

Collective agreements

This refers mainly to any trade unions that the employer recognizes and the right of the employee to join or not. It normally constitutes a statement of the specific terms and conditions by which both employer and employees are bound, and the specific procedures that are to be followed.

Discrimination and equality of opportunity

All organizations are required by law to be equal opportunity employers. It is illegal to discriminate between people when offering employment, promotion, pay, training and development or any other opportunity on any of the following grounds.

- Racial or ethnic origin and religion.
- Gender, including pregnancy, marital status and retirement age.
- Disability (except where the employer's premises do not provide suitable access).

- Membership of a trade union, refusal to join a trade union, insistence on joining or not joining a trade union.
- Spent convictions for previous offences and misdemeanours (although there are many occupations exempted from this including teaching, medicine, law, social work, banking and finance).
- Length of service or hours worked.

Discrimination may be either direct or indirect.

Direct discrimination is overt – the straightforward refusal of work or opportunities on any of the grounds indicated above. Indirect discrimination occurs where a condition or restraint is placed, the effect of which is to bar, restrict or jeopardize the opportunities of people from each of the groups indicated above.

Health and safety

An employer may not order or request an employee to carry out work that is hazardous or unsafe without first providing the correct protective equipment, clothing and training where necessary. An employer may not request, order or coerce an employee to carry out any unsafe or hazardous activity.

It is the duty of employers to provide as far as reasonably practicable a healthy and safe working environment. It is the responsibility and duty of all to ensure that this is maintained and that accidents, hazards and emergencies are notified and rectified immediately.

Maternity

All female employees are entitled to 14 weeks' maternity leave regardless of length of service or hours worked. For those who have more than two years' continuous service the period is 29 weeks.

Pregnant employees are allowed time off with pay for antenatal care.

On returning from maternity leave, the employee has the right to return to her previous job or (if this has ceased) to suitable alternative work.

Time off

Employers must allow reasonable time off from work for employees to carry out the following:

- public duties, including as Justice of the Peace; membership of local authorities, tribunals, health authorities, governing bodies of schools and colleges, boards of prison visitors; jury service if the employee is called;
- duties connected with the activities of recognized trade unions, including representation of members and training;
- looking for work and attending job interviews, retraining, career and

occupational counselling after employees have been declared redundant and before they have left;

- maternity (as above).

Redundancy

Employers may dismiss – make redundant – employees whose work no longer exists or where fewer employees are required to carry out existing levels of work. Where redundancies are declared the employer must disclose the following:

- the reasons for the redundancies;
- the numbers and descriptions of employees affected;
- the criteria for selection;
- the means and dates on which the dismissals are to be carried out.

Employers must consult with any recognized trade unions as soon as it becomes known that redundancies are to occur. This must happen even if only one employee is to be made redundant.

Alternatives – short-time working, short-term lay-offs, transfers, redeployments, early retirements and calling for volunteers – must all be considered and rejected as impractical before compulsory redundancies take place.

The minimum consultation periods are as follows:

- 90 days in the case of 100 or more dismissals in a 90-day period
- 30 days in the case of ten or more dismissals in a 30-day period

otherwise consultation must begin as early as possible.

Employees who are dismissed because of redundancy are normally entitled to a lump sum payment. The amount depends on age, pay and length of service as follows.

For each year of continuous employment:

- from age 41–64, 1.5 weeks' pay,
- from age 22–40, 1 week's pay,
- from age 18–21, 0.5 weeks' pay.

In 1999, £260 was the maximum weekly pay taken into account and 20 years the maximum service. The maximum redundancy payment possible was therefore £7,800 (i.e. 20 years' service between 41 and 64 = 30 × £260).

The amount is reduced by one twelfth for each month of service completed over the age of 64 so that at 65 (the statutory retirement age) no payment is due.

The employer must give the employee a written explanation of a redundancy payment.

Transfers of undertakings

The Transfer of Undertakings (Protection of Employment) Regulations (TUPE) safeguard employees' rights when there is a change of employer following a change of ownership, takeover, merger or privatization. They also apply where there is a change of status – for example, from public to private sector, from building society to Plc.

The effects of the TUPE regulations are:

- the existing contract and terms and conditions of employment are transferred in their entirety to the new employer including continuity of service. The transfer may not take place with the purpose of reducing pay levels and other terms and conditions of employment;
- recognition rights of trade unions are transferred if the new body maintains a distinctive identity;
- dismissals related directly to the transfer of the business are automatically unfair;
- both the old and the new employer must consult and provide advance information to any recognised trade unions and to all employees who are to be affected. This must include: the timing of the transfer; the reasons for the transfer; legal, economic and social implications for those affected.

Industrial action

Industrial action may be conducted in the pursuit of a legitimate trade dispute. A legitimate trade dispute occurs between employer and employees on one or more of the following grounds:

- terms and conditions of employment;
- the physical conditions in which people are required to work;
- dismissal, termination or suspension of employment of one or more employees;
- allocation of work or duties;
- matters of discipline;
- membership or non-membership of a trade union;
- facilities for officials of trade unions;
- machinery for negotiation or consultation and other procedures relating to any of the above matters including the recognition by employers or employers' associations of the right of a trade union to represent employees.

Industrial action must be preceded by a postal ballot independently scrutinized (e.g. by the Electoral Reform Society). Those responsible for conducting a ballot (normally a trade union or staff representative) must give seven days' notice of their intent to hold a ballot. They must notify the employer of the outcome and give seven days' notice of any industrial action intended.

So long as this procedure is followed, trade unions preserve their immunity in law from being sued for damages as the result of losses incurred by the particular employer.

A legitimate trade dispute may take place only at the site where the problem arose. Where the problem has arisen at a multi-site location (e.g. a transport company), then the dispute may be carried out at each site.

Payment

Payment must be made at the intervals stated in the contract and this must consist of the amounts stipulated.

Itemized pay statements must be issued at each interval. These must show the gross pay; the net pay; and the amount of each and every deduction made.

Individual rights

Individual rights at places of work have been clarified and strengthened over recent years (see Summary Box A.1). This has been partly due to UK government legislation and partly due to the European Union (EU). The main individual rights are:

- the right to fair and equal treatment regardless of length of service, hours worked or whether designated a full- or part-time employee;
- the right to employment protection (protection from unfair dismissal) after two years' continuous service regardless of hours worked or whether designated a full- or part-time employee;
- the right to join a recognized trade union or to refuse to join it; the right not to be penalized, victimized or harassed for joining or refusing to join;
- the right to adequate and continuous vocational and job training;
- the right to a healthy and safe working environment;
- the right to information, consultation and participation on key workplace issues and other matters of relevance and importance;
- the right of access to personnel files and other information held (whether on paper or database);
- the right to be represented or accompanied in all dealings with the organization, especially matters of grievance or discipline.

The main laws, and their coverage, are as follows.

LAWS AND REGULATIONS

Equal Pay Act 1970

- *Equal pay:* the right to receive the same pay and other terms of employment as an employee of the opposite sex working for the same or an associated employer if engaged on like work, work rated as

**SUMMARY
BOX A.1**

**Individual
rights**

The great majority of applications made to industrial tribunals are by individual employees. The orientation of the tribunal is therefore towards the individual. Where there is any doubt over the merits and strengths of the case of applicants and respondents, the tribunal normally orders the case to proceed.

Where there is any question that any of the rights indicated above have been either breached or not upheld, the tribunal will normally order the case to proceed.

It is the employer's duty to uphold the rights of individuals. The onus is therefore placed on the employer to be able to prove or demonstrate to the satisfaction of the tribunal that individual rights were upheld. It is the employer's duty to ensure that all employees are informed of their rights.

Employees may not be induced or coerced to sign away all or part of their statutory rights, nor is any such signature legally binding.

equivalent or work of equal value. The question of equal value is supported by the Equal Value Regulations (last amended 1996) which place further onus on employers to ensure that the widest possible view is taken of the equality of the value of the work.

Employment Protection (Consolidation) Act 1978; Employment Rights Act 1996

- *Pay:* the right to receive an itemized pay statement.
- *Maternity rights:* the right not to be unfairly dismissed for reasons connected with pregnancy; the right to paid time off work for antenatal care; the right to return to work following absence because of pregnancy or confinement.
- *Medical suspension:* the right not to be unfairly dismissed on medical grounds; the right to receive pay for suspension on medical grounds.
- *Redundancy:* the right to be consulted by the employer about proposed redundancies; the right of recognized independent trade unions to be consulted by the employer about proposed redundancies; the right to receive payment when made redundant; the right to receive an itemized statement of redundancy payment; the right to pay and time off in the event of redundancy to look for other work or to make arrangements for training.
- *Time off for public duties:* the right to time off for public duties.
- *Trade union membership/non-membership rights:* the right to pay and time off for trade union duties; the right to time off for trade union activities; the right not to suffer dismissal or action short of dismissal for trade union membership or activities or non-membership; the right not to suffer action short of dismissal to compel union membership; the right not to be unfairly dismissed for trade union

membership or activities; the right not to be unfairly dismissed for non-membership of the union; the right not to be chosen for redundancy because of trade union membership or activities, or non-membership of a trade union.

- *Unfair dismissal:* the right not to be unfairly dismissed for any reason; the right to receive a written statement of reasons for dismissal.
- *The right to receive a written statement of terms of employment and any alterations to them.*

Race Relations Act 1976

- *Race relations:* the right not to be discriminated against in employment, training and related fields on grounds of colour, race, nationality, ethnic or national origin.

Sex Discrimination Act 1975

- *Sex discrimination:* the right not to be discriminated against in employment, training and related fields on the grounds of sex, marriage or pregnancy.

Transfer of Undertakings (Protection of Employment) Regulations 1981

- *Transfers:* the right of unions to be informed and consulted about the transfer of an undertaking to a new employer; the right not to be dismissed on the transfer of an undertaking to a new employer.

Employment Act 1980

- *Trade union rights:* the right not to be unreasonably excluded or expelled from a trade union.

Employment Act 1988

- *Trade union rights:* the right not to be unjustifiably disciplined by a trade union; the right of recourse to a tribunal if discriminated or disciplined by an employer concerning trade union rights; the right of trade unions to hold secret ballots on employers' premises; the abolition of the union membership agreement or closed shop.

Wages Act 1986

- *Payment of wages:* the right of all staff not to have deductions made from their wages unless allowed by statute, by the contract of employment or with the individual's prior written agreement; the right of everyone to an itemized pay statement.

Disabled Persons (Employment) Acts 1944 and 1958; Disabled Rights Act 1996

- *Disability:* the general right not to be discriminated against in employment because of a registered disability, the duty of employers with 20 or more employees to employ a minimum of 3 per cent of registered disabled people; the right to complain to tribunal if discriminated against or disadvantaged by virtue of disability.

Rehabilitation of Offenders Act 1974

- *Spent convictions:* job applicants and employees are not under any legal obligation to disclose information about previous convictions; the right to deny a previous offence when the conviction for it is 'spent', i.e. when a person has served their punishment and been rehabilitated (there are a large number of occupations which are exempted from this rule – especially working with money, people and property; and working within the legal, law enforcement and emergency services).

Trade Union Reform and Employment Rights Act 1993; Employment Relations Act 1999

- *Employee rights:* the right not to be dismissed for exercising statutory employment rights regardless of length of service or hours of work; the right of women to 14 weeks' maternity leave regardless of length of service or hours of work; the right to healthy and safe working premises and activities regardless of length of service or hours of work.
- *Transfers of undertakings:* the regulations governing business transfers are extended to cover non-commercial undertakings.
- *Trade unions:* individuals are given the right to join the union of their choice; the deduction of union dues from pay must be authorized in writing by the employees every three years; the duty of an employer to inform and consult union representatives about collective redundancies is re-stated.
- *Industrial action:* strike ballots must be postal and independently scrutinized; unions must give employers seven days' notice of their intention to hold a strike ballot; unions must give employers seven days' notice of the industrial action intended; injunctions may be sought by anybody affected by unlawful or unofficial industrial action to prevent this from taking place.

EXPERT BODIES   ### Advisory, Conciliation and Arbitration Service (ACAS)

ACAS is an independent statutory body funded by government grant. It is the recognized national source of expertise, advice, information and guidance on workplace employee relations and staff management. ACAS

Recent cases that have acquired legal status and set precedent are as follows.

Polkey v. A. E. Dayton Ltd
'Organisations must follow procedures when dismissing an employee' (House of Lords).

The ruling required:

- In a case of incapability an employee must be given fair warning and a chance to improve.
- In a case of misconduct, investigating fully and fairly and hearing what the employee has to say in explanation or mitigation of their conduct.
- In a case of redundancy, warning and consultation with affected employees and adopting a fair basis for selection and taking reasonable steps to redeploy those affected.

The tribunal which considered Polkey's case held that the employer had breached the correct procedure but that the result would have been the same if the procedure had been followed. This was rejected by the House of Lords. The Lord Chancellor stated:

> It is what the employer did that is to be judged, not what he might have done.

Heywood v. Cammell Laird
'Equal pay means *pay* and not equivalent benefits' (House of Lords).

Jean Heywood worked as a cook at Cammell Laird. For this work she was required to have a recognised qualification. She argued that her qualification was of the same level as those of men working elsewhere in the company and that, therefore, her work was equivalent to that of those men. She was paid less than those men.

The company acknowledged that they paid Mrs Heywood less, but because she received a free meal every day, this made her total reward package up to a level equivalent to that of the men with whom she was making the comparison.

The House of Lords rejected this and ordered the company to make up her pay to the same level as that of the men.

Brown v. Stockton-on-Tees Borough Council
'Pregnancy may not be used as a criterion for redundancy' (House of Lords).

Maria Brown worked for Stockton-on-Tees Borough Council. She worked in a group of four female staff. The council made two members of staff redundant and singled out Mrs Brown as one of them because she was pregnant. If 'last in first out' had been used to determined redundancies, Mrs Brown would not have been made redundant; no other criteria for redundancy was published.

The House of Lords upheld the view that pregnancy was not a valid ground for redundancy; and that to make someone redundant because of their pregnancy amounted to discrimination. The Lords went on to state that criteria for redundancy must be published in advance of redundancies; failure to do so means that last in first out (lifo) will apply.

Price v. The Civil Service Commission

'Age constraints must not be indirectly discriminatory on grounds of gender' (Court of Appeal).

Belinda Price worked as a civil servant and, at the age of 36, put in for a promotion to the next grade. The Civil Service Commission turned her down on the grounds that she was too old and that everyone who made the particular grade had to do so by the age of 29.

Ms Price countered this by saying that she could not have achieved this because she was out of the workforce for ten years bringing up children. She was otherwise a good and effective worker; the only thing militating against her promotion was her age; and that because of circumstances, this discriminated indirectly on grounds of gender.

The Court of Appeal upheld this view, stating that the particular age barrier was less favourable to women (and therefore discriminatory) than to men.

Burchell v. British Home Stores

'Allegations of misconduct must be fully investigated before any action is taken against an employee and before an employer comes to a decision as to what is to happen' (Court of Appeal).

Burchell was dismissed for misconduct by British Home Stores without being given the opportunity to state his case. The Court of Appeal laid down three guiding principles to ensure that natural justice would be upheld.

- The employer should show that there was a genuine belief that the employee was guilty of the misconduct under consideration.
- The employer must carry out a reasonable and thorough investigation into the case.
- As the result of the investigation, the employer must have reasonable grounds for maintaining the belief.

Each point is now always cosidered and questioned by tribunals where cases arising from misconduct occur.

publishes guidelines and codes of practice on discipline, grievance, dismissal, employment practices and the content and use of procedures (see Summary Box A.3). These are available from offices of ACAS, either free or for a small charge.

The general role of ACAS is to promote workplace harmony, understanding and well-being.

- *Advice*
  ACAS may be contacted at any time, either by post or by phone, on any aspect of workplace, employee relations or staff management for

general advice and information. ACAS officials also arrange and carry out briefings and training sessions by agreement.

- *Conciliation and mediation*

  ACAS may be contacted at any time to arrange conciliation and mediation in disputes that are likely to become serious if they are not resolved quickly. ACAS searches for common grounds and areas where agreement might be reached and makes proposals for tackling other issues. ACAS also conducts conciliation and mediation in all applications to tribunal as stated above.

- *Arbitration*

  ACAS may be contacted at any time to arrange arbitration in disputes where there is no apparent possibility of resolution. Both parties normally agree to be bound by the arbitrator's findings (though this is not required by law). The arbitrator hears both cases and then makes recommendations based on their assessment of the merits. The result may be wholly in favour of one party or a compromise between the two, or some alternative solution.

In all cases that come to hearing, the tribunal normally requires satisfaction that the advice, proposals, recommendations and guidance of ACAS have been followed. Where this has not occurred, good reason must be shown. Where both parties agree to be bound by the findings of an arbitrator, good reason must be shown if one party then decides not to accept these findings.

Health and Safety Executive (HSE)

The HSE is also an independent body funded by government grant. It is the recognized source of expertise, advice, information and guidance on all matters concerning health and safety at work.

The HSE publishes advice and guidelines on general health and safety matters. It has a statutory right of access to all work premises. It carries out inspections, advises on safety matters and, in extreme cases, may close down premises or parts of premises where these are considered to be unsafe or unhealthy. Where a case arises concerning health and safety matters the tribunal always requires satisfaction that the advice, proposals, recommendations and guidance of the HSE have been followed. If this has not occurred, good reason must be shown.

Department for Education and Employment (DfEE)

The DfEE publishes booklets and leaflets giving advice and information on changes to the law and the implementation of regulations. It is the duty of employers to ensure that they keep themselves up to date with current employment legislation.

A tribunal does not accept ignorance of the law as a defence – whether on the part of applicant or respondent.

Commission for Racial Equality; Equal Opportunities Commission; Disablement Resettlement Officer

These bodies provide independent advice and guidance, and act as sources of information on employment law and related matters. Their advice and guidance is normally considered to be the highest form of expertise available.

In tribunal cases, where the advice and guidance of these bodies has been sought the tribunal will normally place great emphasis on their recommendations.

Trade unions; employers' associations; professional associations; independent associations

These bodies provide advice and guidance and act as sources of information on employment law and related matters to their members. Their advice and guidance carries no particular presumption of expertise. It is, however, generally of high quality and represents the state of knowledge and information available.

Tribunals may choose to place emphasis on the recommendations, advice and guidance given by these bodies.

SUMMARY BOX A.3

Procedures

Procedures exist to set standards of performance, conduct and behaviour at places of work and to ensure that everyone knows what is expected of them and that they conform to this. They ensure fairness and equality of treatment for everyone.

All organizations must have procedures for handling and managing all staff matters, and especially discipline, grievance, disputes and dismissal. These have to meet standards prescribed by ACAS and the Department for Education and Employment. They must:

- be in writing;
- state to whom they apply;
- be applied evenly to everyone concerned regardless of rank or occupation;
- be accessible, available for inspection and available for use at any time;
- be capable of being understood and followed;
- be fair and reasonable;
- indicate the nature and range of actions which may be taken in given sets of circumstances;
- indicate the levels of management which may take particular actions;
- provide for matters to be dealt with quickly.

EUROPEAN UNION LAW

European Union law is broadly superior to UK law; any case that reaches the European Court of Justice will be judged by this as the conclusion to the matter in hand.

The particular concern of European Union law is the strengthening and upholding of individual rights in all aspects of life – and this includes employment. The main areas of concern are:

- freedom of movement for workers and self-employed persons across the European Union;
- protection of employment and remuneration;
- adequate vocational training;
- freedom of association, especially the right to join trade unions and associations, or not to join trade unions and associations;
- information, consultation and participation of employees on major workplace issues;
- health and safety at work;
- specific protection for stated groups of employees, especially children, adolescents, elderly persons, disabled persons; equal treatment for men and women.

The general principle is that current UK legislation reflects the demands of EU law and standards. It is especially important to note that any case that does reach the European Court of Justice will be judged by persons who take a European perspective (see Summary Box A.4).

SUMMARY BOX A.4

The European Court of Justice

The following judgments were issued by the European Court of Justice after the tribunal and UK legal systems had been exhausted.

Swift v. British Rail
'Retirement age and the opportunity to retire must be the same for all employees regardless of gender.'

British Rail v. National Union of Railwaymen
'Union membership agreements – the closed shop – are illegal and may not be enforced; no-one should be forced to join a trade union or any other organisation against their will (nor should they be prevented from joining a trade union or any other organisation if they so wish).'

European Union law has its basis in: the treaties by which it was created and developed; the Social Charter; the different legal instruments at its disposal; and the decisions and judgments of the European Commission, the Council of the European Union, and the European Court of Justice.

Treaties

The treaties by which the European Union was established and developed are as follows.

- *Treaty of Rome 1957:* which gave the European Economic Community a distinct legal personality and set up institutions to administer the system. The position of employees, trade unions and other employee representatives, and of employers and their representatives, as 'social partners' was reinforced, through the 'Social Chapter' of the treaty.

- *Single European Act 1987:* this was implemented in each of the domestic legislatures of the Member States, following agreement across the European Community. Its main provisions were: free movement of labour so that people from member nations could obtain employment and live in any Member State; and to receive unemployment and other social security benefits in their chosen country of residence. The common recognition of the qualifications of workers was also to be advanced.

- *Maastricht Treaty 1992:* from an IR point of view, the main contribution of the Maastricht Treaty was to formalize the Social Charter as the basis on which all employment (and also wider human) rights would be established within the Member States of the EU. At this point, the UK negotiated an 'opt-out', because the prevailing political view at the time was that the adoption of the Social Charter would lead to increased labour costs and therefore a lack of competitiveness.

- *Amsterdam Treaty 1997:* this recognized the problems inherent in the continued high levels of unemployment within the Member States of the EU (at the time that it was signed, there were a total of 18 million people out of work within the Member States). The Amsterdam Treaty required Member States to put the fight against unemployment at the top of Europe's agenda. For the first time, it required governments to coordinate their strategies for creating employment and promoting a skilled, trained and adaptable workforce. It also required the Member States to produce an annual report on the employment situation in the EU, detailing the effectiveness of actions taken (see Summary Box A.5).

SUMMARY BOX A.5

The Treaty of Amsterdam and employment rights

The Maastricht Treaty 1992 gave every person holding UK citizenship, citizenship of the European Union. Union citizenship complements national citizenship by giving individuals rights in all Member States. It does not replace national citizenship, nor does it impose new obligations.

The Amsterdam Treaty builds on this and gives further prominence to the rights of individuals as follows:

- the Council is permitted to take action by unanimity to combat discrimination based on sex, race or ethnic origin; religion or belief; disability; age; and sexual orientation;
- it is committed to eliminate inequalities between men and women in matters of pay, opportunities and wider social responsibility;
- protection against the misuse of personal data held by the Community institutions and Member States;
- a commitment taken by the European Commission to consult widely among Member States and all those interested parties within Member States before proposing legislation. This again clearly reinforces the position of all interested parties in places of work as 'social partners'.

The European Union Social Charter enshrined all of the areas of concern – freedom of movement; protection of employment and remuneration; vocational training; freedom of association; information, consultation and participation of employees; health and safety at work; and specific protection for stated groups of employees (see Summary Box A.6). The specific coverage of the Social Charter is as follows.

THE EUROPEAN UNION SOCIAL CHARTER

1. Everyone shall have the opportunity to earn his or her living in an occupation freely entered upon.
2. All workers have the right to just conditions of work.
3. All workers gave the right to safe and healthy working conditions.
4. All workers have the right to a fair remuneration sufficient for a decent standard of living for themselves and their families.
5. All workers and employers have the right to freedom of association in national or international organizations for the protection of their economic and social interests.
6. All workers and employers have the right to bargain collectively.
7. Children and young persons have the right to a special protection against the physical and moral hazards to which they are exposed.
8. Employed women, in cases of maternity, have the right to a special protection.
9. Everyone has the right to appropriate facilities for vocational guidance with a view to helping him or her choose an occupation suited to his or her personal aptitude and interests.
10. Everyone has the right to appropriate facilities for vocational training.
11. Everyone has the right to benefit from any measures enabling him or her to enjoy the highest possible standard of health attainable.
12. All workers and their dependants have the right to social security.
13. Anyone without adequate resources has the right to social and medical assistance.
14. Everyone has the right to benefit from social welfare services.
15. Disabled persons have the right to independence, social integration and participation in the life of the community.
16. The family as a fundamental unit of society has the right to appropriate social, legal and economic protection to ensure its full development.
17. Children and young persons have the right to appropriate social, legal and economic protection.
18. The nationals of any one of the Parties have the right to engage in any gainful occupation in the territory of any one of the others on a footing of equality with the nationals of the latter, subject to restrictions based on cogent economic or social reasons.
19. Migrant workers who are nationals of a Party and their families have the right to protection and assistance in the territory of any other Party.

20. All workers have the right to equal opportunities and equal treatment in matters of employment and occupation without discrimination on the grounds of sex.
21. Workers have the right to be informed and to be consulted within the undertaking.
22. Workers have the right to take part in the determination and improvement of the working conditions and working environment in the undertaking.
23. Every elderly person has the right to social protection.
24. All workers have the right to protection in cases of termination of employment.
25. All workers have the right to protection of their claims in the event of the insolvency of their employer.
26. All workers have the right to dignity at work.
27. All persons with family responsibilities and who are engaged or wish to engage in employment have a right to do so without being subject to discrimination and as far as possible without conflict between their employment and family responsibilities.
28. Workers' representatives in undertakings have the right to protection against acts prejudicial to them and should be afforded appropriate facilities to carry out their functions.
29. All workers have the right to be informed and consulted in collective redundancy procedures.
30. Everyone has the right to protection against poverty and social exclusion.
31. Everyone has the right to housing.

The legal instruments of the European Union

- *Treaty Articles:* binding on all Member States and employers immediately.
- *Regulations and Statutes:* laws that apply immediately and equally in all Member States.
- *Directives:* binding on public sector employers immediately; binding on other employers when enacted by the particular government of the Member State in question.
- *Decisions of the European Court of Justice:* which set precedent and therefore have the same effect as Regulations and Directives.
- *Decisions of the European Commission:* which also set precedent and become binding immediately.
- *Recommendations of the European Commission:* which are not legally binding but detail the Commission's views and opinions about how specific issues should be dealt with.
- *Codes of practice and guidance:* issued by the European Commission and its Directorate-General (its administrative establishment).

SUMMARY
BOX A.6

The UK and
the European
Union Social
Charter

The UK government opted out of signing the Social Charter under the Maastricht Treaty in 1992. In 1997, the UK Labour government signed the Social Charter, at the same time as it signed the Treaty of Amsterdam. In this, it committed itself to the following.

- *The introduction of a minimum wage:* this principle is now established. A minimum wage of £3.60 per hour was introduced in 1999. There are not so far any plans to review this figure – on a sectoral, occupational or annual basis. Any review process introduced in future will have to take account of pay leagues, payment structures and differentials.
- *Working hours:* the broad principle of the maximum 48-hour working week was adopted by the UK Conservative government under the terms of the Trade Union Reform and Employment Rights Act 1993.
- *Health and safety at work:* broadly speaking, the Health and Safety at Work Act 1974 is regarded as model legislation by the European Union. It sets high standards of practice, and then requires that these be enforced at individual places of work according to the particular circumstances. In turn, the Social Charter reinforces the absolute right of all those on work premises to the highest possible standards of health, safety and protection at work.
- *Maternity and parental leave:* the Trade Union Reform and Employment Rights Act 1993 gave every woman the right to 14 weeks' maternity leave regardless of length of service or hours worked; this was in accordance with the adoption of the Social Charter and European Union law. The principle of paternal leave is also enshrined. Fathers may claim up to a maximum of three months over the first five years of the child's life (though this is certain to be amended in the future).

Note

The Subsidiarity Principle: The view adopted by the EU is that enforcement of particular matters should take place at the most local level possible. Therefore, the enforcement of much European Union legislation is left in the hands of the employment tribunal and courts systems of the UK (see Figure A. 1). Only when there is a specific gap in the laws or regulations of a particular Member State is the European Union view enforced at a higher level.

Employee relations and European Union Directives

In this context the main EU Directives to note are as follows.

The Acquired Rights Directive 1977 (amended 1997)

The Acquired Rights Directive 1977 ensures the right of all staff to full employment protection, including fairness and equality of treatment, the right to continuity of employment, the right to security of wage payments, and the right to benefits provided by the organization in question, regardless of length of service or hours worked. It also protects employees

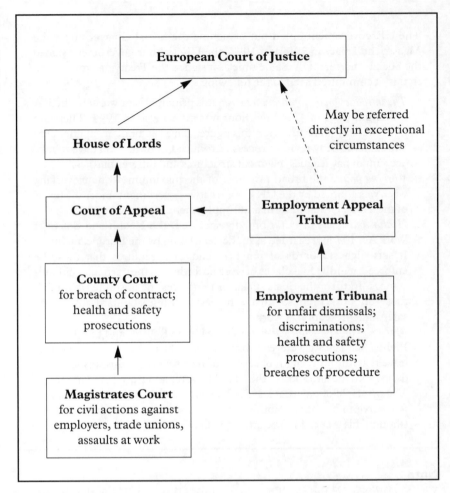

from dismissal, downgrading or loss of material benefits in the event of
the organization's change of status (e.g. nationalized to privatized); or in
the event of a merger, takeover, demerger or sale.

The European Works Council Directive 1994
The European Works Council Directive 1994 enshrines the principle of
pre-eminence of all those at a particular organization - and in particular,
requires adequate representation on organizational and managerial decision-making from all sectors of the staff. It is certain that the requirement
to constitute works councils will be broadened; and where this is not possible (e.g. in very small organizations), the right to information,
consultation and participation will nevertheless be enshrined.

The Working Hours Directive 1994
As stated above, this enshrines the principle of the maximum 48-hour
working week. It does make allowances for those whose work is carried

out in irregular patterns - for example, airline crews; other transport sectors; public security and emergency services.

The Working Hours Directive also enshrines the principles of:

- the entitlement to rest periods at work;
- the entitlement to minimum rest periods between periods of work;
- the right to paid holidays – at present there is no statutory minimum requirement for paid holidays for organizations working out of the UK.

Underpinning all this is the concept of 'the humanization of work' - the recognition that work is to be carried out from the point of view of mutual interest and harmony; that this is only possible in the long term if work is set in the context of the wider spectrum of life; and that people at places of work are to be treated with ordinary decent humanity.

The draft European Company Statute

The proposed European Company Statute recommends the creation of a special form of European organization to be known as a Societas Europeas or SE (if created, the letters SE would replace Plc or Ltd at the end of the company name in the UK).

The proposal was first recommended in 1970. However, it has made little further progress, because the European Commission continues to insist that SEs have compulsory employee participation in management decisions. Between one third and one half of its board of directors must consist of employee representatives, unless the organization constitutes a works council which has this form of executive authority and control. It therefore raises the level and influence of staff to that of shareholders.

Employees would also have to be consulted about acquisitions, mergers and takeovers; and at any disposal of a part of the business valued at more than 5 per cent of the SE's share capital.

If implemented, SEs will be governed by a set of fresh rules and regulations applicable throughout the EU, rather than by the laws of Member States. Such organizations will however be able to offset profits and losses between activities in various member countries; and this will apply also to subsidiaries. If implemented, therefore, those hitherto responsible only for employment relations would also be required to take much greater account of strategic, operational and commercial issues when devising and implementing human resource management and IR policies.

CONCLUSION

The purpose of this appendix has been to indicate the legal basis and framework that exists for the regulation of employee relations in the UK. The importance of the European dimension cannot at present be understated. It is essential that all of those involved in the devising and implementing of IR strategies, formats, standards, procedures and man-uals understand this as the framework within which they must work. Only then can adequate and effective – and successful – IR activity be contem-plated.

Appendix 2

Sanyo Industries (UK) Ltd: Staff Handbook

AGREEMENT

THIS AGREEMENT is made the tenth day of June 1982 BETWEEN:-

(1) SANYO INDUSTRIES (UK) LIMITED
of Oulton Works, School Road, Lowestoft, Suffolk NR33 9NA

(hereinafter referred to as "the Company")

(2) THE ELECTRICAL ELECTRONIC TELECOMMUNICA-
TIONS AND PLUMBING UNION
of Hayes Court, West Common Road, Hayes, Bromley, Kent BR2
7AH

(hereinafter referred to as "the Union").

The Company and the Union have agreed to enter this Agreement for the
purpose of recognising various mutual and other objectives which is in
the interests of both parties and of the employees of the Company to
achieve and accordingly the Company and the Union have agreed the following matters:-

1. (1) The independence of the practices and procedures laid down in
respect of the factory premises at Oulton Works, School Road,
Lowestoft ('the Establishment') from time to time
   (2) The non-federated status of the Establishment established by
this Agreement
   (3) Each of the terms and provisions of this Agreement is dependent
upon the observance of all the other terms and provisions, individual provisions cannot be acted upon without consideration of
all other relevant provisions in the Agreement
   (4) For the duration of this Agreement the Union shall have sole
recognition and bargaining rights for all employees covered by
this Agreement

2. In order to achieve the above objectives it is agreed that:-
   (1) All aspects of the Establishment and its operations will be so
organised as to achieve the highest possible level of efficiency
performance and job satisfaction so that the Company shall:-
       (i) be competitive and thus remain in business

(ii) provide continuity and security of employment for an effective work force

(iii) establish and maintain good working conditions

(iv) establish and maintain good employee relations and communications by supporting the agreed consultative negotiating, grievance and disciplinary procedures set out in this Agreement

(2) Both parties accept an obligation to ensure that the Establishment will operate with effective working methods with the best utilisation of manpower and without the introduction of wasteful and restrictive working practices and this objective will be achieved by:-

(i)   the selection, training, retraining and supplementary training of employees, wherever necessary, to enable such employees to carry out any job

(ii) the maximum co-operation with and support from all employees for measures and techniques used in any area to improve organisation and individual efficiency and to provide objective information with which to control and appraise the performance of individual employees and the Establishment

(iii) the maximum co-operation and support from all employees in achieving a completely flexible well motivated work force capable of transferring on a temporary or permanent basis into work of any nature that is within the capability of such employee having due regard to the provision of adequate training and safety arrangements

(3) Both parties recognise that the well-being of the employees is dependent upon the Company's success and that the high standards of product quality and reliability are essential if the products produced at the Establishment are to become and remain competitive and that therefore the maximum co-operation and support must be given to measures designed to achieve, maintain and improve quality and reliability standards.

3. The following matters have been agreed in connection with the Union:-

(1) Employees will not be required to become union members but the Company will encourage all employees covered by this Agreement to become a member of the Union and participate in Union affairs and in this connection the Company will provide a check off arrangement for the deduction of union subscriptions

(2) Union representation will be established in the following manner:-

(i)   The number of representatives of the Union together with the constituencies which they will represent will be agreed between the Union and the Company

(ii) The representatives will be elected in accordance with the Union Rules by union members in each constituency

(iii) Each such representative ('the Constituency Representative') will be accredited by the Union and the Union will then send details of the credentials of such representative for approval to the Head of Personnel who will confirm such approval with the Union and thereafter inform the appropriate line management concerned of the appointment

(3) The elected representatives will elect from amongst themselves a senior representative ('the Senior Representative') in accordance with the Union Rules

(4) The Senior Representative will be responsible for controlling and co-ordinating the activities of the Union in accordance with the terms and conditions of this Agreement and within the Union Rules and Regulations and will ensure that each elected representative shall have a working knowledge of the Union Rules and Regulations and in this connection in conjunction with the Personnel Department of the Company the Senior Representative shall ensure that the representatives shall have a comprehensive understanding of the employee relations procedures and practices of the Establishment and of general employee relations procedures and practices and it is agreed that all communication between the representatives and the full-time official(s) of the Union will be made through the Senior Representative

(5) Each elected representative must be employed in the constituency which he represents

(6) The Company will provide adequate facilities to ensure that all Union elections and ballots of members shall be carried out in secret and by the use of voting papers and not by way of a show of hands

4. It is agreed by the Company and the Union that all matters of difference should wherever possible be resolved at the source of such difference as speedily as practicable and it is the intention of the parties that all such matters will be dealt with in accordance with the agreed procedure and in this connection:-

(1) Where a matter relates to an individual employee covered by this Agreement such employee must in the first instance raise the same with the supervisor who will then be given the appropriate time necessary to resolve the situation PROVIDED ALWAYS that:-

    (i)   if the employee is not satisfied with the solution proposed by the supervisor then the employee may request the services of the constituency representative to reach a solution with the supervisor

    (ii) if the constituency representative and the supervisor shall fail to reach agreement then the constituency representative will discuss the matter with the Department Manager or his representative

    (iii) if after careful deliberation a satisfactory solution cannot be found then the constituency representative shall be entitled to raise the issue with the Senior Representative who will then decide if the grievance should be discussed at a higher level of management within the Company and the services of the Personnel Officer may then be called upon if it is considered that this will help to resolve the matter

    (iv) failing such resolution discussions will then take place between the Senior Representatives of the Company normally including the Head of Personnel together with the Senior Union Representative and the constituency representatives on the Joint Negotiation Council ('JNC') referred to in Clause (5) below

    (v) in exceptional circumstances the services of the National Officer of the Union may be requested to assist in the matter either by the Union or by the Company and in such circumstances the Company will arrange an appropriate meeting to be attended by senior representatives of the Company and the Union as well as the National Officer or the Full-time Official

(2) Insofar as differences shall arise in connection with issues of a Departmental nature then the procedure shall commence with a meeting between the constituency representative and the Department Manager or his representative

(3) In the case of an issue concerning the Establishment or the Company as a whole the matter will commence on the same basis as is set out in Sub-Clause (iii) above

5. The Company and the Union will establish a Joint Negotiation Council ('JNC') for the purpose of providing a forum through which discussions regarding improvements to employment conditions and other major matters can be discussed and in this connection:-

(1) The JNC will consist of representatives from the Company including the Head of Personnel and Senior Company Representatives and on behalf of the Union the Senior Representative from Production/Warehousing and one constituency representative from Administration

(2) Discussions regarding substantive improvements to employment conditions will normally be held on an annual basis during December in each year and such discussions will not include changes arising as a result of promotions, transfers or changes to job content which can be implemented at any time as agreed

(3) Matters agreed by the JNC will constitute one of the terms and conditions of employment for each employee covered by this Agreement

(4) The Senior Representative will be given appropriate facilities to consult with Union Members, Constituency Representatives and the Full-time Official or National Officer of the Union to enable the Senior Representative to conduct a meaningful collective bargaining exercise

(5) All claims on behalf of Union Members must be made in writing by the Senior Representative to the Head of Personnel who will convene the appropriate meeting of the JNC

(6) It is recognised by both parties that whilst discussions are taking place all business and negotiations discussed at the JNC will remain confidential to its members and the Company recognises its responsibility to ensure clear communication to employees of the results of such discussions and negotiations and in this connection the Head of Personnel will be responsible in consultation with the members of the JNC for announcing the details of any offer to be made to employees following such discussions and negotiations as aforesaid

(7) In exceptional circumstances the services of the National Officer or the Full-time Official of the Union may be requested by the JNC and in such circumstances the Company will arrange an appropriate meeting to be attended by representatives of the Company and the Union and the National Officer

6. In addition to the JNC the Company will establish a Joint Consultative Council ('JCC') and the following provisions shall apply thereto:-

(1) The membership of the JCC shall consist of the Head of Personnel (as Chairman) and appropriate members of the Company's Senior Executives and the Senior Representative together with one constituency representative from each of Production, Engineering and Administration and a further constituency representative on a rotating basis as a co-opted member and in addition the Managing Director of the Company shall act as President of the JCC and shall attend meetings from time to time

(2) The JCC shall meet on a monthly basis for the purposes of discussing issues of a mutual nature and one week prior to each JCC meeting the Personnel Officer will publish an Agenda agreed with the Senior Representative who will be responsible

for submitting items for discussion on behalf of the Union in time for such items to be included on the Agenda

(3) Items to be included for discussion at JCC meetings will include:-

    (i)   manufacturing performance

    (ii) operating efficiency

    (iii) manufacturing planning

    (iv) employment levels

    (v)   market information

    (vi) establishment environment

    (vii) employment legislation

    (viii) union policies and procedure

    (ix) level of union membership

(4) Following each meeting of the JCC the Head of Personnel will be responsible for communicating to all employees the nature and content of the discussions and in this connection the Company and the Union recognise the need to conduct meetings of the JCC in constructive manner for the benefit of the Company and all its employees

7. In the event that the Company and the Union shall be unable ultimately to resolve between themselves any discussions or disputes they may jointly agree to appoint an arbitrator and in this connection:-

(1) The Arbitrator will consider evidence presented to him by the Company and the Union and any factors that he believes to be appropriate

(2) The Arbitrator will decide in favour of one party

(3) The decision of the Arbitrator will be final and binding and will represent the final solution to the issue

8. DISCIPLINARY MEASURES

It is in the interest of the Company and its employees to maintain fair and consistent standards of conduct and performance. This procedure is designed to clarify the rights and responsibilities of the Company, the Union and employees with regard to disciplinary measures

Principles

The following principles will be followed in applying this procedure:

8.1 In the normal course of their duties, the Company will make employees aware of any shortcomings in performance or conduct. This counselling stage is separate from the disciplinary procedure as such

8.2 When the disciplinary procedure is invoked, the intention is to make the employee aware that the Company is concerned with their conduct or performance and to assist the person to improve to a satisfactory level

8.3 When any disciplinary case is being considered, the Company will be responsible for fully investigating the facts and circumstances of the case

8.4 The procedure will operate as quickly as possible, consistent with the thorough investigation of the case

8.5 The employee will always be informed of any disciplinary action to be taken and the reasons for it, indicating the specific areas for improvement

8.6 Normally the formal procedure will commence with the issuing of the first formal warning, however, the disciplinary procedure may be invoked at any stage depending on the seriousness of the case

8.7 Each formal warning will apply for 12 months. Should the employee improve their conduct or performance to an acceptable level and maintain the improvement for the duration of the warning, this will result in the deletion of the warning from their record

9. DISCIPLINARY PROCEDURE

The stages of the disciplinary procedure as follows:-

9.1 *First Formal Warning*

A formal warning at this stage represents the outcome of investigation and discussion into an employee's conduct or performance. If a first formal warning is issued, the individual concerned will be advised to this effect both verbally and in writing by the Company representative conducting the hearing, indicating the duration of the warning (which will be 12 months), the reasons for the warning and the specific areas for improvement

9.2 *Final Warning*

If there is no significant and sustained improvement in the employee's conduct or performance, then the next stage of the procedure is the final warning. If a final warning is issued, the individual concerned will be advised to this effect by the Company representative conducting the hearing, both verbally and in writing, indicating the duration of the warning (which will be 12 months), the grounds for the warning and the specific areas for improvement

9.3 *Dismissal*

If there is no significant and sustained improvement in the employee's conduct or performance during the period of the final warning, then following thorough investigation by the Company, the next stage of the procedure will be the dismissal stage. This stage will also be invoked in cases of gross misconduct. If an employee is dismissed he will be advised in writing of the principal reasons for the dismissal, and the notice periods which will apply to him

9.4 *Union Representation*

At all stages of this procedure and consistent with the circumstances of the issue the Company will ensure the involvement of the appropriate constituency representative. When, following careful investigation, disciplinary action is contemplated by the Company, the Union members concerned will be afforded the services of the Union constituency representative

10. APPEALS

Appeals against disciplinary action will follow the procedure as outlined below

10.1 All appeals will be in writing by the Senior Representative within two working days after the disciplinary action shall have been taken by the Company

10.2 The appeal will be made to the Personnel Officer who will arrange the formal appeal hearing within two working days of the appeal

10.3 The appeal will be heard by a Senior Personnel representative and a Senior Manager of the Department concerned who has not been involved in the case

10.4 The appeal will be conducted on the employee's behalf by the Senior Representative accompanied by the Department representative

10.5 The employee appealing, his Supervisor and other appropriate employees may be called to give evidence if it is thought their involvement is essential to the outcome of the hearing

10.6 The decision of the hearing is final. It is recognised that the Union may wish to discuss the matter as a collective issue

11. INDUSTRIAL ACTION

The Company and the Union undertake to follow the procedures agreed to and recognise that this Agreement provides adequate and speedy procedures for the discussion of Company related affairs and the resolution of problems and as such precludes the necessity for recourse to any form of industrial action by either the Company, the Union or the Employees.

Signed by

M. SADA
N.T. SALMON

duly authorised for and on behalf of
SANYO INDUSTRIES (UK) LIMITED

SIGNED by

R. SANDERSON

L. CHITTOCK

duly authorised for and on behalf of
THE ELECTRICAL ELECTRONIC
TELECOMMUNICATIONS AND PLUMBING UNION

Dated this 10th day of June 1982.

Source: Sanyo (UK) Ltd. (1982). Used with permission of Sanyo Industries (UK) Limited, Oulton Works, School Road, Lowestoft, Suffolk NR33 9NA

Bibliography

Adair, J. (1975) *Effective Leadership*, Kogan Page, London.

Argyris, C. (1990) *Understanding Organisational Behaviour*, John Wiley, New York.

Armstrong, M. (1996) *Personnel Management*, Kogan Page, London.

Ash, M. K. (1985) *On People Management*, McDonald, New York.

Baddeley, J. (1981) *Understanding Industry*, Butterworths/Industrial Society, London.

Bennett, R. (1996) *European Management*, FT Pitman, London.

Bercusson, B. (1997) *European Labour Law*, Butterworths, London.

Blake, R. and Mouton, J. (1986) *The New Managerial Grid*, Gulf, New York.

Brewster, C. (1990) *Industrial Relations*, Pan, London.

Brewster, C. (1991) *Management of Ex-Patriots*, Kogan Page, London.

Cartwright, D. (ed.) (1959) *Studies in Social Power*, University of Michigan Press, Ann Arbor.

Cartwright, R. (1995) *In Charge of Human Resource Management*, Blackwell, Oxford.

Cartwright, R. (1997) *In Charge: Managing Oneself*, Blackwell, Oxford.

Cheatle, K. (1996) *Human Resource Management*, NCVCCO, London.

Cheatle, K. (1999) *Mastering Human Resource Management*, Macmillan, London.

Commission of the European Union (1997a) *The European Social Charter*, EU, Brussels.

Commission of the European Union (1997b) *The Treaty of Amsterdam*, EU, Brussels.

Donovan, D. (1968) *Report of the Royal Commission on Trades Unions and Employers' Associations*, HMSO, London.

Drucker, P. F. (1986) *The Practice of Management*, Heinemann, London.

Drucker, P. F. (1999) *Management Challenges for the 21st Century*, Harper Collins, London.

Drummond, J. and Carmichael, S. (1989) *Good Business: A Guide to Corporate Responsibility*, Hutchinson, London.

Etzioni, A. (1964) *Power and Organisations*, McGraw-Hill, London.

Evenden, A. and Biddle, D. (1992) *The Human Side of Enterprise*, Routledge, London.

Farnham, D. (1994) *Employee Relations*, IPD, London.

Farnham, D. and Pimlott, J. (1992) *Industrial Relations*, Prentice Hall, Hemel Hempstead.

French, J. and Raven, B. (1959) 'The bases of social power', in D. Cartwright (ed.) *Studies in Social Power*, University of Michigan Press, Ann Arbor.

Furner, A. and Hyman, R. (eds) (1992) *Industrial Relations in the New Europe*, Blackwell, Oxford.

Furnham, A. (1997) *The Psychology of Managerial Incompetence*, Whurr, London.

Goldthorpe, J. *et al.* (1968) *The Affluent Worker*, Vols 1, 2 and 3, Cambridge University Press, Cambridge.

Griseri, P. (1998) *Managing Values*, Macmillan, London.

Handy, C. B. (1990) *Understanding Organisations*, Penguin, Harmondsworth.

Handy, C. B. (1994a) *The Age of Unreason*, Macmillan, London.

Handy, C. B. (1994b) *Understanding Organisations*, Penguin, Harmondsworth.

Handy, C. B. (1996) *Understanding Organisations*, Penguin, Harmondsworth.

Hantrais, L. (1996) *European Social Policy*, Macmillan, London.

Harrison, R. (1987) *Organisation and Culture*, Prentice Hall, Hemel Hempstead.

Harvey-Jones, J. (1982) *Making It Happen*. London: Fontana.

Henderson, J. (1997) *A Guide to the Employment Acts*, Routledge, London.

Herzberg, F. (1962) *Work and the Nature of Man*, Pelican, London.

Herzberg, F. (1970) *Work and the Nature of Man*, Free Press, New York.

Kanter, R. M. (1990) *The Change Masters*, Free Press, New York.

Kessler, S. (1999) *Employment Relations in Public Services at the end of the 20th Century*, Templeton/IPD, Oxford and London.

Kessler, S. and Bayliss, F. (1996) *Contemporary British Industrial Relations*, Macmillan, Basingstoke.

Legge, K. (1992) *Human Resource Management*, Macmillan, London.

Lessem, R. S. (1987) *Intrapreneurship*, Wildwood House, London.

Lessem, R. S. (1989) *Managing Corporate Culture*, Gower, London.

Likert, R. (1961) *New Patterns of Management*, McGraw-Hill, London.

Livy, B. (1989) *Corporate Personnel Management*, Pitman, London.

McCarthy, W. E. J. (1962) *Trade Unions*, Penguin, Harmondsworth.

McGregor, D. (1980) *The Human Side of Enterprise*, McGraw-Hill, London.

Maslow, A. (1960) *Motivation and Personality*, Harper & Row, New York.

Mayo, E. (1943) *The Hawthorne Studies: The Human Problems of an Industrial Civilisation*, Macmillan, New York.

Morita, A. (1987) *Made in Japan: The Sony Story*, Fontana, London.

Mumford, A. (1989) *Management Development*, IPD, London.

Ouchi, W. G. (1993) *Theory Z*, Free Press, New York.

Pascale, R. and Athos, A. (1983) *The Art of Japanese Management*, Fontana, London.

Peter, L. J. (1970) *The Peter Principle*. London and New York: Bantam.

Peters, T. and Austin, N. (1985) *A Passion for Excellence*, Collins, London.

Peters, T. and Waterman, R. (1980) *In Search of Excellence*, Free Press, New York.

Pettinger, R. (1997) *Introduction to Management*, Macmillan, London.

Pettinger, R. (1998a) *The European Social Charter: A Manager's Guide*, Kogan Page, London.

Pettinger, R. (1998b) *Managing the Flexible Workforce*, Cassell, London.

Pettinger, R. and Frith, R. (1996a) *The Management of Discipline and Grievances*, Technical Communications Ltd, Oxford.

Pettinger, R. and Frith, R. (1996b) *Preparing and Handling Industrial Tribunal Cases*, Technical Communications Ltd, Oxford.

Phelps-Brown, H. E (1967) *The Rise of Trade Union Power*, Penguin, London.

Reddin, W. (1970) *Managerial Effectiveness*, McGraw-Hill, Maidenhead.

Rice, J. (1995) *Doing Business in Japan*, Penguin, Harmondsworth.

Roddick, A. (1992) *Body and Soul: The Body Shop Story*, Ebury, York.

Salamon, M. (1992) *Industrial Relations*, Prentice Hall International, Hemel Hempstead.

Salomon, G. (1992) *Human Resource Strategies*, Open University Press, Milton Keynes.

Schein, E. (1990) *Organisational Psychology*, Prentice Hall, Hemel Hempstead.

Semler, R. (1992) *Maverick*, Free Press, New York.

Senge, P. M. (1997) *The Fifth Discipline*, Harper & Row, New York.

Sieff, M. (1990) *Humanity and Managment: The Marks & Spencer Approach*, McGraw-Hill, Maidenhead.

Sisson, K. (1991) *Personnel Management in Britain*, Blackwell, Oxford.

Sternberg, E. (1995) *Just Business*, Warner, London.

Stewart, R. (1991) *Managing Today and Tomorrow*, Macmillan, London.

Storey, J. (1996) *New Perspectives on Human Resource Management*, Blackwell, Oxford.

Taylor, F. W. (1947) *Scientific Management*, Harper & Row, New York.

Thomason, G. (1986) *A Textbook of Human Resource Management*, IPD, London.

Thomason, G. (1987) *A Textbook of Industrial Relations*, IPD, London.

Torrington, D. and Hall, L. (1992) *Personnel Management: A New Approach*, Prentice Hall International, Hemel Hempstead.

Trevor, M. (1992) *Toshiba's New British Company*, Policy Studies Institute, London.

Trice, H. M. and Beyer, J. M. (1985) 'Using six organisational rites to change culture', in R. H. Kilman *et al.* (eds) *Gaining Control of the Corporate Culture*, Jossey-Bass, San Francisco, pp. 374–5.

Vroom, V. (1964) *Work and Motivation*, John Wiley, Chichester.

Vroom, V. and Deci, E. L. (1992) *Management and Motivation*, Penguin, Harmondsworth.

Walton, D. and McKersie, A. (1965) *A Behavioural Theory of Labour Negotiations*, McGraw-Hill, Maidenhead.

Warr, P. (1987) *Psychology at Work*, Penguin, Harmondsworth.

Weber, M. (1986) *Social and Economic Organisation*, Free Press, New York.

Wickens, P. (1996) *The Road to Nissan*, Macmillan, London.

Wickens, P. (1999) *Culture and Transformation*, Macmillan, London.

Williams, A. and Dobson, P. (1995) *Changing Culture*, IPD, London.

Woodward, J. (1970) *Industrial Organisation: Behaviour and Control*, Oxford University Press, Oxford.

Index